CONTENTS

York Minster

Produced by the Publications Division of the
Automobile Association

Editor: Michael Cady   Art editor: Peter Davies

Contributors: David Austin, Julia Brittain,
Michael Buttler, Ross Finlay, Bob Johnson,
Barbara Littlewood, Roger Prebble,
Rebecca Snelling, Pat Rowlinson

Phototypeset by Vantage Photosetting Co Ltd,
Eastleigh and London
Printed and bound by New Interlitho S.p.A.,
Milan

The contents of this book are believed correct at the
time of printing. Nevertheless, the publisher can ac-
cept no responsibility for errors or omissions or for
changes in the details given.

ISBN 0 86145 195 3

**Published by The Automobile Association
Fanum House, Basingstoke, Hampshire
RG21 2EA**

THE STORY OF TOWNS

York, one of Britain's most historic towns

The story of most British towns begins many hundreds of years ago. Some of our most treasured cities, such as Chichester, Bath or Lincoln, were already important centres in Roman times; others, like Winchester and Canterbury, can be traced back even further. But no town has reached the end of its story; rarely does a year elapse without a townscape being changed in some way. The 20th century is leaving its legacy – not always destructive or ugly – just as the many centuries before it have left theirs, making our best townscapes a fascinating patchwork of ingredients from every age.

Town roots
It is not always easy to define what makes a place a town. Is it size, or position, or importance as local centre for trade and commerce? In most cases it is probably a mixture of all these things. Still less is it easy to say when towns came into being in Britain. The generally accepted view has been that the Romans introduced the idea of urban life. But the prehistoric hillforts which are to be found throughout the country, and are especially numerous on the chalk downs of southern England, represent complex and centralised living, for they are usually packed with the traces of huts

and other buildings, and were surrounded by many satellite homesteads. It is no longer thought that the hillforts were occupied only in times of crisis; it is much more likely that they had permanent populations.

In contrast to the exposed hillforts, several low-land tribal centres have been identified. These were probably developed by Belgic peoples, who arrived from the Continent in the century before the Roman conquest. One of the best-known of these centres is at Wheathampstead, Hertfordshire, where huge earthworks can still be seen. Very few of these early centres have since become towns. This is markedly different from the Roman centres – out of their principal towns only two (Wroxeter and Silchester) are not urban sites today.

Life in Roman towns
The Romans were highly centralised, and based their empire on organisation and discipline. Within a few years of their foundation, most Roman towns had such sophisticated embellishments as public baths, public lavatories and amphitheatres.

All towns had, as a matter of course, a forum (or market place) and a basilica, which served all the functions of a civic centre.

There were also theatres, shops providing every kind of service, Christian churches, temples, inns, and less savoury kinds of establishments like brothels – all neatly laid out along made-up streets. Of course, Roman towns were largely filled with private houses. These usually took the form of long terraces, probably with shops or workrooms below and living quarters above. Such places were small and unambitious. Richer and more important citizens had detached, substantially built villas – often with central heating and sometimes with private baths.

Life in the Roman towns and cities was calm and prosperous for most – a state of affairs that lasted for centuries. Britain was a comfortable province of an empire which included most of the civilised world – it must have seemed that nothing could change. But Rome was stretched to its limits. The Empire was no longer controllable; some parts were in a state of unrest; some in open rebellion. Rome began to pull in its tentacles, and troops were recalled from Britain to curb uprisings on the continent.

In the towns and cities of Britain life went on virtually unchanged for a long time. Some commodities became unobtainable; the veneer of sophistication began to rub off. Saxon mercenaries were brought in by the authorities to replace the legions. It was a mistake, for the Saxons soon began to arrive unasked. Gradually, the great Roman towns fell into decline, became overgrown, fell into ruins. The fortifications were usually re-used however, even when the original walls had fallen into ruins. It seems that although they did not maintain the buildings, the Saxons re-used most of the town sites.

Silchester as it was in Roman times

Vikings and Saxons

At York the continuity of settlement is perhaps more clearly seen than anywhere else. Here the line of the Roman defences is marked by original masonry in parts, and elsewhere the Roman line is followed by Saxon and later fortifications. Still in York, excavations have shown that the Roman military buildings were still in use in the 9th century. It is in York that most survives of the Viking influence on British towns. It was capital of a Viking kingdom until 954, and much of the history of that era has been brought to light and displayed in recent years.

New towns were established in Saxon times – Southampton and Bury St Edmunds are examples. Some were created as commercial centres, some as 'burghs' or fortified settlements, and some began life as religious communities around which towns grew up. By the 10th century most of the Roman townscapes had disappeared, and had been replaced by Saxon towns, many of whose street plans can still be traced. The initial destruction of the Norman Conquest that followed eventually consolidated urban life.

After the Conquest

The Norman Conquest brought to Britain a more stable government and a gradual increase in trade and prosperity. With this came a growing need for market and cultural centres. Some villages began to expand to serve this need, and many of the Roman towns – so often strategically sited at route centres or important river crossings – were revived. Most medieval towns were not planned all at once; they evolved over the centuries to serve the changing needs of their community. This meant that they often acquired haphazard-looking street patterns and the higgledy-piggledy groups of buildings that are still so appealing in medieval corners of our towns today.

Medieval towns were not really disorganised, however. The focal point was nearly always the market place – hardly surprising, since in many cases that was the reason for the town's existence. The arrangement of streets was such that the market place could be easily reached from all the streets in the central area. Many towns had two or more open spaces like this, which were very important, being used not only for the principal market but also for fairs, public gatherings, plays or specialised markets for local products such as leather, wool or flax. Sometimes there was a town hall or guildhall, which survives at many places including Exeter and Norwich. Almost always the town's mother church stood nearby. This had pride of place, being one of the few 'permanent' buildings in the town, and unusual in having been constructed by skilled men.

Castles and fortified towns

The other notable permanent structure in many medieval towns was the castle. Famed as castle-builders, the Normans generally made use of natural high ground for their most important fortifications. Often they built a special castle mound, or motte, to give extra height to the main keep – as at Lincoln. Many Norman castles were of wood at first, but these were gradually replaced by stone structures.

The 12th and 13th centuries also saw the construction of many purpose-built military townships in Europe. The military role of such towns was always uppermost: castle, walls, gates and watchtowers usually dwarfed a modest settlement, as at Conwy and Caernarfon, both constructed by the great castle-builder Edward I, and the finest surviving examples in Britain of this kind of town.

Medieval homes

King, church and noblemen may have had the means to build in stone, but what of the ordinary people? In almost unimaginable contrast to the massive castles and the vast, richly decorated churches and cathedrals of stone, most of them had to build for themselves tiny, dark houses out of whatever materials they could find. The building plots allotted to them were usually long and very narrow; even today, many town shops and houses have a narrow frontage – a legacy of medieval building arrangements. The people had to use local materials, and only the rich could afford stone, even when it was available locally. So most of the houses were timber-framed with wattle-and-daub infill and a thatched roof. Later, brick infill and tiled roofs became more widespread. The narrow plot meant floor space was limited, which gave rise to the characteristic overhanging or 'jettied' first floor – a quaint feature that betrays many a house's medieval origins. An obvious threat to any town built mostly of timber, with thatch as well in many places, was the risk of fire. Once started, a fire could sweep through a street in no time – as was seen most notoriously in the Great Fire of London in 1666. By this time, however, new trends in town-building were already well under way.

The first architects

London very nearly became the complete Renaissance capital. Its rise throughout medieval and Tudor times had been phenomenal. In size alone it far outstrode every other city in Britain. It dominated all aspects of culture as well as being the seat of government, and beside it all other towns had the air of rural backwaters. When the monarch ceased to make long journeys around the country with a huge entourage of followers, the centralisation thrust was complete.

The Great Fire had destroyed nearly everything – houses, churches, even the huge and sprawling St Paul's Cathedral. Plans were mooted for a new city, a city fit for a great nation, a city built along Classical and Renaissance lines.

The architectural schemes of the Renaissance were hardly new. Palladio, the Italian architect who was their greatest exponent, had lived a century before. Inigo Jones, Britain's first true architect, had introduced Renaissance ideas in the early 17th century (his greatest achievement was the Banqueting House, built in 1619), but it was to be more than a century until his ideas were generally accepted. It was another new architect – Sir Christopher Wren – who is most often associated with the rebuilding of London, though his revolutionary plan for a complete new city was not taken up, because it would have taken too long to build. So a new London rose from the ashes of the old, largely on the old street pattern. Wren designed its churches and some other public buildings. But what made the new London so different from its predecessors, and from all other towns, was its lack of timber buildings. These were banned to reduce the risk of another fire.

Renaissance ideas spread gradually to most provincial towns. King's Lynn gained its delightful Custom House in 1683, and many small towns gained town or market halls in the new style. The university towns of Oxford and Cambridge were the site of much building work; Oxford's Sheldonian Theatre was Wren's first project. But despite the gradual spread of the new ideas, wholesale redevelopment was hitherto almost unheard of. Now, for the first time, there were striking exceptions to this. Bath is perhaps the finest. No fire destroyed its old shape, and it had been a town since Roman times at least, flourishing again with the cloth trade in the Middle Ages. It had been founded partly on account of its medicinal springs, and it was these which attracted royalty and high society again in the early 18th century. Bath became fashionable and was transformed into an elegant city with sweeping stone crescents, long vistas and dignified squares.

The styles propounded by Wren and his followers – basically simple shapes lent character by classical doorways, windows and pilasters – were easily copied by local builders (indeed there were special pattern books for the purpose), so rows of similar houses began to spring up in many towns. The style was refined over the next hundred years into what we now know as Georgian – a very familiar element in town architecture. The Georgian style became so popular that Georgian façades were often placed on very much older buildings – a tell-tale sign of this today is a surviving steeply pitched medieval roofline.

The Georgian age enhanced the look of many towns; later, Regency architecture went still further. Its principal architect was John Nash. He worked at Brighton, helping to create a fashionable resort from a quiet fishing village. Other seaside towns were quick to follow Brighton's lead, and soon crescents and elegant terraces grew up alongside many a newly created promenade. Many of the new townscapes were now planned on very large scales. Great areas of London were redeveloped on Regency lines. But the buildings were not as tightly packed together as before: roads were wider, to take the increasing carriage

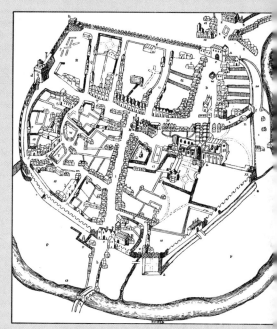

The pictures on these pages show Bath's growth over 400 years. Above: the city in Tudor times, its limits defined by walls originally built by the Romans

traffic; new parks and squares were created; old parks were kept, but made an integral part of new designs. It was all very civilised and calm in comparison with what was to follow.

The industrial era

The first factories began to make their impact on Britain's towns from the mid 18th century, when mechanised cotton and woollen mills, pottery works, iron works and breweries became more widespread. Canals, the arteries of the Industrial Revolution, had also made their mark. For the first time raw materials and manufactured goods could be moved in large quantities around the country with comparative ease, and commerical opportunities increased.

Taking over where the canals left off, the railways had a much more dramatic effect on the way towns looked. It was not only a question of demolishing swathes of earlier buildings to make way for railway lines, stations, workshops and marshalling yards. The railways added speed to the advantages of the canals – and this boost to the supply and distribution lines did much to encourage an even greater industrial boom. As factories grew larger to house bigger and more efficient machinery, so more and more workers were needed to man them, and they too had to be housed. Most factory-owners built the cheapest housing possible for their employees, and the absence of any controls until the later part of the 19th century led to the building of thousands of tiny, dark, unhealthy terraces which became the slums of the early 20th century and have mostly been demolished, though some rows of high-density terraced housing from this period survive in our towns.

A more direct effect of the railways at this time was on the use of local building materials. Mass-produced bricks could now be moved around the country so easily and cheaply that local building materials were neglected altogether, and little thought was given to choosing the best building material for a particular job. Fortunately, as time wore on, wealthy industrialists and their architects grew bored with the monotony and began to seek new styles of building, turning to decorative brickwork and to flint, stone and even half-timbering to liven up their towns.

As the towns filled up with their employees, and became grimy, noisy and polluted by the effects of their factories, so the mill-owners and better-off

In 1750 (above), although redevelopment was already taking place, Bath was still almost confined within its ancient walls. Today (right) it sprawls for miles

middle classes found town living distasteful and began to move out of their town houses. They built for themselves Victorian villas and mansions in what became the suburbs. The money they had made also allowed them to indulge their civic pride and improve their standing in the community by building churches, town halls, museums, law courts, libraries and other public buildings. In many cases, earlier churches were 'restored', often with disastrous results. These public buildings, built or rebuilt by the Victorians, are the most obvious legacy they have left us in many of our towns. Every conceivable architectural style was used for these buildings, with increasing flamboyance – perhaps in reaction to the drab rows of monotonous houses which had been built for the factory workers. Completely new kinds of building were required, such as railway stations and waterworks – very much hallmarks of the Victorian and Edwardian period. Iron and glass, produced by the new industries, were used in building as never before, to construct everything from shopping arcades to warehouses, and, not least, the seaside pier. The seaside gained dramatically in popularity in the 19th century – again, largely because it was now easy to reach by rail. Houses became more and more exotic, sprouting every conceivable kind of decoration. Warehouses, banks and hotels appeared in Moorish, Chinese or Egyptian styles – there were no holds barred.

Into the modern age
The 20th century has not, on the whole, been good for Britain's townscapes. Many were bombed almost flat during World War II, many more have been flattened since by town planners and get-rich-quick developers.

Monumental buildings, first in an overbearing style based on classical motifs, and then in the '60s non-style often called 'brutal', mushroomed in virtually every town in the country, pushing older buildings out and overshadowing those they stood beside. Attractive shop fronts were ripped out in their thousands and replaced by featureless panes of glass. In many a town street the only way to see what remains of older buildings is to look above the glass and the garish trade signs to the unaltered upper floors.

All this is not to say that there had been no destruction in previous centuries. Towns are by their nature in a state of perpetual change – one of the things that give them vitality and character. But the 20th century had little respect for anything that had gone before, and not much respect for itself. Whole town centres which had evolved as living, working environments over centuries were bulldozed, only to be replaced by the 'precinct' or the 'new town centre'. Worse still, thousands of acres were flattened – not to build anything on them, but to serve as car parks.

Cars generally have had a dramatic effect on Britain's towns. Ring roads have cut great swathes through many, destroying all in their path and making a nonsense of traditional street plans. In the worst cases it is virtually impossible to travel across town except in a car. Fortunate towns have by-passes which keep large volumes of through-traffic out of old streets that were not built for it. Less lucky towns have to cope with juggernauts that constantly increase in size. In recent years there have been signs of a change, a realisation that much that was irreplaceable has been destroyed, but that it is not too late to save and enhance. For example, pedestrianised areas are on the increase, an especially welcome innovation in interesting old streets which lose much of their character if they are blocked by traffic, and which demand to be explored on foot – the only way to discover the legacy our towns have acquired through the ages.

I | ABERDEEN

Although Aberdeen is the busiest place in north-east Scotland, the centre-point of the North Sea oil industry, it remains a city of many unexpectedly quiet corners. One of these is Old Aberdeen, based on the University which started in 1500 with only five students, and on St Machar's Cathedral. Much of Old Aberdeen is now University property. The very modern departments, like the Natural Philosophy building, are carefully designed and placed, so that in the tree-lined streets and lanes they do not clash with the mellowed Georgian houses which give Old Aberdeen its air of graceful permanence.

ROUTE DIRECTIONS
Start in University Rd. Turn r. into College Bounds (1) and continue into High St passing Kings College (2). Turn r. into Grant's Pl (3) and at end of houses turn l. and immediately l. again into Wrights' and Coopers' Pl to return to High St and turn r. Bear l. at Town House (4) and cross St Machar Dr into The Chanonry (5), with the Cruickshank Botanic Gardens (6) on l. Bear r. into St Machar's Cathedral (7). Return to entrance, turn r. then bear r. into Seaton Park (8). Follow main pathway to l. downhill. Keep r. at car park then bear l. off tarmac along riverside. Bear r. uphill on main path above bend in river. Leave through gate and turn l. downhill on road to Brig o'Balgownie (9). Return from bridge, then opposite entrance to Hillhead Halls of Residence take footpath on l. and follow for some distance before crossing Don St to re-enter Seaton Park through gate with 'no through road' signs. Immediately turn l. along path, then leave park at exit behind St Machar's Cathedral. Turn l. at cathedral entrance into The Chanonry passing Chaplain's Court (10), then turn r. back onto Don St to reach the Bede House (11). Cross St Machar Dr, keep l. of the Town House and return to University Rd.

1 COLLEGE BOUNDS
Once a boundary of the area within which students of the University had to live, this is the main approach to the High Street of Old Aberdeen. One architectural eccentricity is the Powis Lodge gateway, built in 1834 for the landowner John Leslie of Powis. Its high minarets bring an unexpected touch of the Near East to this old Scottish burgh.

2 KING'S COLLEGE
Named after James IV, in whose reign it was founded by Bishop William Elphinstone, King's College – in both architecture and sentiment – is the heart of the University. Built between 1500 and 1505, it is topped by a superb crown tower. King's College Chapel has irreplaceable 16th-century woodwork and some fine modern stained glass. Bishop Elphinstone died in 1514. He was buried in the Chapel itself. But in the 1920s a new sarcophagus was set up on the College lawn. In 1860 King's was merged with Marischal College in the city to form the modern Aberdeen University. Fears that Old Aberdeen would be forced into a decline have proved false. In fact, most university expansion has been here, rather than in the main part of the city.

3 GRANT'S PLACE
Just off the High Street, Grant's Place is a row of cottages built around 1732. Beyond it, Wrights' and Coopers' Place – named after one of the Incorporated Trades of the old burgh – is a row of two-storey houses of a few years later. Both were restored with the greatest care in 1965, in a project financed by the MacRobert Trust. Where they meet is a memorial garden to Lady MacRobert and her four sons.

King's College Chapel

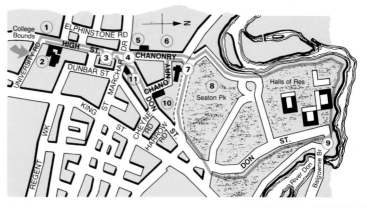

4 TOWN HOUSE

This is a reminder that Old Aberdeen – originally Aberdon, taking its name from the nearer river – was an independent burgh from 1498 to 1891, when it voted to merge with the City of Aberdeen. The Georgian Town House was built about 1790. Above the door are the arms of Old Aberdeen, featuring three lilies and three salmon. Until 1922 it stood in the middle of a Y-junction. But in that year St Machar Drive was opened, leaving it on the island site it occupies today.

5 THE CHANONRY

This street, three-sided and with a northern extension, takes its name from the manses where the canons of St Machar's Cathedral once lived. None of those original buildings remains, but the granite houses of the University professors, in elegant Georgian style, are still called manses. Chanonry Lodge is the residence of the Principal of the University. But there are non-University buildings too, like Mitchell's Hospital, laid out on three sides of a courtyard in the 19th century for widows and spinsters of Old Aberdeen.

6 CRUICKSHANK BOTANIC GARDENS

Laid out in the grounds of the University Department of Botany, this eight-acre garden was created in 1898. There are two rock gardens, a water garden and pathways by shrub-lined lawns.

Robert the Bruce was responsible for the completion of lovely Brig o' Balgownie in the early 14th century

7 ST MACHAR'S CATHEDRAL

The original Cathedral of St Machar was built in the middle of the 12th century. But the present building, still used for worship by a Church of Scotland congregation, was completed in 1513 by Bishop Elphinstone, who founded the University. A few years later, Bishop Gavin Dunbar commissioned the splendid heraldic ceiling, with its 48 coats of arms – of Pope Leo X, archbishops and bishops, kings, dukes and earls, of the University and of the burghs of Aberdeen and Old Aberdeen. Other treasures of St Machar's include a collection of medieval charters and another of silver chalices. A 20th-century change was the removal of all the plaster from the interior walls, revealing the original sturdy stonework. In the churchyard is the grave of George Sinclair, the last Provost of Old Aberdeen, who died in 1914.

8 SEATON PARK

Bounded by a double curve of the River Don, with woodlands and playing fields, this was once the grounds of Seaton House, the mansion of the Hay family. They sold the park to the City of Aberdeen. The house itself was burned out in 1963. At the north end of the park are the University's Hillhead Halls of Residence.

9 BRIG O'BALGOWNIE

With completely restored houses by the roadside on both approaches, but now closed to vehicle traffic, this is perhaps the most famous medieval bridge in Scotland. Based on the shape of a Gothic arch, it was opened in 1329 to take the main road north from Aberdeen.

10 CHAPLAIN'S COURT

Back in The Chanonry, Chaplain's Court is another of the University houses. At its heart is the original 'court', built by Bishop Dunbar in 1519 to give accommodation to the chaplains of St Machar's Cathedral. His coat of arms is preserved on the outer wall looking onto The Chanonry.

11 BEDE HOUSE

Far quieter than when it took all the traffic to and from the Brig o'Balgownie, Don Street finishes at the Bede House of Old Aberdeen. This was a charitable refuge for elderly men of the burgh. Recently restored, the Bede House itself has been turned into flats.

EARLY CLOSING: *Wed & Sat.*

MARKET DAYS: *Fri.*

PARKING: *University Rd.*

OPENING TIMES:

King's College Chapel: *Open all year. Mon–Fri, and for Sunday services.*

Cruickshank Botanic Gardens: *Open all year. Mon–Fri. Weekends May–Sept.*

ROUTE DIRECTIONS

Start the walk at the railway station, terminus of the branch line from Shrewsbury and of the Vale of Rheidol Railway (1). Walk west along Alexandra Rd, reach a roundabout and continue forward into Mill St. Just before reaching a bridge turn l. then r. to walk beneath its arches. From here there are views of the harbour (2). Ascend steps on r. beyond a warehouse, then turn r again and at the end turn l. into Bridge St. Turn l. into Princess St and keep forward into Vulcan St. Pass Enoc Huws Shop (3). Continue into Sea View Pl, join South Rd and reach New Promenade. Turn r. and enter the grounds of Aberystwyth Castle (4). Leave the castle by the main gate and take a path beside a children's playground, with the University College of Wales (5) away to the l. Reach St Michael's Church (6). Walk through the churchyard into Laura Pl (7). Keep forward into New St, Eastgate and Portland St, then turn l. into Terrace Rd, passing the Ceredigion Museum (8). Turn l. again into Corporation St, go past the library and turn r. down Crynfryn Row, a narrow passage which leads to the sea front. To the left is the pier (9). Turn r. along Marine Terr (10), then turn r. into Albert Pl and r. again into Queen's Rd, passing the Town Hall (11). Reach the end of Queen's Rd and continue into Thespian St. Turn r. into Alexandra Rd for the return to the railway station.

An air of bygone-gentility still clings to the hotels, guesthouses, churches and chapels which line the streets of Aberystwyth. It is a quiet and unassuming seaside resort foremost, but it is also an administrative centre and the setting for the modern buildings of the University of Wales.

1 VALE OF RHEIDOL RAILWAY

The only narrow-guage railway owned and operated by British Rail, the Vale of Rheidol runs for 12 miles through lovely scenery up to Devil's Bridge. The line was opened in 1902 to carry lead from several upland mines. At the same time its builders had an eye on the increasing numbers of tourists visiting the area, and it is these which have kept the railway going through thick and thin ever since.

2 HARBOUR

When Daniel Defoe visited Aberystwyth in 1724 he reported that both town and harbour were very dirty and smoky from the huge quantities of coal and lead that were exported from here. Things are far different today, and the harbour is a quiet backwater with a few fishing boats and pleasure craft. Reminders of old industries survive in the shape of a disused brewery and crumbling lime kilns.

3 ENOC HUWS SHOP

Set at the corner of Prospect Street, Enoc Huws' is a peculiar establishment – in its window display are items of millinery and haberdashery that have not been available for many years. In fact, this is not a real shop at all, but a cleverly mounted exhibition set up for entertainment and amusement.

4 ABERYSTWYTH CASTLE

When Edward I decided to crush Welsh insurgency once and for all he built powerful castles in the most strategically important places, and Aberystwyth was one of them. It was completed in 1277, captured and destroyed by the

Built in the 1860s, the old University College building is a remarkable exercise in Victorian design

Welsh five years later, and rebuilt by the king two years after that. Wales' last great guerilla leader, Owain Glyndwr, captured it in 1404 and held it for four years. The castle's final appearance in history came when it was taken, after a long siege, by Parliamentary forces during the Civil War and destroyed by them.

5 UNIVERSITY COLLEGE OF WALES

By any standards this is an impressive building. It is an architectural extravaganza which only the Victorian age could have created. It was built for a railway magnate as a hotel for the thousands of tourists he hoped to entice to the town, but during its construction he became bankrupt and the building was subsequently purchased by a group of Welsh businessmen as home for a new Welsh university. The building which stands here today is in fact only the south wing of the original; the rest was burned down in a fire in 1885. The main university buildings overlook the town from Penglais. These include the National Library of Wales, a repository for rare Welsh books and manusripts and the recipient of a copy of every book published in Britain.

6 ST MICHAEL'S CHURCH

A massive stone tower built in 1906 dominates this church, which itself dates from 20 years before that. The large churchyard is dotted with slate gravestones, some of which bear touchingly naive memorials. Inside, there is a reredos which

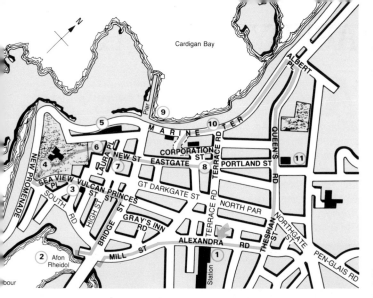

Cardigan Bay

place, and in 1938 it was severely damaged by a storm. Today it still stands on the sea front, truncated and battered, but a powerful reminder of Edwardian holidays.

10 MARINE TERRACE
Hotels and guesthouses line this thoroughfare and look out over the waters of Cardigan Bay. It leads to Constitution Hill, where a funicular railway built in 1895 carries passengers up and down the 1-in-2 slope. Originally operated by water balance tanks, it was electrified in 1922.

11 TOWN HALL
Set at the end of Portland Street, the town hall was built in 1961 and opened a year later. It is a white building with a Palladian front to the centre block and two plain Georgian-style wings. It gained a Civic Trust award in 1962. The previous building here originated from 1842 and was burned down in 1957.

EARLY CLOSING: *Wed.*

MARKET DAY: *Mon.*

PARKING: *railway station, Maesyrafon.*

OPENING TIMES:

Vale of Rheidol Railway: open Easter – Oct.

Ceredigion Museum: open all year. Weekdays.

is a copy of Leonardo da Vinci's *Last Supper*.

7 LAURA PLACE
Aberystwyth began to become popular as a seaside resort at the beginning of the 19th century, even though it was then a remote and inaccessible place. Most of the buildings from that period disappeared when the railway arrived in the 1860s, but Georgian architecture can still be seen scattered through the town, and the best collection is to be found in Laura Place.

Facing the sweep of Cardigan Bay, Aberystwyth stands among the gentle hills of mid Wales

8 CEREDIGION MUSEUM
A converted theatre is the setting for this fascinating museum. In it can be found agricultural implements, farm carts, weights and measures, a dairy, carpenters' workshop, pharmacy, and a complete one-room cottage interior equipped with curtained four-poster bed, fire-place, furniture and utensils.

9 THE PIER
When it was opened to the public in 1865 the pier was 800ft long, but very shortly afterwards 100ft of it was washed away by the sea. Further deterioration took

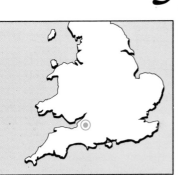

Although a Celtic and a Roman watering place, Bath is a true Georgian city, the creation of the local postmaster Ralph Allen and his architects, John Wood and his son. Allen financed the building of the new squares, streets and crescents, and the Woods designed the elegant stone terraces and fine public buildings that grace them, using the warm-toned local stone from Allen's Coombe Down quarries. The result is one of the finest planned townscapes in Britain. Many of Bath's loveliest streets, gay with window boxes and hanging baskets of flowers, are now pedestrian areas which have transformed the city centre into a traffic-free haven.

ROUTE DIRECTIONS

Start at Bath Abbey (1), then cross to the Pump Room and Roman Baths (2). Leave by Stall St, turn l. and l. again into York St to the Toy Museum (3). Continue along the street, then turn r. into Abbey St leading to Abbey Grn and l. into North Parade Pass, passing Sally Lunn's House (4). Turn l. along Terrace Walk (at the end of North Par), cross Orange Grove and keep r. along Grand Par. Ahead is Pulteney Br (5). Turn l. through the market. (On Sundays continue, turn l. into Bridge St, and l. again into High St for Guildhall.) On the l. is the Guildhall (6). Cross High St to Northumberland Pl and walk through to Union St. Turn r. and cross Upper Borough Walls to go along Old Bond St into Milsom St (7). On the r. is the Octagon. At George St turn r., cross over and walk up Bartlett St and Saville Row to Bennett St. Turn l. and walk to The Circus, passing the mews where the Carriage Museum (8) is situated. Leave The Circus along Brock St which leads to the Royal Cresc and the period house (9). Return to Margaret's Bldngs and turn l. to reach Catherine Pl. Turn r. along Rivers St, and at the end cross Julian Rd to the Camden Works Museum (10). Return to Bennett St via Russel St. Turn r. and cross over to the Assembly Rooms (11). On leaving, turn l. down the alleyway, then turn r., leading to Miles Bldngs. At George St, turn r., then l. down Gay St to Queen Sq. Turn l. along Wood St, r. down Queen St, l. into Trim St, then turn l. into Upper Borough Walls and turn r. into Union St for the return to the abbey.

At night Bath's majestic abbey is made even more dramatic by floodlighting

1 BATH ABBEY

The building of Bath Abbey, called from the size and number of its windows 'the lantern of the west', is a story of continual checks and setbacks. The first Norman cathedral, replacing the Saxon abbey church, was gutted by fire in 1137, then abandoned until 1499 when Bishop Oliver King began work on the present structure. The Dissolution of the Monasteries in 1539 caused another interruption, but when Elizabeth I visited Bath in 1574, she urged them to complete the abbey. Even so, it was not until the 17th century that the nave was roofed, and then only with timber. The splendid stone fan vaulting that the visitor sees today was not completed until 1864. Inside, the abbey is filled with elaborate 18th-century memorials to the fashionable inhabitants of the city in its heyday.

2 PUMP ROOM AND ROMAN BATHS

In the elegant Pump Room, completed at the end of the 18th century, a statue of Beau Nash celebrates the man who made Bath the most fashionable spa in the country. Here visitors to Bath gathered to taste the waters and to meet each other – a scene eloquently described by Jane Austen in *Northanger Abbey*.

An 18th-century sedan chair displayed in the Pump Room

Coffee and afternoon tea are now served in these gracious surroundings, and music is provided by the Pump Room ensemble. The Roman Baths were lost to view for centuries, and the Great Bath was only re-discovered in 1878. It is lined with lead sheets, dating from the Roman period, which are still intact. Other small baths, cold plunges and the hypocaust room can also be seen, and the museum adjoining the baths contains a superb collection of Roman remains.

3 BURROWS TOY MUSEUM

Closed 1987

This delightful little museum houses a staggering array of children's toys of the past three centuries from all over the world. There are examples of everything from cheap penny toys to exquisite dolls and beautifully made dolls' houses.

4 SALLY LUNN'S HOUSE

Situated in picturesque Old Lilliput Alley, which connects the charming old square of Abbey Green with North Parade, Sally Lunn's House dates from 1482 and is reputedly the oldest inhabited house in Bath. Sally Lunn, who gave her name to the teacakes she made (which are still sold locally), lived here around 1680. Her house is, fittingly, a tea shop.

5 PULTENEY BRIDGE
The design of Pulteney Bridge, built by Robert Adam in 1770, was inspired by the famous Ponte Vecchio in Florence, but does not look at all out of place in Bath. It is the only bridge in England completely lined with shops on both sides.

6 GUILDHALL
Next door to the fine old covered market, the Guildhall, designed by Thomas Baldwin and completed in 1775, contains a magnificent Banqueting Hall, with walls and ceilings decorated with plasterwork in the Adam style.

7 MILSOM STREET
In Jane Austen's day, young ladies spent much of their time and money in Milsom Street, then as now the main shopping street of Bath. The grand stone buildings were designed by John Wood the elder, and like Gay Street, Milsom Street links the lower and the upper parts of the city. Just off Milsom Street, the 18th-century Octagon building, once a private chapel, is now the museum of the Royal Photographic Society and exhibits a remarkable collection of historic photographs and photographic equipment.

Carriage and patient horse at the Carriage Museum

8 CARRIAGE MUSEUM
Visitors can give themselves a taste of 18th-century life by taking a carriage ride from the museum in Circus Mews. There are more than 30 carriages on display in the old stables, which once served the residents of the elegant terraces in The Circus.

9 THE CIRCUS AND ROYAL CRESCENT
These two superb architectural compositions were created by John Wood the elder and his son, John Wood the younger. The father died in 1754, just as work was starting on The Circus, which he had planned as a perfect circle. From the Circus, Brock Street leads into the magnificent curve of Royal Crescent, placed high on the hillside overlooking Royal Victoria Park and the surrounding Avon countryside. No. 1 Royal Crescent, the house designed by John Wood the younger for his father-in-law, Thomas Brock, has been meticulously restored by the Bath Preservation Trust, and contains beautiful period furniture, displayed in its original setting.

10 CAMDEN WORKS MUSEUM
This fascinating museum preserves and displays an almost forgotten side of Bath – its Victorian industrial heritage. J. B. Bowler was a small family firm of engineers and brass founders, with a profitable sideline in mineral waters, which remained in business from the 1870s to 1969. The museum is laid out as the original works – which were demolished in 1972. As visitors enter, they see the old shop counter, with its boxes of nails, screws, door handles, light bulbs and general ironmongery – Mr Bowler never threw anything away. The collection is a unique record of the daily running of a 19th-century business and the part it played in town life.

11 ASSEMBLY ROOMS AND MUSEUM OF COSTUME
Completed in 1771 by John Wood the younger, these elegant reception rooms were known as the Upper Rooms to distinguish them from the earlier assembly rooms in North Parade (the Lower Rooms). Fashionable society met here for concerts and other genteel evening entertainments. In the basement is the Museum of Costume, based on the collection of Mrs Doris Langley Moore. It covers the fashions of four centuries, from 1580 to the present day. Most sumptuous are the royal and ceremonial clothes in the Modern Room.

PARKING: *Broad St, Manvers St, Walcot St.*

OPENING TIMES:

Roman Baths & Pump Room: open all year.

Burrows Toy Museum: open all year.

Guildhall: open all year. Mon–Fri all day.

Octagon (National Centre of Photography): open all year.

Carriage Museum: as above.

1 Royal Crescent: open summer only. Tue–Sat all day, Sun pm only.

Camden Works: open all year. Mon–Sun pm only. (Closed Fri – winter only.)

Assembly Rooms and Museum of Costume: as above.

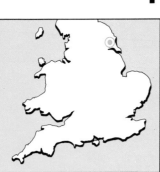

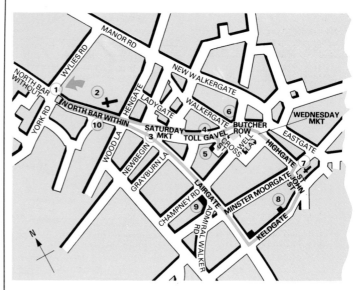

ROUTE DIRECTIONS

Start at North Bar (1) and walk along North Bar Within towards the town centre, passing St Mary's Church (2). Enter Saturday Mkt (3) and keep left, passing the Corn Exchange, and then continue into Toll Gavel (4). Cross Toll Gavel and enter Cross St to reach the Guildhall (5). Return to Toll Gavel and turn r. to enter Butcher Row, where the Regimental Museum (6) stands, and enter Wednesday Mkt. Leave by Highgate to reach the Minster (7). Leave the Minster by the Highgate entrance, and turn l. into Minster Moorgate, then turn l. along St John St, turning r. into Keldgate (8), passing Ann Routh's Hospital and the Old School House, before turning r. into Lairgate, where The Hall (9) is, and return along North Bar Within (10) to North Bar.

FRID STOOL

Older than the Minster itself, the Frid (or Frith Stool) is the great church's rarest possession, dating back to pre-Conquest England. The stool is a simple stone seat that gave the right of sanctuary. For centuries fugitives found refuge here, and thus won 30 days grace during which time the canons of the Minster attempted to reconcile the opposing parties.

Beverley has not just one, but two magnificent Gothic churches; both the pinnacled tower of St Mary's at one end of the main street, and the twin towers of the Minster at the other, are familiar landmarks for miles around. Between these two great buildings narrow medieval streets and pleasant market squares are graced by red-brick Georgian houses built by the landed gentry of the East Riding during the town's heyday as a fashionable resort.

1 NORTH BAR AND BAR HOUSE

At one time a deep, wide ditch encircled the town and the only way into it was over one of the five drawbridges which were each defended by a gateway or Bar. North Bar, the only survivor of these, was built in 1409 and is consequently one of the earliest surviving examples of English brickwork. Adjoining the west side of the Bar is Bar House – a pleasant mid 19th century building where local artist F. W. Elwell lived for 42 years from 1870.

2 ST MARY'S CHURCH

Were it not for the beautiful Minster, St Mary's Parish Church would easily be the most magnificent building in the town. The splendid West Front with its pinnacled towers was completed in 1420. In 1520, during morning service, the original Norman tower collapsed, killing many members of the congregation, and was replaced by a magnificent Tudor tower. The merchant guilds favoured the church which meant there were many contributions to its rebuilding, and inscriptions on the 'Minstrels Pillar' record these benefactors. Of particular note are the misericords, and the ceiling, which consists of painted panels depicting 40 English kings; and there is a carving by Robert Thompson of a rabbit believed to have given Lewis Carroll the inspiration for the White Rabbit in *Alice in Wonderland*.

3 SATURDAY MARKET

This irregularly-shaped market place replaced the older market place – Wednesday Market – when the town spread northwards. It is dominated by the Market Cross which was built in 1711 to replace an earlier one. Its stone pillars were supposed to be far enough apart to allow carriages to be driven through. Two of the town's MPs, Sir Charles Hotham and Sir Michael Warton, contributed to the cost and their coats of arms, together with those of both Queen Anne and Beverley, can be seen on the cross. Handsome town shops surround it.

Beverley Minster was founded in the 8th century, but the present building is mostly in the superb gothic style of the 12th to 15th centuries

4 TOLL GAVEL

The curious name of this street dates from the days when tolls were collected. It is one of the town's busiest modern shopping areas now, but there are one or two old buildings of interest to look out for. Number 44 used to be a chemist's shop, as the snakes entwined around the door posts show – snakes are the symbol of Aesculapius, the god of medicine. Further along at No.65 is the former home of the 18th-century benefactress, Ann Routh.

5 THE GUILDHALL

A guildhall has stood on this site since about 1500, but it was largely rebuilt in 1762 by William Middleton. Later, the Mayor's Parlour and public gallery were added – the latter's pillars being taken from the Minster in 1826. The impressive and elegant courtroom has a royal coat of arms and a rococo ceiling depicting Justice unblindfolded. The borough's ancient seals and civic treasures are also kept here and may be viewed by arrangement.

6 THE REGIMENTAL MUSEUM

Started in 1920, this was one of the first infantry museums to be established in Britain and since 1963 has been housed at 11 Butcher Row. The exhibits are displayed in six rooms of this pleasant old house and include regimental silver, medals, uniforms, badges and trophies.

The Market Cross in Saturday Market Place. The Minster stands behind

7 THE MINSTER

Twin towers soar up above the rooftops of the town as a constant reminder that here is one of the most beautiful pieces of Gothic architecture in Europe. The church was actually begun during the 13th century and although several phases of rebuilding followed, the whole harmonises completely. The wealth of beauty and detail throughout the Minster is immense, but carving both in stone and wood is one of its most outstanding features, and nowhere is this more apparent than in the choir, where the collection of misericords is incomparable. Another great treasure is the famous Percy Shrine, probably built for Lady Eleanor, wife of the first Lord Percy. Its canopy, one of the richest and most elaborately carved monuments in Britain, displays a profusion of angels, cherubs, knights, flowers and vines. The Minster clock is unique in that it strikes in both towers at once.

8 KELDGATE

Ann Routh built an almshouse (now known as Ann Routh's Hospital) to the right of Keldgate in 1749 and the plaque in the middle of the building is a memorial to philanthropy in Georgian Beverley. Old School House, a little further along this pleasant street, dates from the 17th century when it was built for Beverley Grammar School.

9 THE HALL

Built in 1700, this fine house has tended to be named after its occupiers and was first known as Pennyman House when Sir James Pennyman, a mayor and MP, lived there. He was responsible for major alterations – particularly the reception rooms designed by Carr. Both the Chinese room and dining room have splendid stucco ceilings and the design of the former incorporates musical instruments and has beautiful hand-painted Chinese wallpaper. Later, the house was known as Admiral Walker House after Admiral Walker who lived here until 1925 when the Borough Council bought it.

10 NORTH BAR WITHIN

Standing on the left-hand side of the road is an 18th-century pub now called the Beverley Arms but formerly known as the Blue Bell. The novelist Anthony Trollope stayed here when he stood as a parliamentary candidate for the town in 1868. Another 18th-century coaching inn, the Tiger, has been converted into a row of small shops.

EARLY CLOSING: *Thu.*

MARKET DAY: *Sat.*

PARKING: *Saturday Mkt, Wilbert La.*

OPENING TIMES:

Regimental Museum: open all year. Tue – Fri pm only.

5 | BRIGHTON

In 1754 Dr Richard Russell moved to Brighton. His belief in curing most ills by bathing in and drinking sea water transformed the rather poor fishing village of Brighthelmstone into one of the most fashionable resorts along the south coast. Now, the legacies from its past – the fascinating old Lanes, the amazing Pavilion, the pier – combined with the modern shopping and entertainment facilities that have developed, draw more visitors than ever to this historic seaside town.

ROUTE DIRECTIONS

The walk starts by the George IV statue, near the junction of Marlborough Pl and Church St. Turn l. along Church St past the entrances to the Royal Pavilion (1) and the Dome (2). Continue along Church St over Queens Rd and turn l. into the churchyard of St Nicholas Church (3). Leave by a footpath to the l. of the church which joins Dyke Rd. Continue to the traffic lights and negotiate the junction around the clock tower (4) by crossing Queens Rd and North St into West St. Turn l. into Duke St, r. into Middle St and shortly turn l. again into Dukes La which enters The Lanes (5). Continue through an arcade into Ship St and turn l. Immediately turn r. into Union St (a footpath through The Lanes) and at the end turn r. into Meeting House La and follow it round to the l. Continue through the narrow passageway into a paved square. Cross the square, descend the steps, and turn r., passing the Druid's Head. Continue until the lane opens out and cross into Market St. On reaching the Sussex public house, take the footpath alongside it which emerges in East St. Turn l. and then r. into Steine La and continue to Old Steine (6). Turn r. here and continue to Pool Valley and turn r. At the Bus Station bear l. and cross over to the sea-front. Turn l. and continue along Grand Junction Rd to Palace Pier (7). Continue into Madeira Dr, passing the Aquarium and Dolphinarium (8) on the l., to reach the Volks Railway (9) terminus. From here ascend the staircase at the end of the shopping arcade up to Marine Par. Turn sharp l. here and then turn r. into Camelford St. At the end turn l. into St James's St then r. into Dorset Gdns. Turn l. at the end into Edward St and on reaching Grand Par, cross by the pedestrian crossing and turn r. along by the Royal Pavilion then turn l. back to the George IV statue.

1 ROYAL PAVILION

When, in 1783, the Prince Regent, soon to become George IV, made his first visit to the town, he rented a small farmhouse in The Steine which was destined to become one of the most famous buildings in Britain. In 1785 the Prince married and brought his bride to Brighton where they gathered around them a court of high society friends. As the farmhouse soon became too small for the Prince's requirements, he commissioned his architect, Henry Holland, to rebuild it as an elegant, classical villa, which was later transformed by John Nash into the exotic and bizarre extravaganza that can be seen today. The addition of domes, minarets and cupolas turned it into an Indian mogul's palace, and this oriental exterior is more than equalled by its sumptuous interior.

2 THE DOME

The Dome, built in the same style as the Pavilion between 1803 and 1805 as stables and a riding school for use by the Prince Regent, has since been divided into an art gallery and museum, a concert hall and an exhibition hall. Of particular interest to the visitor to Brighton is the seaside exhibition on the upper floor of the art gallery and museum. This traces the history of the seaside resort in general, but spotlights Brighton in particular, and features models of the Old Chain Pier, terraces of Regency houses and Brighton as it was in 1805, together with examples of period bathing costumes and accessories and vintage slot machines, including a famous 'what the butler saw'.

3 ST NICHOLAS CHURCH

This largely 14th-century church contains an elaborately carved Norman font depicting the last supper and scenes from the life of St Nicholas. Among those buried in the churchyard is Martha Gunn, 'queen' of the 'Dippers' – the attendants who looked after women bathers in the 18th century. She became a favourite of George IV, and a portrait of her now hangs in Buckingham Palace.

4 THE CLOCK TOWER

Like many ornate clock towers, this one was erected in 1888 to commemorate Queen Victoria's Jubilee the previous year. The clock face has gilt Roman numerals, and a gilt time-ball which can rise and fall precisely on the hour.

5 THE LANES

This attractive corner of the town is all that is left of the 17th-century fishing village of Brighthelmstone. The Lanes were the focal area of the village and although few of the present buildings are older than the 18th century, the existing network of alleys represents the town's medieval street pattern. Today the narrow passageways connect the many antique shops, jewellery shops, picture galleries, pubs and cafés which are housed in the bow-fronted 18th-century cottages.

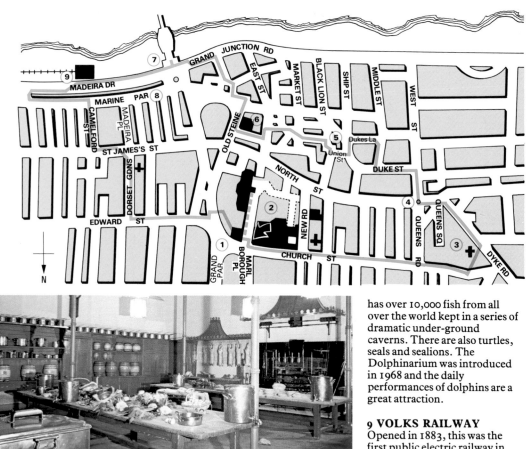

Copper equipment in the kitchen at
Brighton Pavilion

6 THE STEINE
Around The Steine are a
number of the elegant houses
typical of Regency Brighton.
Next to Steine House, once the
home of Mrs Fitzherbert, the
Prince Regent's lover, stands
the most important of these –
Marlborough House, now the
tourist information centre.
Originally built for the 4th
Duke of Marlborough, it was
sold in 1786 and subsequently
transformed by Robert Adam.

Palace Pier revives memories of
Edwardian England

7 PALACE PIER
Built in 1899 and opened to the
public in 1901, Palace Pier
stands just west of the site of the
old Chain Pier, which was the
first pleasure pier ever built in
England. The original pier,
which resembled a suspension
bridge, was destroyed by a
storm in 1896. Palace Pier
measures a third of a mile in
length, and boasts an elaborate
dome and pagoda-shaped roof
which echoes the style of the
Royal Pavilion.

8 AQUARIUM AND
DOLPHINARIUM
Established by a private
company in 1869, the Aquarium
has over 10,000 fish from all
over the world kept in a series of
dramatic under-ground
caverns. There are also turtles,
seals and sealions. The
Dolphinarium was introduced
in 1968 and the daily
performances of dolphins are a
great attraction.

9 VOLKS RAILWAY
Opened in 1883, this was the
first public electric railway in
Britain. The engineer
responsible for it was Magnus
Volk, a leading pioneer in the
use of electricity at the time.
The carriages have a smart
chocolate brown and yellow
livery, and are monogrammed
with the initials VR – which
craftily implies royal patronage
as Queen Victoria was a regular
visitor to the town when the
railway opened.

PARKING: *King St, Dyke Rd,*
Bread St, Market St.

OPENING TIMES:

Royal Pavilion: open all year, except
Christmas.

Art Gallery & Museum: open all
year, except Good Fri & Christmas.
Tue–Sat all day, Sun pm only.

Aquarium & Dolphinarium: open
all year.

Volks Railway: open daily, summer
only.

6 | BRISTOL

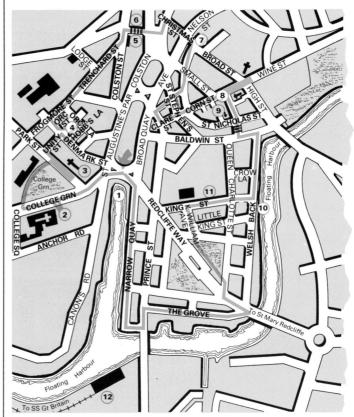

ROUTE DIRECTIONS

Start from Neptune's statue at the head of St Augustine's Reach of the Floating Harbour (1). Cross Canon's Rd and turn l. up College Grn to the cathedral (2). Leave the cathedral and walk across College Grn to Park St. A few yards down on the r. is the Lord Mayor's Chapel (3). Go down Unity St, turn r. into Denmark St and l. into Hobb's La past Harvey's Wine Museum (4). Turn l. into Orchard La, l. into Orchard St and r. into Denmark Ave. By the Hatchet pub, turn r. into Frogmore St and continue into Trenchard St. Cross into Colston St and turn l., passing The Foster Almshouses (5) before turning r. down Christmas Steps (6). Cross the dual carriageway, turning l. and r. into Christmas St, at the end of which is St John's Church and the old city gate (7). Through the gate, turn r. into Bell La, crossing Small St to Leonard La. Opposite the craft centre is an alley leading to St Stephen's St. Turn l. and soon turn r. down the alley to St Stephen's Ave. Turn l. and at the crossroads, turn l. into Clare St. Continue into Corn St (8) past the Corn Exchange to Christ Church at the end of Corn St. Return along Corn St and turn l. down All Saints La, passing the church, to reach St Nicholas Mkt. Continue into St Nicholas St and cross to St Nicholas Church (9). Go down the steps to Baldwin St and cross to Welsh Back (10), walking alongside the harbour to King St. Turn r. along King St (11) passing the Llandoger Trow, and the Theatre Royal then l. into King William Ave to Queen Sq. Cross the square to Redcliffe Way, turning l. then sharp r. to The Grove. (For a detour to St Mary Redcliffe, keep on to Redcliffe Br and cross over to the church.) Walk alongside the Harbour beside the car park, then rejoin The Grove. At Prince St turn l. For a detour to the Industrial Museum and the SS Great Britain (12), cross the Swing Bridge and turn r. along Prince's Wharf. The main walk turns r. before the Swing Bridge to reach Narrow Quay, which brings you back to the start.

O riginally known as Bricgstow – the place by the bridge – Bristol began to grow during Anglo-Saxon times and rapidly developed into an important trading community and port that had gained city status by the 16th century. Today, it is still an important port and commercial centre and although the 20th century has invaded the city, its rich heritage has survived. Historic inns, beautiful churches, restored warehouses and fine 18th-century houses all recall a prosperous and fascinating past.

1 THE FLOATING HARBOUR

Neptune's statue, close to the famous Hippodrome Theatre, stands in small gardens at the head of the Floating Harbour. Nearby are a number of plaques which serve as reminders of Bristol's maritime history: one records that John Cabot sailed from Bristol to the New World in 1497; another notes Captain Thomas James's expedition to explore the North-West Passage, and yet another commemorates Bristol-born Samuel Plimsoll, originator of the famous load line for ships.

2 BRISTOL CATHEDRAL

Founded as the Abbey Church of St Augustine, Bristol Cathedral was built in various stages from the 12th to 15th centuries. The interior is rich in fine carving, both in wood and stone, especially in the Elder Lady Chapel and the choir, where there is a fine organ case carved by Grinling Gibbons. The cloisters, leading to the beautiful Norman chapter house, have fine stained-glass windows along their entire length.

VIRTUTE·ET·INDUSTRIA

3 LORD MAYOR'S CHAPEL

The only chapel in the country owned by a city corporation – it was given to them by Henry VIII – this delightful little church was part of the Hospital of the Gaunts, founded in 1220 by Maurice Gaunt, an ancestor of the Lord of Berkeley.

4 HARVEY'S WINE MUSEUM

As the home of some of Britain's foremost wine shippers, Bristol contains many wine bonds. Beneath Harvey's solid stone warehouse on Hobb's Lane, the

13th-century cellars of Gaunt's Hospital have been converted into an interesting wine museum. Visits must be pre-arranged.

5 FOSTER ALMSHOUSES
Founded by a 15th-century mayor of Bristol, John Foster, the almshouses were rebuilt in the 19th century with pleasing little pointed turrets in the Burgundian Gothic style. The houses are grouped around a galleried courtyard, on one side of which is the Chapel of the Three Kings of Cologne, which dates from the original foundation.

6 CHRISTMAS STEPS
The well-to-do wine merchant and local benefactor Jonathan Blackwell had this steep, narrow alley stepped at his own expense in 1669, and also thoughtfully provided seats.

7 ST JOHN'S CHURCH AND GATE
St John's is the last of the nine gates that once gave access to the walled city, and the church above its archway is the last of five that were originally incorporated into the city walls.

8 CORN STREET
The heart of Bristol's business area, Corn Street contains many flamboyant Victorian buildings. Outside the magnificent 18th-century Corn Exchange are the four bronze pillars known as the 'nails', on which merchants used to make cash transactions, hence the expression 'to pay on the nail', i.e. in cash.

9 ST NICHOLAS CHURCH AND MUSEUM
Only the crypt, with its exceptional roof bosses, remains of the medieval church, which was rebuilt in the 18th century, and again after the last war. The main part of the church now houses a fascinating museum of the history of Bristol, and also exhibits many church treasures.

10 WELSH BACK
This part of the quay was, in medieval times, the old port of Bristol and the place where Welsh market produce, shipped in coastal vessels, was unloaded. A rock music centre is housed in the old Granary, a remarkable structure, built in a style known as 'Bristol Byzantine'.

11 KING STREET
Here stands the Llandoger Trow public house, the best 17th-century timbered house in Bristol, three storeys high, gabled and with many picturesque oriels. Higher up, near St Nicholas's Almshouses, the Theatre Royal, home of the Bristol Old Vic, is the oldest theatre in the country. It was built in 1746.

Carving on the prow of SS Great Britain

ST MARY REDCLIFFE (detour)
From the spacious, 18th-century Queen Square, it is a short walk across the Redcliffe swing bridge to this 'fairest, goodliest, and most famous parish church in England', as Queen Elizabeth I described St Mary's. The inner north porch is the oldest part of the church, and the outer porch, in a rare hexagonal shape, features an intricate carved arch.

12 BRISTOL INDUSTRIAL MUSEUM AND THE SS *GREAT BRITAIN* (detour)
From Prince Street, a short detour across the swing bridge leads to the industrial museum and adjoining National Lifeboat Museum, and a rather longer riverside walk to the SS *Great Britain*. In the museum can be seen displays relating to the history of land transport, horse-drawn and mechanised, and shipping. Also, exhibits of machinery and manufacturing tell the story of Bristol's development as an engineering and aviation centre. The SS *Great Britain*, designed by Brunel, was the first ocean-going propeller-driven iron ship.

EARLY CLOSING: *Wed, Sat.*

PARKING: *Canon's Marsh (off Canon's Rd, opp. Bristol Exhibition Complex).*

OPENING TIMES:

St Mark's Chapel (Lord Mayor's Chapel): open all year except Aug. Sun – Fri all day.

St Nicholas Church Museum: open all year except Christmas, New Year, Easter & May BH. Mon – Sat all day.

Bristol Industrial Museum: open all year except Christmas, New Year, and Good Fri. Sat – Wed all day.

National Lifeboat Museum: open Mon – Sun summer only.

SS Great Britain: open all year except Christmas.

The capital of the old county of West Suffolk, this ancient market and cathedral town takes its name from the Saxon King of East Anglia who was martyred by the Danes in AD 870 and whose remains were eventually buried in the monastery here. The town plan today is essentially that laid out in the late 11th century by Abbot Baldwin, creating a square for God (Angel Hill) and a square for man (the market place in Cornhill).

ROUTE DIRECTIONS

Start at the market place in Cornhill beside Moyse's Hall Museum (1). Cross Cornhill to the Traverse, with the Market Cross (2) on the r., and continue past the Cupola House (3) to the end of the street. Turn l. into Abbeygate St, then at end r. into Angel Hill past the Angel Hotel (4) to reach the Athenaeum (5). Return across Angel Hill past Abbeygate St to Angel Corner (6). Cross to the Abbey Gate (7) then through the arch into the Abbey Gardens (8). Take the path to l. turning r. at gate marked 'private' then keep l. and cross to Abbots' Br (9). Follow riverside path and by footbridge turn r. passing the Abbey ruins (10). Take outer path l. around formal gardens to sundial and turn l. past rose garden. Leave the gardens by gate at the east end of the cathedral (11) and turn r. to the Norman Tower then l. through Chequer Sq into Crown St for St Mary's Church (12). Walk on down Crown St past the brewery to Theatre Royal (13). Turn r. into Westgate St then second r. into College St, then l. into Churchgate St past the Pentecostal Church (14) At the end of the street, turn r. into Guildhall St. Cross the junction with Abbeygate St and return to Cornhill.

1 MOYSE'S HALL

Built in 1180, Moyse's Hall is thought to be the oldest Norman house in East Anglia. It is popularly said to have been built as a Jew's hall, or synagogue, but there is no documentary evidence, and Moyse is an old-established Suffolk surname. Before it was adapted as the Borough Museum in 1899, it had served as a workhouse and house of correction. In the lower room, partitioned in the 15th century, the old Norman arches can still be seen. The museum is devoted to the history and natural history of Suffolk; collections include Bronze Age weapons and finds from a Saxon village.

2 THE MARKET CROSS

Formerly the old town hall, the market cross is a 17th-century building, badly damaged by fire in 1608 and rebuilt in 1774 to designs by Robert Adam. The upper floor is now an art gallery, used for temporary exhibitions.

3 THE CUPOLA HOUSE

This fine late 17th-century building takes its name from the cupola which surmounts the roof. It was the home of Cox Macro, a local antiquarian and alderman. The façade, with its projecting second-floor balcony and attractive ground-floor bow windows, is unusually decorative. Nearby is the Nutshell, reputed to be the smallest public house in Britain.

4 & 5 ANGEL HILL

Despite its name, this is a spacious, elegant square, laid out on the slope leading up from the abbey gateway. The Angel Hotel, built in 1779, is where Charles Dickens stayed in 1859 and 1861, immortalising it in *Pickwick Papers* as the place where Mr Pickwick received news of the breach-of-promise action against him by Mrs Bardell. Beyond the hotel is the Athenaeum, a magnificent late 18th-century building. The interior has a fine ballroom.

This fine clock echoes the elegance of Angel Hill

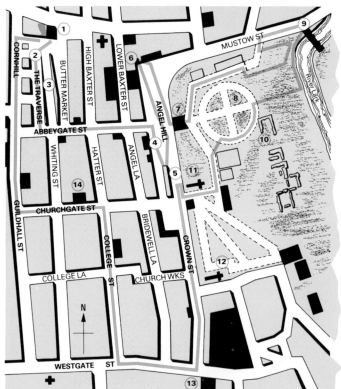

The Nutshell pub is Britain's smallest public house

Inside the Theatre Royal

11 CATHEDRAL CHURCH OF ST JAMES

There were once three parish churches on the perimeter of the abbey – St Mary's and St James (the cathedral church), being the only two that have survived. St James was considerably extended in 1959 to make it more fitting as a cathedral. Of particular interest is the attractive hammerbeam roof with its painted angels holding shields with the insignia of St James, St Edmund and St George. The statue of St Edmund outside the south side is a bronze by the modern sculptress Elizabeth Frink. The tower, an outstanding example of Norman architecture, originally served as one of the gateways to the abbey precinct. It was built in the 12th century and restored in 1864; it is still used as the cathedral belfry.

12 ST MARY'S CHURCH

One of the largest parish churches in England, St Mary's dates from the 15th century. The nave is famous for its angel roof, and the waggon roof of the chancel is also noteworthy. That of the Baret chantry chapel is charmingly decorated with stars, each containing mirror glass to reflect the sunlight.

13 THEATRE ROYAL

Built in 1819, this delightful Regency theatre stands hard by the Greene King Brewery which dominates Crown Street and is still a family-run concern. The theatre, the third oldest in England, has now been immaculately restored to its former elegance by the National Trust and is once again in use as a theatre after many ignominious years when it served as a barrel store.

14 PENTECOSTAL CHURCH

Formerly the Unitarian Chapel, this Queen Anne building, erected in 1711, follows closely the style of Sir Christopher Wren and is regarded as one of the finest examples of a Nonconformist chapel in Britain. It contains a double-decker pulpit and its original 'horse-box pews' which have been moved up into the gallery. Set in the wall above the entrance is a charming sundial.

6 ANGEL CORNER

This fine Queen Anne house, on the far side of Angel Hill, contains the John Gersham-Parkington Memorial Collection of clocks and watches, one of the most important collections outside London. There are timepieces by many of the famous craftsmen, some dating back to the 16th century, as well as a range of associated instruments, such as sundials, quadrants and compasses; all are immaculately kept and displayed.

7 ABBEY GATE

Built in about 1347 following the destruction by the townspeople of the previous gateway in an uprising against the Abbot, this typical example of the Decorated style of architecture formed the principal entrance to the monastic buildings. Its massive battlemented structure was designed as much for defence as for ornament. The niches which decorate the facade would once have contained sculpted figures.

8, 9 & 10 ABBEY GARDENS AND RUINS

Beautifully laid-out formal gardens form the centrepiece of the grounds, and lead down to the Abbot's Bridge, which was built in the early 13th century to give access to the monks' vineyards which lay beyond the River Lark. The buttresses on the north side are pierced with holes that once held poles supporting a wooden bridge by which the townspeople were able to cross the river without entering the abbey grounds. A riverside path leads past a hexagonal dovecot to the abbey ruins. The monastery, originally founded in the 7th century, became an important place of pilgrimage after Edmund's body was placed here in about 900. At the High Altar, rebellious barons met in 1214 to swear an oath to raise arms against King John if he would not sign *Magna Carta*. The town's motto, 'Shrine of a King, Cradle of the Law', derives partly from this momentous gathering and partly from the Shrine of St Edmund which drew many pilgrims to the abbey. By the gate at the east end of the cathedral is all that has survived of the immense west front of the abbey church. Stripped of its facing stone after the Dissolution of the Monasteries, there are Tudor, Georgian and Victorian houses built into it, giving it the appearance of a folly.

EARLY CLOSING: *Thu.*

MARKET DAYS: *Wed, Sat.*

PARKING: *Angel Hill.*

OPENING TIMES:

Moyse's Hall Museum: *open all year except Christmas, New Year & Good Fri. Mon–Sat all day.*

Art Gallery: *open all year except as above. Tue–Sat all day, Sun pm only.*

Angel Corner: *open all year except as above. Mon–Sat all day.*

Abbey Gardens: *open all year.*

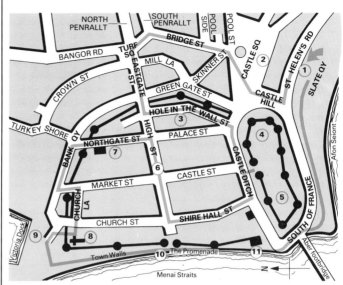

ROUTE DIRECTIONS

Start from the Slate Quay (1). Go up Castle Hill (to the r. of the castle) then r. into Castle Sq (2). Turn l. along Bridge St and turn l. into Turf Sq. Continue into Eastgate St to the arch in the town wall. Go through this and turn immediately l. into Hole in the Wall St (3). At the end turn r. into Castle Ditch to reach the Castle (4) where the Royal Welch Fusiliers Museum (5) is housed. Continue the walk along Castle Ditch and turn r. into Shire Hall St then r. again into the High St (6). Turn l. into Northgate St (7), past the Blackboy Inn, and continue through the town-wall arch then turn l. into Bank Quay. Turn l. into Market St through another arch and turn immediately r. into Church La which leads to St Mary's Church (8) in Church St. Leave the churchyard by turning l. through another wall arch to Victoria Dock (9). Continue towards the sea and turn l. along the Promenade (10), following the town walls to the Anglesey Hotel (11). (A short detour can be made from here across Aber Bridge. A walk to the l. affords fine views of the castle.) Continue from the hotel for the return to Slate Quay.

Caernarfon's grimly impressive castle and massive 13th-century town walls overshadow the town in every sense of the word. Even though the town attracts thousands of visitors every year, it still retains something of the atmosphere established during the Middle Ages. Tiny, terraced houses, ancient inns and quaint shops, crowding together in narrow streets against the giant walls, contrast strikingly with the awe-inspiring grandeur of the greatest fortress in Wales.

1 SLATE QUAY

During the late 19th century this must have been constantly busy with cargo ships plying in and out of the harbour with their loads of slate and coal. Recalling Caernarfon's days as an important port is the stone Harbour Master's Office, built in 1840. Today the river is alive with fishing and pleasure craft, and during the summer there are boat trips from the quay.

2 CASTLE SQUARE

The Welsh call this Y Maer, which means The Field, and although the square is far from being a meadow, it is a pleasant open space that teems with traders and shoppers every market day. Dark bronze

statues of two of Wales' most famous figures – Lloyd George and Sir Hugh Owen – stand in the square, along with a small fountain commemorating several cholera victims who died before the disease was conquered in Britain.

3 HOLE IN THE WALL STREET
Terraces of colour-washed houses lying in the shadow of the town wall rise up on either side of this narrow street which represents the heart of the ancient town of Caernarfon. On the right is the stone market building dating from 1832, which houses a variety of attractive gift and clothes shops.

4 CAERNARFON CASTLE
Frequently called the finest castle in Britain, this massive fortress has dominated the town since Edward I built it as the chief stronghold in his chain of defensive castles around Wales. Today, although little more than an empty shell, its brown and cream stone walls and tall turreted towers present a façade which is as impressive as ever. It was here that the first Prince of Wales – Edward II – was born, and centuries later two other princes – Prince Edward (later Edward VIII) and Prince Charles were invested with the same title

during ceremonies held on the grassy wards within the castle walls. One of the most fascinating defensive features of the castle is its continuous system of wall passages around the inner faces of the towers.

5 ROYAL WELCH FUSILIERS REGIMENTAL MUSEUM
Housed in the Queen's Tower of the castle, the museum was set up in 1960 by the trustees of the regiment. The exhibits represent almost 300 years of the regiment's history and include relics from the Napoleonic Wars, the Crimean War, the Indian Mutiny, the Boer War and the two World Wars, as well as numerous uniforms, medals, swords and personal relics.

6 HIGH STREET
A channel runs beneath the street carrying the Afon Cadnant, which was diverted underground to make way for traffic, into Victoria Dock. West Gate, at one end of the street, is known as the Golden Gate – possibly because lovely sunsets over the Menai Strait can be seen through it. East Gate at the other end had a large tower on it until 1963 when it was removed for safety reasons. At the base of the arch in Bank Quay there is a very small cell which was used as the town lock-up until 1835.

7 NORTHGATE STREET
A colourful tale is associated with the name of this street. The Welsh call it 'Stryd Pedwar a Chwech', meaning Four and Six Street, which apparently dates back to the time when sailors could have a hammock for the night here for fourpence; an extra sixpence would secure female company as well. Near the town wall is the famous Blackboy Inn, officially dated 17th-century but possibly as much as 300 years older.

8 ST MARY'S CHURCH
Henry de Allerton, assistant master mason at the castle, founded St Mary's in 1307 for the garrison, but although its origins are so ancient, much of the present building was reconstructed in the 19th century. The church seems to grow out of the town wall and one of the drum towers is used as a vestry.

9 VICTORIA DOCK
This was built during the 1870s as part of a much larger development plan for the entire quayside which never materialised. A small maritime museum, run by volunteers, has recently opened here in a whitewashed stone building. Moored alongside is the SS *Seiont II*, which belongs to the museum. It was purchased in 1980 for restoration.

10 THE PROMENADE
Dating from the 13th century, the walls are virtually still complete and form a dramatic and striking feature of the town. The Promenade follows the seaward length of the walls and provides a very pleasant walk, with Anglesey just visible across the Menai Strait.

11 ANGLESEY HOTEL AND HANGING TOWER
A customs house before 1822, when it was turned into a public house, the Anglesey Hotel is the last secular building in the town still attached to the castle walls. Behind the bar is a bottle of water from the Sargasso Sea, containing a few of the millions of elvers that hatch there every year. The squat round tower next to the hotel is known as the hanging tower because it used to be a place of execution.

EARLY CLOSING: *Thu.*

MARKET DAY: *Sat.*

PARKING: *Slate Quay, Bank Quay.*

OPENING TIMES:

Castle: open all year. Sun am only Oct – Mar.

Maritime Museum: open summer pm's only.

The unforgettable sight of Cambridge is the view of The Backs, the river, and the magnificent Gothic chapel of King's College, dominating the surrounding buildings. Although the town was and is an important market centre, it owes its fame and its prosperity to the University, which was established in the 13th century and soon became one of the most celebrated centres of learning in Europe.

ROUTE DIRECTIONS

Start in the market square and walk to r. of the Guildhall into Peas Hill, then turn r. into Bene't St, passing St Bene't's Church (1), and l. into King's Parade (2). Walk past Corpus Christi College, and St Catherine's, opposite, and continue past St Botolph's Church into Trumpington St (3) for the Fitzwilliam Museum (4), next door to which is Peterhouse. Walk back to Little St Mary's La and turn l. to pass Little St Mary's Church (5). Continue up the lane to Granta Pl, and turn r. to reach Laundress La. At the end cross Silver St and turn r. then l. into Queen's La which leads to Queens' College (6 & 7). Return to Silver St and turn r. to cross the River Cam and take the path r., keeping r. at the fork, to cross The Backs (8) to Queens' Rd. Turn r. and r. again through the back gate of King's College, recrossing the river and turning l. to reach the chapel (9). On leaving, turn r. around the west end of the chapel and go through the gate, passing Clare College on l. Keep on, past the Old Schools, Senate House Passage and Trinity Hall down Trinity La and turn l. at the end down Trinity St. Pass Trinity College (10) and keep on into St John's St, turning l. through the gate of St John's College (11). Walk through to Third Court and go through the arch on the l. to cross the river by the Kitchen Bridge. Keep forward, passing New Court of St John's College to the gateway leading onto Queens' Rd. Turn r., then keep r. into Northampton St and cross into Kettle's Yd for the Art Gallery (12). Walk down the steps and turn r. for the Folk Museum (13). Cross to Magdalene St for Magdalene College (14) and the Round Church (15) and keep on into Sidney St, past Sidney Sussex College. Cross over, turn r. into Market St for Gt St Mary's Church (16) and the return to the Market Sq.

College key:
A Corpus Christi B St Catherine's C Pembroke D Peterhouse E Queens' F King's G Clare H Trinity Hall I Trinity J St John's K Magdalene L Sidney Sussex

1 ST BENE'T'S CHURCH
The oldest building in Cambridgeshire, St Bene't's is believed to have been built about 1025, in the reign of King Cnut. Although the church itself has been considerably altered since Saxon times, the massive tower is virtually unchanged.

2 KING'S PARADE
Once the main street of Cambridge, the Parade retains on the east side a number of interesting 18th-and 19th-century buildings, mostly converted into shops. A fine row of Victorian town houses leads up to Corpus Christi College. Next door stands St Botolph's Church, dedicated to the patron saint of wayfarers, near the site of one of the old town gates.

3 TRUMPINGTON STREET
Beyond St Botolph's, King's Parade becomes Trumpington Street. At the junction with Pembroke Street, notice the wide gutter, usually filled with water. This is part of a 17th-century scheme designed to clean the city ditch which then formed the southern and eastern town boundary. The chapel of Pembroke College, nearby, was designed by Christopher Wren and was the first of his designs to be completed; it was built in 1663–6. Diagonally opposite, Peterhouse is Cambridge's oldest college, founded in 1284 by the Bishop of Ely.

4 FITZWILLIAM MUSEUM
Egyptian, Greek, and Roman antiquities, oriental porcelain and ceramics, armour, coins, medals, manuscripts and European paintings are all gathered together in this magnificent 19th-century building.

5 LITTLE ST MARY'S CHURCH
The original church on this site was dedicated to St Peter, and gave its name to Peterhouse College, which it served as a chapel. In 1350, however, the church collapsed, and when it was rebuilt in 1352 it was dedicated to the Virgin Mary.

6 QUEENS' COLLEGE
Queens' College was founded by two queens. The first patroness was Margaret of Anjou, wife of

Historic King's College has an air of tranquillity in direct contrast to this busy market outside the college.

Henry VI, who wished to emulate his foundation of King's College, and took over a small, medieval college for the purpose. Later, it was re-founded by Elizabeth Woodville, wife of Edward IV. Beyond the main court, with its charming 17th-century sundial, lies the delightful Cloister Court, built at the end of the

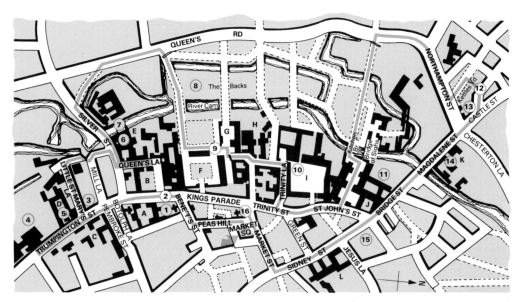

15th century. This was the first court with cloistered walks to be built in Cambridge.

7 THE MATHEMATICAL BRIDGE
This wooden bridge is one of the great curiosities of Cambridge. It was built for Queens' in 1749 on geometric principles, entirely without the use of nails. When it was dismantled in 1867, it proved impossible to reassemble without bolts.

8 THE BACKS
These green lawns bordering the River Cam provide a perfect setting for the college architecture. The land was once a common, on which the townspeople pastured their animals, but from the 16th century onwards it was gradually bought up by the colleges that backed on to the river to make gardens and pleasant walks for their scholars.

9 KING'S COLLEGE CHAPEL
One of the finest Gothic churches in England, the chapel was built in three stages, from 1446 to 1515. To this last phase belongs the magnificent fan-vaulted ceiling. The intricately carved screen and choir stalls, fine examples of Renaissance craftsmanship, date from the mid 16th century. The stained glass forms the most complete set of Renaissance windows to survive in any church in the country.

10 TRINITY COLLEGE
The largest of all Cambridge's colleges, Trinity was created by Henry VIII from three medieval establishments, King's Hall, founded by Edward III, Michaelhouse, and Physwick Hostel. However, by the time of Henry's death only the imposing Great Gate had been completed, and the Great Court, with its spectacular domed fountain, was not built until the reign of Elizabeth I.

Punting on the River Cam

Trinity's finest building, the classical library, was the work of Sir Christopher Wren.

11 ST JOHN'S COLLEGE
Founded in 1511 by Lady Margaret Beaufort, St John's displays architecture of all the succeeding centuries. It has a magnificent three-storey gatehouse, ornamented with carvings of heraldic beasts. The famous 'Bridge of Sighs', modelled on its more famous namesake in Venice, was built in 1831 to link Third Court and New Court on the other side of the River Cam.

12 KETTLE'S YARD ART GALLERY
This fascinating private collection was given to the university in 1960. On display are works by many important modern painters and there are also temporary exhibitions.

13 THE FOLK MUSEUM
The exhibits of local craft and industry feature domestic equipment, tools, farm implements, furniture and children's toys.

14 MAGDALENE COLLEGE
The showpiece of Magdalene is the Pepys Library. Samuel Pepys studied here from 1650 to 1653, and the bookcases and desk were part of his personal library. The famous shorthand diaries in which he recorded daily events are on display here.

15 CHURCH OF THE HOLY SEPULCHRE
Only four round churches remain in England, and nearly all, like this one, founded in 1130 by the Knights Templars, had connections with the Crusades. The shape is based on that of the Church of the Holy Sepulchre at Jerusalem, but during the 14th century a square chancel and north aisle were added to the Norman church.

16 GREAT ST MARY'S
The university church, St Mary's is a fine example of the Perpendicular style, with slender, soaring columns supporting a vaulted roof with massive, carved bosses. From the top of the tower, which was completed in the 17th century, there is a splendid view across the rooftops of the city.

EARLY CLOSING: *Thu.*

MARKET DAYS: *Mon–Sat.*

PARKING: *Park St (off Bridge St), Corn Exchange St.*

OPENING TIMES:
Fitzwilliam Museum: open all year except Good Fri, Christmas & New Year. Tue–Sat all day, Sun pm only.

Kettle's Yard Art Gallery: open all year, pm only.

Folk Museum: open all year except Bank Hols. Tue–Sat all day, Sun pm only.

The Colleges: Most of the colleges admit visitors during daylight hours, though not all their buildings are open to the public. During term-time, especially when examinations are being held, opening hours may be restricted.

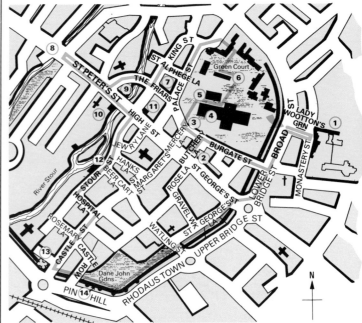

ROUTE DIRECTIONS

Start from the City Wall by the Quenin Gate car park in Broad St. Cross Broad St and go down Lady Wootton's Grn to St Augustine's Abbey (1). Return to Broad St, turn l. (SW) to Burgate St, and turn r. Shortly turn l. along Butchery La for Roman Pavement (2). Return to Burgate St, go through Christchurch Gate (3) and keep to the l. side of Cathedral precincts past the west end of the Cathedral (4). Follow the path through the Cathedral Cloisters (5), turning r. after the Chapter House and l. through Dark Entry into Green Court of the King's School (6). Go l. round Green Court and l. through Green Court Gate into Mint Yd. Mint Yd Gate leads into Palace St, and there turn l. Take first r. down St Alphage La to St Alphage's Church (7), then l. along King St and r. down The Friars. Turn r. along St Peter's St to Westgate (8) then return down St Peter's St to the Weavers House (9) and St Thomas's Hospital (10), opposite. Turn r. down Stour St, with the Royal Museum (11) on l. Pass Poor Priests' Hospital (12) on r. Turn l. into Hospital La and r. down Castle St. Opposite the Castle (13), a footpath (SP East Station and Wincheap) leads to Castle Row. Cross into Dane John Gdns and go up the path to the City Walls (14). Follow the walls round to St George's St and return to Broad St.

Despite the ravages of World War II, Canterbury still retains its medieval character with narrow streets and ancient buildings. Dominating them all is the incomparable cathedral, storehouse of priceless treasures and the setting for many dramatic events in past centuries. The present day has brought the city a modern shopping centre, a new university on the hill to the north and a wealth of local businesses and crafts which make it as varied and colourful as it has ever been.

1 ST AUGUSTINE'S ABBEY

The impressive gateway of St Augustine's Abbey, the Fyndon Gate, stands at the top of Lady Wootton's Green. The abbey entrance is to the left of the gate and leads through to the abbey ruins. The abbey was founded by St Augustine in AD 602, but did not reach its peak until the Middle Ages when it became one of the richest and most influential communities in Britain until Henry VIII dissolved the monastery in 1538 and most of the buildings fell into ruin. By 1848 the

The Old Weaver's House

remaining buildings were turned into a religious training college and they are now an annexe of the King's School.

2 ROMAN PAVEMENT

Beneath one of the new shops in the Longmarket precinct is a well-preserved Roman tessellated pavement which came from one of the rooms in a large courtyard building dating from AD 100. Also on display are other remains of the building and various finds from Roman Canterbury.

A gardener puts the finishing touches to a display at Westgate Gardens

3 CHRISTCHURCH GATE

An elaborate example of Perpendicular architecture, this impressive gateway was built between 1502 and 1519. The fine carved oak doors are closed every evening at 9 pm.

4 CHRISTCHURCH CATHEDRAL

This superbly impressive cathedral must be one of the best-known buildings in the world and has been regarded as the mother church of British Christianity since the 12th century. The oldest part of the present structure, the crypt, dates from 1100, although there are traces of earlier work. St Augustine built a church here in AD 602 but most of the building work was carried out by Archbishop Lanfranc from 1070, and later by Archbishop Anselm. In 1170 the famous and dramatic murder of Archbishop Thomas Becket took place here and from that time onwards the cathedral became the setting for the shrine of the martyr, attracting thousands of pilgrims. The nave, one of the glories of western architecture, was rebuilt in 1400, and Bell Harry tower, which dominates the exterior of the cathedral, was added in 1500. Of all the cathedral's many riches, perhaps none is so priceless as its collection of stained glass. Some of the oldest can be seen in the west window and south-west transept, while a series of 13th-century windows in the Trinity Chapel illustrate miracles performed at Becket's shrine. Contrasting with these are some brilliant modern windows in the south-east transept. Perhaps the most famous tomb in a building full of remarkable memorials is that of Edward, the Black Prince.

5 CATHEDRAL CLOISTERS

Originally the Great Cloister was the centre of the monastery that used to stand next to the cathedral. The cloisters were built in the 14th century and one of their outstanding features is the collection of over 800 colourful roof bosses.

6 THE KING'S SCHOOL

A large courtyard, Green Court, is the centre of this famous public school. Along the north side are ranged the old monastery buildings that house many of the classrooms. The lovely external staircase in the north-west corner is one of the best-known pieces of Norman architecture in Britain.

7 ST ALPHEGE'S CHURCH

Even in 1166 this church was described as 'old', but its actual age is uncertain. It contains several excellent brasses.

8 WESTGATE

Said to be the finest city gate in England, this massive fortification was built by Archbishop Simon of Sudbury in 1380. It served for a time as the city gaol, but now contains a small museum.

9 WEAVER'S HOUSE

Attractively set beside the River Stour, this house was built for a rich merchant in 1561 and accommodated refugee weavers escaping from persecution in the Netherlands.

10 ST THOMAS'S (EASTBRIDGE) HOSPITAL

Hidden in this unpretentious building is a superb Norman undercroft, a 12th-century refectory and a beautiful 14th-century chapel.

11 ROYAL MUSEUM (BEANEY INSTITUTE)

An imposing Victorian building housing a good collection of Roman, Saxon and medieval finds including a 5th-century hoard of silver spoons.

12 POOR PRIESTS' HOSPITAL

This medieval building has had many uses. Originally, in 1220, it was a hospice for the poor and infirm. Later it was a poor house and a school and is now a museum of Canterbury's heritage. Preserved here is one of the oldest railway engines in the world, the *Invicta*. It was built by George and Robert Stephenson and was used on the world's first regular steam passenger service, between Canterbury and Whitstable.

13 CANTERBURY CASTLE

All that now remains of Canterbury's Norman castle is the keep. It was originally taller than it now appears, but even so, it is one of the largest (and earliest) keeps in the country.

14 CITY WALLS

About half of Canterbury's original Roman and medieval wall survives today. A ramp leads to the high-level walk along the parapet, which in this first section consists of restored 14th-century bastions.

EARLY CLOSING: *Thu.*

MARKET DAY: *Wed.*

PARKING: *Quenin Gate off Broad St, Lower Chantry La, St George's La.*

OPENING TIMES:

St Augustine's Abbey: open all year. Mon–Sat all day, Sun pm only.

Roman Pavement: open all year. Summer all day. Winter pm only.

Westgate Museum: open as above.

St Thomas's Hospital: open all year.

Royal Museum: open all year. Mon–Sat.

II | CARDIFF

World-famous as the home of Welsh rugby football, Cardiff was officially designated a city in 1905 and created capital of Wales exactly 50 years later. Although recognition of its status is comparatively recent, its history goes back to Roman times, and it owed its first importance to its flourishing port. Expansion came after the Industrial Revolution, when the South Wales coalfields were developed and an iron and steel industry was established. Much of the medieval town was swept away in this period of rapid change, but the romantic castle, the Victorian arcades, the dignified and impressive Civic Centre complex and the acres of parks, combine to make an attractive and rewarding city walk.

ROUTE DIRECTIONS

Start in Castle St by the main gate of the castle (1) After visiting the castle and the Regimental Museum (2), cross the road, then turn r. and l. into Castle Arcade (3), at the end of which turn r. into High St. At Church St turn l. to reach St John's Church (4). Leave the church, turning l. along Trinity St and l. again up the path opposite the market. Turn l. on Working St, then r. into Queen Arcade. (If the arcade is closed, continue along Working St into St John St, turn r. into Queen St, and l. into the Friary.) Cross Queen St into the Friary, then turn r. into Greyfriars Rd, and r. into Park Pl. At Queen St turn l. and l. again into Windsor Pl and cross the dual carriageway into St Andrew's Cresc. Turn l. into St Andrew's Pl, crossing Park Pl into Gorsedd Gdns and Cathays Park (5). Across the road on the right is the National Museum of Wales (6). From here continue to City Hall (7) then return to Museum Ave and turn l. then l. again into City Hall Rd for Alexandra Gdns on the r. Walk through to the end of the gardens and turn l. into College Rd, then l. into King Edward VII Ave. By the statue at the end of the ave turn r. then cross by subway, walk up steps (r.) and turn l. into Bute Pk. Follow castle wall to Blackfriars Priory ruins (8) and turn l. to reach the gate into Cowbridge Rd East, turning l. for the return to Castle St.

1 CARDIFF CASTLE

The history of Cardiff Castle stretches back to the time of the Romans. On the site of their fort the Normans raised a formidable keep to subdue the rebellious Welsh, and this polygonal structure can still be seen within the castle walls. There are lovely views over the city from its walls. In medieval times the castle was extended and made more comfortable, but it had fallen into disrepair by the Tudor period. In the 19th century, however, the 3rd Marquess of Bute, one of the richest men of his age, decided to rebuild it. He employed a young architect, William Burges, to construct a medieval dream-castle for him. Work began in 1865 and the result is a Romantic *tour de force*, a many-towered Camelot. The most distinctive feature of the exterior is the tall clock tower, decorated with a series of coloured figures portraying the planets. The interiors are sumptuous, rich with carved wood, patterned tiles, stained glass and colourful murals depicting scenes from the castle's history. The detail of the rooms is incredible. For example, the chimneypiece in the banqueting hall represents a mock castle. On its battlements heralds are blowing trumpets and three ladies watch a knight in armour riding out.

2 WELCH REGIMENT MUSEUM

Housed in the Black Tower of Cardiff Castle, the Welch Regiment Museum was opened by the Prince of Wales in 1978. The proud history of this South Wales regiment, formed in the 18th century, is portrayed through paintings, uniforms, weapons and battle trophies.

THE VICTORIAN ROMANTIC

The dazzling, exotic interior of Cardiff Castle is the work of a brilliant, if eccentric, architect and designer called William Burges. He gained inspiration for his ideas by travelling all over the world – to Europe, Japan, India, North Africa and Arabia – and the amalgamation of these influences resulted in his desire to recreate the lost romanticism of the Middle Ages. In the apartments which Burges created, every inch is covered by a riot of colour and pattern.

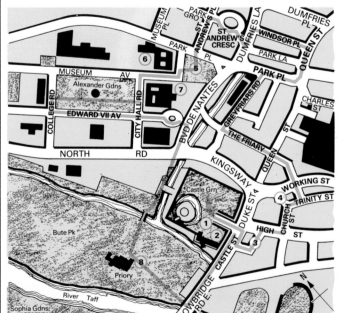

National Museum of Wales (see below), the National War Memorial and the Temple of Peace and Health were added to this distinguished quadrangle.

6 NATIONAL MUSEUM OF WALES
Many famous European works of art can be seen here, including Renoir's *La Parisienne*, highlight of an outstanding collection of Impressionist and post-Impressionist paintings. The most important objects in the archaeology section are the inscribed stones, an unrivalled collection dating from Roman and Romano-British times. The museum also features impressive displays of industrial and natural history and the sciences.

7 CITY HALL
A flamboyant Welsh dragon surmounts the great baroque dome of City Hall. The interior, with its immense marble hall, is equally magnificent.

8 BLACKFRIARS PRIORY
The remains of the medieval Dominican priory were excavated by the 3rd Marquess of Bute. Walls were added to mark out the shape of the various buildings and the church area is tiled with copies he had made of the orginal medieval tiles found on the site.

3 CASTLE ARCADE
One of Cardiff's many shopping arcades, this is a superb, late Victorian, glass-roofed construction, three storeys high, with elegant iron balconies and a fine range of interesting shops.

4 ST JOHN'S CHURCH
The only medieval church still left in the city centre, St John's dates back to 1453. Its chief glory is the splendid, 130ft-high Somerset Tower; so-called because it is in the same style as church towers commonly found in that county. It was erected in 1473 by Lady Ann Nevill, wife

The Castle Arcade is a shopper's delight

of Richard of Gloucester. Inside, the Jacobean Herbert Chapel is of special interest and beauty.

5 CATHAYS PARK
Wide, tree-lined avenues and gardens set off the dazzling white buildings of Cardiff's Civic Centre. The land was purchased for the municipality at the end of the last century, and work started on the first of the buildings, the City Hall (see below), in 1901. Next came the Assize Courts, then at various periods over the next half-century, the Register Office, County Hall, the Welsh Office, the University College of Cardiff, the College of Advanced Technology, the

EARLY CLOSING: *Wed.*

MARKET DAY: *Mon & Sat.*

PARKING: *Quay St (off Westgate St).*

OPENING TIMES:

Cardiff Castle: open all year.

National Museum of Wales: open all year except Christmas, New Year and Good Fri. Mon – Sat all day, Sun pm only.

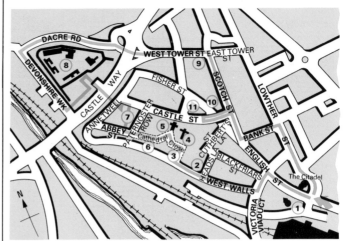

ROUTE DIRECTIONS

Start from the Citadel (1), near the railway station. Walk along English Street, between the two Citadel towers, and turn first l. down Victoria Viaduct. Turn second r. along West Walls to the Tithe Barn (2). Continue along West Walls (3) to the next turning r. to reach St Cuthbert's Church (4). From the church walk past the Resources Centre into the Cathedral Close for the Cathedral (5). Opposite the Cathedral is the Fratry (6). Walk north-west through Prior Slee's Gateway into Abbey St, and turn r. to Tullie House, Carlisle's museum and art gallery (7). Continue north-eastwards through the gardens into Castle St and turn l. At Annetwell St use the subway to reach the castle (8). After leaving the castle, turn r. and next r. down Devonshire Walk to follow the castle walls round the perimeter of castle. Meet Castle Way and use the subway to reach West Tower St. Continue past Market Hall (9) and turn r. up Scotch St to Old Town Hall (10). Visit the nearby Guildhall (11), then return to Scotch St and turn r. Continue to Bank St, turn l. and next r. into Lowther St. Follow Lowther St to return to the start point.

Carlisle's pink-washed old town hall is an important feature of the town

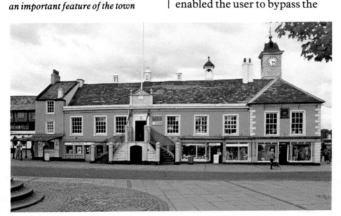

Within a relatively small area, the city of Carlisle contains a richness and diversity unusual in northern England. It has been a place of changing fortune for many centuries, thanks largely to its geographical position and the historical antipathy between English and Scots. There are still visible reminders of those ancient conflicts, but today Carlisle is a peaceful place with a unique character which has been enhanced by the restoration of many fine old buildings in recent years.

1 CITADEL
The original Citadel was built by Henry VIII in 1543 as part of a general programme of defence following his dispute with the Pope. The present building, now divided by a road, was built on the ancient foundations in 1810.

2 TITHE BARN
After many years of dereliction, this historic tithe barn has been restored to serve as a parish hall. It was built towards the end of the 15th century by Prior Gondibour as a large barn to house the tithes from the city and the Carlisle Plain. It is not generally open to the public, but the inside can be seen through the side-windows.

3 WEST WALLS
The section of walls near the tithe barn is the largest continuous section to survive today. At this point, the flight of steps still in evidence recalls the former sally-port, which was an entrance into the town that enabled the user to bypass the city toll gates, or escape from the city in times of siege.

4 ST CUTHBERT'S CHURCH
The present building dates from 1779, although a church has stood on this site since the 7th century. The pleasing Georgian interior has an upper gallery supported on Tuscan columns, and marked by the royal coat of arms, introduced after the Jacobite Rebellion. The most unusual feature of the church is its movable pulpit, allowing the people sitting in the gallery to see the preacher.

5 CATHEDRAL
The cathedral is undoubtedly the most beautiful building in the city. Its origin is Norman and there are still traces of this ancestry. Some of the arches in the south transept have been affected by subsidence as a result of a severe drought in the 13th century. The bulk of the church is made up of the 14th-century chancel, whose splendid barrel roof has been excellently restored. The wooden choir stalls have detailed 15th-century carvings on one side and a set of fascinating paintings on the reverse. The lovely east window retains most of its original 14th-century glass.

6 FRATRY AND PRIOR'S TOWER
Opposite the cathedral's south door is the Fratry, or refectory, the best-preserved of a once extensive series of priory buildings. Its 14th-century undercroft now houses a visitor

Much of the cathedral dates from the 14th century

centre and bookshop. Nearby is Prior's Tower, a 13th-century pele tower domesticated in the 15th century and given a remarkable painted ceiling on the first floor.

7 TULLIE HOUSE – CARLISLE MUSEUM AND ART GALLERY

Carlisle's finest Jacobean house contains the city's main museum. Its strength is the Roman collection drawn from excavations along Hadrian's Wall as well as in the city itself. There is also an extensive natural history collection, and an art gallery.

8 CASTLE

Sturdy and impressive fortifications reflect Carlisle's importance as a strategic centre. Its position so close to the Scottish border occasioned more violence than most other English castles have seen. The oldest part is the keep, which dates from 1150. On the second floor is an exhibition room, showing a remarkable and macabre wall taken from one of the prisoners' cells, covered with a variety of carvings of great imagination and vitality. Also within the Inner Ward is the Military Museum of the Border regiments.

9 MARKET HALL

Stretching between West Tower St and Fisher St is the large expanse of the covered market, built 1887–9. The butcher's stalls have attractive pedimented heads and replace the stalls they used to have in Market Square. Many different meats were sold in the market and animal's heads carved in the capitals on the Fisher St side reflect the variety.

10 OLD TOWN HALL

The Old Town Hall, housing the tourist information centre, was built in 1717 and is now attractively finished in pink

Jacobean Tullie House

stucco. Facing it is the Carlisle Cross, a historic monument that marks the centre of the original Roman city here. The present cross was erected in 1682 and is the spot where all the important declarations in the city's history were proclaimed.

11 GUILDHALL

Medieval trade guilds used to meet in this guildhall which survived, neglected, until 1977. Since then, the building has been restored so well that all aspects of its original construction and use can be understood.

EARLY CLOSING: *Thu.*

MARKET DAY: *Wed & Sat.*

PARKING: *Victoria Viaduct, West Walls, Tait St.*

OPENING TIMES:

Prior's Tower: open all year. May – Sep all day; Sep – May pm only.

Tullie House, Carlisle Museum and Art Gallery: open all year. Mon – Sat all day, Sun pm only. Oct – Mar, closed Sun.

Castle: open all year. Mon – Sat all day, Sun pm only.

Guildhall: open all year, Mon – Sat all day. Sun (Jun – Aug) pm only.

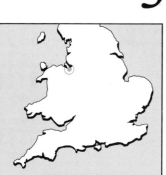

Chester began life as a Roman military camp, the base for nearly 200 years of the famous 20th Legion, the Valeria Victrix. The Romans called it Deva, meaning 'holy place', after the goddess of the River Dee. For centuries after the Romans left, the city owed its wealth and importance to river traffic, and until the Dee silted up it was one of the country's leading ports. Within the walls, which have survived almost intact, the streets are lined with timbered buildings, mostly Victorian reconstructions of Tudor architecture, through which run the famous Rows, the raised walkways along the old Roman streets which are Chester's unique feature.

ROUTE DIRECTIONS

Start at the Eastgate (I) and walk down the left-hand side of the Rows (2) past Bishop Lloyd's House (3) to Weaver St. Cross and return down the opposite side of the Rows to Northgate St. Turn l. to reach the Market Sq and Town Hall (4), then cross to St Werburgh St and the cathedral (5). Leave the cathedral through the Slype and walk across to Abbey St, turning l. to reach Abbey Sq. Go through the arch, turn r. and cross over Northgate St. Continue to the Pied Bull, turning l. into King St. Cross Water Tower St to ascend the City Walls at St Martin's Gt. Detour l. along walls to the Bonewaldesthorne and Water Towers (6), then return and walk along walls past the Bluecoat Hospital (7) and King Charles' Tower (8). At Newgate descend for Amphitheatre (9) and British Heritage Exhibition (10). Return to the walls and ascend, then shortly descend the Wishing Steps and the Recorder's Steps to the street beside the River Dee. Turn r. at the Old Dee Bridge, cross over Lower Bridge St, then turn l. into Shipgate St and up St Mary's Hill. Walk l. down Castle St to castle (II). Return by Grosvenor St past the museum (I2) to Bridge St and cross to the Chester Heritage Centre (I3). Walk back up the Bridge St Rows to Eastgate St and back down the right-hand side of the Rows to complete the walk.

I THE EASTGATE
Although the street which runs beneath it is now closed to traffic, the Eastgate was from Roman times right up to the present day the principal gate into the city and Eastgate Street formed part of the Roman *Via Principalis* or Main Street.

2 THE ROWS
The Rows are a feature unique to Chester and there are no records of them existing in any other English city or town. They are raised galleries with shops at first-floor level and they date back at least as far as the 13th century, but beyond that their origin is unknown. In time, shopkeepers built extra storeys to their houses, projecting out over the Rows, thus roofing them in, and the ground-level space, originally used for stalls, also became filled in with shops, creating a two-tier system.

THE JUBILEE CLOCK
Surmounting the Eastgate is one of Chester's most distinctive landmarks, the ornate and gaily coloured Jubilee clock, which was presented to the city by Edward Evans-Lloyd, a citizen and freeman of Chester, to commemorate Queen Victoria's Diamond Jubilee in 1897.

Watergate Street has been a picturesque roadway for centuries

3 BISHOP LLOYD'S HOUSE
Many of Chester's most distinctive black-and-white timbered buildings are the product of 19th-century romanticism, and date from the revival of interest in the Tudor period that began in the 1850s. Several on Watergate Street, however, date back to the 16th and 17th centuries, and the most fascinating is Bishop Lloyd's house, built in the early 17th century (open only by appointment).

4 TOWN HALL
The Victorian Gothic town hall dominates the market place and is best visited by arrangement with the Mayor's secretary so that all the items of interest – including official insignia and silver plate – can be seen.

5 ST WERBURGH'S CATHEDRAL
The origins of the cathedral, heavily restored in the 19th century, go back to the Anglo-Saxon foundation of the Abbey of St Werburgh, and it remained an abbey church until the reign of Henry VIII, when a diocese was established at Chester. The cathedral is famous for its remarkably beautiful choir stalls, with their intricately carved canopies,

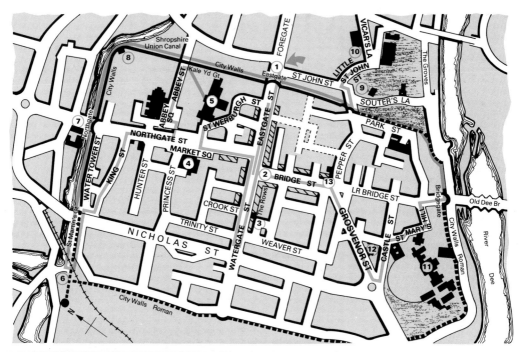

corbels, bench ends and misericords, and unusual in that it has a detached modern bell tower, built in 1974.

CITY WALLS
Chester's city walls are the most complete anywhere in the country, and are remarkably well preserved. They date from Roman times, but throughout the medieval period they were strengthened and extended. On the west, the line of the walls is now at road level, but on the other three sides the walk around the top of the walls is an ideal way to view the city and to reach many places of interest.

6 WATER TOWER AND BONEWALDESTHORNE'S TOWER
These two medieval towers at the north-west corner of the walls were built to guard the river when Chester was a port. As early as the 14th century the Dee was silting up, and the Water Tower, which now contains a small museum of Chester's history, was built on an outlying spur of wall at that time. The course of the Dee lies even further away today and is no longer navigable.

7 BLUECOAT HOSPITAL
Below the Northgate can be seen the handsome Bluecoat Hospital, built in 1717 to house the 46 pupils of the school founded in 1700 by Ranulph Blundeville.

8 KING CHARLES' TOWER
From here Charles I watched the disastrous defeat of his army at the Battle of Rowton Moor in 1645. Next day, he fled to Denbigh, asking the citizens of Chester to hold out for ten more days to cover his retreat. In fact, the resistance lasted for four months, until the people were reduced to eating rats and mice.

9 & 10 AMPHITHEATRE AND BRITISH HERITAGE EXHIBITION
By Newgate, steps lead to two relics of Roman *Deva*, the amphitheatre and the Roman Garden. The amphitheatre is one of the largest yet discovered in Britain – it could seat up to 7,000 spectators. The heritage exhibition is in Vicar's Lane opposite St John's Church. It shows films of Chester's history, and has a delightful reconstruction of the Rows.

11 CHESTER CASTLE
Little remains of Chester Castle except the mound and one of the towers of the inner bailey. The complex of buildings which stands here today was erected in the late 18th century to house offices, courts and barracks.

12 GROSVENOR MUSEUM
The outstanding features of the museum are the models illustrating life in a Roman fort, and the remarkable remains of the Roman period which have been discovered everywhere in Chester, including many sculpted tombstones.

13 CHESTER HERITAGE CENTRE
St Michael's Church in Bridge Street, declared redundant for religious purposes, was given a new lease of life in 1975 when it became the country's first Heritage Centre. Chester's history and the work of conserving it are related through a series of photographic displays and a short film show.

EARLY CLOSING: *Wed.*

MARKET DAY: *Mon – Sat.*

PARKING: *Pepper St, Frodsham St, Newgate St, Castle Dr, New Crae St.*

OPENING TIMES:

Water Tower: open summer only. Mon – Sat all day, Sun pm only.

King Charles' Tower: open as above.

British Heritage Exhibition: open all year. Closed Sun in winter.

Grosvenor Museum: open all year. Mon – Sat all day, Sun pm only.

Chester Heritage Centre: open all year. Closed Wed, and Sun pm.

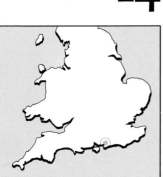

I4 | CHICHESTER

Chichester's compact city centre still lies within the walls built by the Romans in about AD200, when the town was laid out to the basic plan that has survived ever since. The Middle Ages saw the building of the cathedral and its precincts, then, in the 18th century, shipping and the corn trade drew wealthy merchants who paid for many of the elegant houses and civic buildings that still enhance Chichester's streets.

ROUTE DIRECTIONS
Start at the cathedral belltower (1) and cross to the west door of the cathedral (2). Follow the walkway into the cloisters (3) and turn r. into St Richard's Wk then r. again to reach the Bishop's Palace Garden (4). Return along Canon La (5) and turn r. into South St. Turn l. into Theatre La and l. again into South Pallant to reach Pallant House (6), then turn r. into East Pallant. Turn l. into Baffins La and cross East St into Little London. By the District Museum (7) turn r. into East Row and turn l. and l. again into Priory Rd. Turn r. into Priory Pk (8) and keep r., following the city walls, then crossing the castle mound, to reach the Church of the Greyfriars. Leave the park by the main gate and turn l. into Priory La and continue to St Martin's Sq and St Mary's Hospital (9). From here walk along Lion St past the Council House (10) and turn l. into North St. At the City Cross (11) turn r. into West St for the return to the belltower.

1 THE BELLTOWER
Built in the late 14th or early 15th century, this is the only surviving, detached cathedral belltower in England, and contains a ring of eight bells.

2 CHICHESTER CATHEDRAL
Chichester has been a cathedral city since 1075. A section of Roman mosaic pavement visible beneath the floor of the south choir aisle is a reminder that the site was in use long before that, but the oldest parts of the present building are Norman. Outstanding works of art here range from two priceless 12th-century carved stone panels to the brilliantly coloured altar tapestry designed by John Piper and hung in 1966. Other modern works include a painting by Graham Sutherland and a stained-glass window designed by Marc Chagall.

3 THE CLOISTERS
These are unusual in that they never formed part of a monastic house, and were always used more as a thoroughfare than as a place for monks to study. They still form part of a useful pedestrian route between West Street and South Street.

4 THE BISHOP'S PALACE GARDEN AND CITY WALLS
A delightful formal garden enclosed by high walls of mellow red brick leads into the main garden, bounded on two sides by the city walls. Originally built by the Romans, but strengthened and improved in medieval times, the walls enclosed an area of about 100 acres and can still be seen round much of the city. They form part of the landscaping in the Bishop's Palace Garden, and by walking round the perimeter of the garden you will follow a grassy path along the top of them. One of the medieval bastions can still be seen, and there are views over Westgate Fields below.

5 CANON LANE
Opposite the end of St Richard's Walk are the fine wrought iron gates of the Deanery. The original Deanery was destroyed by the Parliamentary Army in 1643, and the present building

This venerable old man guards the flowers in Priory Park

dates from 1725. A little further along, tucked behind a rose garden on the right, is the Chantry, one of the oldest domestic buildings in Chichester. Parts of it date from the 13th century, though it has been extensively altered over the centuries. Just before reaching the end of Canon Lane, do not miss Vicar's Close, a row of four charming 15th-century cottages with neat gardens, set on the left at right-angles to Canon Lane.

6 THE PALLANTS
The four Pallants – North, South, East and West – form a complete townscape in the south-east quadrant of the city. South Pallant is a pleasant, narrow street of harmonious buildings, old and new blending perfectly. It leads to the crossroads where the four Pallants meet. The grand building on the north-east corner is Pallant House, sometimes nicknamed locally Dodo House because of the ungainly stone birds on the gatepiers. They are intended to be ostriches – a motif featured in the family crest of Henry Peckham, for whom the house was built in 1712.

7 DISTRICT MUSEUM
The museum is housed in a converted 18th-century corn-store. The city's history since Roman times is traced by means of many fascinating exhibits, including pottery from a medieval kiln found in Orchard St, and a strange Victorian mobile oven that belonged to Joe Faro, a colourful local character known as the 'City Pie Man'. One section of the museum is devoted to the Royal Sussex Regiment.

A combined mobile stocks and whipping post in the District Museum

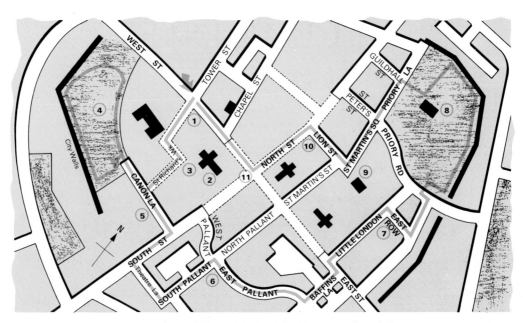

8 PRIORY PARK

A pleasant, tree-shaded promenade follows the city walls round two sides of the park, with views to the left over the cricket pitch towards Greyfriars Church, and to the right over the flower gardens of Jubilee Park. Follow the small path down to the left, when you reach the children's playground near the bowling green, to a small hillock clothed in evergreens which is the mound of Chichester Castle. Probably there was never a stone castle here, but just a wooden structure of the kind that was common in Norman times. It was demolished in 1217. Beyond the castle is the old Church of the Greyfriars. This Early English church was restored in 1933 and is now the Guildhall Museum, housing archaeological finds from the area, including Roman remains.

Brass rubbing at the cathedral

9 ST MARY'S HOSPITAL

This unique almshouse is one of Chichester's most rewarding places to visit, both as a historic building and as a striking example of a centuries-old institution that still plays an important part in the life of the city. The hospital dates from 1269 and, like many similar medieval establishments, consisted of a hospital and chapel in one large hall. It is England's only surviving example of such a building. The hall was completed in 1290 and, apart from the tall chimneys which were added later, still looks much as it did then. Inside, it looks similar to a church: the chapel corresponds to the chancel and the infirmary area to the nave. Between them still stands the original beautifully carved screen, and the 14th-century misericords beneath the choir stalls show craftsmanship worthy of any cathedral. In the 1660s the

hospital area, where the sick had been tended for almost 400 years, was converted into eight little two-roomed dwelling units and became an almshouse. But this remarkable and historic building is no museum piece, for to this day it is home to eight elderly ladies of the city, who still receive free lodging and a small pension from the original trust set up some 700 years ago.

10 THE COUNCIL HOUSE

The Palladian façade of the Council House, built in 1731, is topped by a huge stone lion. Set into the front wall, to the left of the door, is a famous Roman stone. Dug up here in 1723, its Latin inscription records the dedication of a Roman temple to Neptune and Minerva. Inside the Council House will be found the tourist information office and, on the first floor, the elegant Council Chamber and the main Assembly Room.

11 THE CITY CROSS

Chichester's most famous landmark, the City Cross was built in 1501 at the hub of the city's Roman street plan. It is a handsome octagonal structure, 50ft high, and has beautiful carved decorations, including a series of fine roof bosses. A bronze statue of Charles I is set into the east side.

EARLY CLOSING: *Thu.*

MARKET DAY: *Wed.*

PARKING: *Orchard St, South Pallant, St Martin's St.*

OPENING TIMES:

Bishop's Palace Garden: open all year.

District Museum: open all year.

Guildhall Museum: open summer only. Tue–Sat pm only. (May be shut at short notice.)

St Mary's Hospital: open all year. Tue–Sat only. Visitors should ring the bell outside the porter's lodge for the caretaker, who will show them round.

SHOPS AND PUBS

Bread and ale, the basic fare of medieval Britons, were the most important commodities in early shops and alehouses. Unlike other necessities, exchanged in markets, they were under price control. Though a far cry from present-day shops and pubs, it was here that it all began.

The public house is a unique English hybrid descended from related parents. The alehouse (called a tavern in the town) dispensed ale which was brewed on the premises, while the inn (or hostelry) as well as providing ale, offered food, shelter and stabling for the horses.

The earliest alehouses, called *tabernae*, were wooden huts built alongside the old Roman roads during the Saxon period for the sale of victuals. The ale sold was probably brewed in a nearby dwelling. A long pole identified the *taberna* and an evergreen bush hanging from the pole indicated that wine was also available. By 959, King Edgar, concerned by the increasing number of alehouses, decreed that this number should be limited to only one per village. They had become renowned for roistering by this time and it is likely that refreshments and entertainment were a feature in many of them.

Around 1400, a Flemish import known as beer began to challenge ale as the national beverage. Ale was brewed from malt and water, was sweet and sometimes flavoured with honey. Beer, brewed from malt, hops and water, had a much stronger flavour. Many people were violently opposed to it and pronounced that all manner of ailments and illnesses were caused by drinking the 'tainted liquor'.

By 1500 tippling houses had become established. These differed from home-brewed alehouses, being private houses where a cask of beer was put up for resale in retail quantities. Trade was usually carried on under the guise of giving beer away to friends and genuine alehouse traders agitated for legislation to curb tippling houses. A census taken in 1577 revealed 14,202 alehouses, 1,631 inns and 329 taverns in England and Wales.

The first inns were established in medieval times by the Church. A fine example is the New Inn, Gloucester, which was built in 1440 by the monks of Gloucester Abbey. The murder of King Edward II had occurred close by in 1327 and the pilgrims who flocked to see this martyr's tomb

Top: a traditional grocers'
Above: revelry in an 18th-century pub

required shelter and refreshment after their dusty journeys. Knowing most pilgrims to be rich, the monks anticipated that they would be paid generously for their hospitality. The inn is little changed since 1440 and, with its ornate pillared galleries overlooking the flagged courtyard, offers an irresistible glimpse into the past.

Mother's ruin

An increase in the duty on beer encouraged the drinking of brandy and of spirits distilled from English-grown corn. By 1736 there were about 7,000 regular shops in London and Westminster, and gin became the most popular of the spirits. At the height of the gin era, between 1740 and 1742, consumption of gin was believed to be the principal reason why the death rate increased to twice the birth rate.

Though gin-drinking declined in the 19th century, many 'gin palaces' are still to be seen, particularly in London. These flamboyant Victorian pubs are characterised by dark furniture, elaborate wood-carvings, large gift-framed mirrors with advertising motifs, and ornate lighting.

Probably the most frequently seen urban pubs are either the attractively vulgar Victorian street-corner establishments, or the picturesque Tudor coaching inns. An unpretentious example of the former is the Goose and Firkin on Borough Road in Southwark.

Below London Bridge, beside the Thames, is a quaint old inn with its balcony overhanging the water. When it was built in 1520 it was called the Devil's Tavern, but now it is known as the Pros-

*Top: in Victorian times pubs reached new levels of
flamboyant extravagance*
Above: pub signs are a minor art form

pect of Whitby. The more recent name was taken
from a boat which brought coal from Whitby on
the north-east coast. Many famous people have
frequented this pub, including Samuel Pepys and
Judge Jeffreys. The 'Hanging Judge' used to
watch condemned robbers squirming in their
chairs as they were left hanging over 'Execution
Dock' while he ate his dinner.

In the market place

The earliest shops and markets were concerned
with bare necessities, in great contrast to those of
the 20th century. Now a vast array of goods and
luxuries crams our shops, markets and boutiques.

The first shops were exchange markets. Even
from early medieval times, laws were in operation
to ensure that the 'prices' of goods being 'sold'
were fair – even though virtually no coinage was
available. For instance, how many eggs were fair
exchange for a cooking pot? Doubtless a lot of
private bartering took place in the hope that seller
and purchaser could reach agreement without the
constraints of the law.

Initially markets were simply open-air gatherings, where some traders had improvised stalls
while others simply displayed their goods on
carts. A market could not be set up without
permission, and dues had to be paid by the traders
to the king or local lord. Once a market was
established, the right of a town to hold it could not
be taken away, nor its day changed.

Market crosses were built to remind traders of
the importance of honest dealings. Later, when
markets became covered, the crosses were often
placed on the roof. Many famous covered markets
were established in and around London as early as
the 13th century. First was the famous fish market
at Billingsgate, which was held until 1982. Other
single commodity markets established early include Leadenhall (poultry), Smithfield (meat)
and, most renowned of all, the elegant Italianate
Covent Garden (fruit and vegetables). While markets became more sophisticated, the fronts of
houses in town streets were being adapted for the
sale of some goods. Certain items, such as drap-
ery, could clearly be stored more safely in the
complete cover of a permanent building.

The smartest shops in 17th-century London
were in Cheapside and on London Bridge. Fashionable Cheapside boasted goldsmiths, silk mer-
cers, milliners, booksellers, stationers, drugsters,
linen drapers and haberdashers. The wives of
Cheapside merchants would sit outside their
shops, chat to passers-by and entice them inside.
In especially cold winters, shops, stalls and entertainments were set up on the frozen River Thames
for the London Frost Fair.

On with the price tag

Bargaining was still the order of the day in shops
until 1750, when a Mr Palmer opened a haberdashery shop on London Bridge and sold goods at
a fixed price. Every item was marked with a price
ticket, but the idea took over a hundred years to
catch on! Unashamed knick-knacks were offered
for sale in the early 19th century at Fullers 'Temple of Farey'. This was the forerunner of bazaars
and souvenir shops, which have never looked
back and which have culminated recently in the
conversion of the old Covent Garden market to its
present chic image.

The mid-19th century saw the birth of the first
multiple stores: W H Smiths, John Menzies, International Tea Company and Freeman, Hardy
and Willis. This development followed the
growth of a national rail network, which made
goods much easier to distribute. Trends in shopping, and the nature of shops in general, changed
as the goods in them changed.

Until the emergence of the departmental chain
stores, specialist shops reigned supreme. Then, in
the 1890s, Michael Marks started the Penny
Bazaars in Manchester. The American company,
F. W. Woolworth, established the first British
branch of Woolworths in Liverpool in 1909. Early
Marks and Spencer stores were little changed
from covered markets – the difference being that
all the stalls had the same owner.

The friendly, colourful corner shop with its
jumble of groceries, hardware, toiletries and confectionery held its ground for several decades
against the competition of the chain stores. Then,
in the 1960s, the supermarket trend took over the
high street. Self-service cut down overheads, so
that goods were priced more cheaply than in
neighbourhood shops, and hygiene gained priority over cosiness. Assembly-line shopping became
the accepted method of buying, appealing particularly to working mothers who had little time to
spend exchanging pleasantries with the local
shopkeepers.

The Brave New World of supermarkets and
hypermarkets does not appeal to all, and it is
reassuring to escape down narrow lanes and
squares where picturesque street markets still
thrive and garrulous stall-owners still peddle their
special brand of gallantry.

*Advertising has had a tremendous impact on shops and
shopping. Early examples have a nostalgic charm*

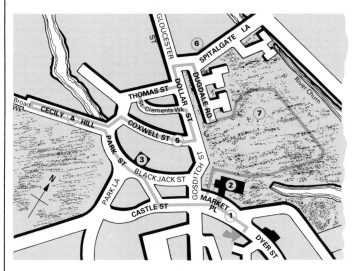

ROUTE DIRECTIONS

Start at the Corn Hall in Dyer St and turn l. into Market Pl (1) to reach St John's Church (2). Continue into Castle St and turn r. into Silver St. Keep l. into Park St, passing the Corinium Museum (3) on the r. Bear r. with Park St, then l. up Cecily Hill (4) to Cirencester Pk. Return to Park St and turn l. then r. into Coxwell St (5) past the Woolgathers. At the end turn l. then l. again along St Clements Wk. Follow this to Thomas St and turn r., then l. then r. into Spitalgate La past The Hospital and Chantry of St John the Evangelist (6). Turn r. into Dugdale Rd and on reaching the Abbey Grounds (7) keep l. Leave the park by the church and turn l. to return to the Corn Hall.

Part of the Jupiter Capital in the Corinium Museum

N ineteen centuries ago, Cirencester, then called Corinium Dubunnorum, was built by the Romans as the chief administrative centre for the West Country at the junction of two of their greatest highways – Ermine Street and Fosse Way. The town became the second largest in Britain, but after the Romans left it fell into obscurity until the Middle Ages when it became an important wool town. It was during this phase of prosperity that the great parish church was built by wealthy merchants and, with twisting streets, gabled cottages and elegant limestone buildings, the character of the town was established.

1 MARKET PLACE

The square plan of the Roman forum that preceded Market Place is far removed from the irregular shape that evolved during medieval times when Cirencester was virtually rebuilt. The present imposing character of the Market Place is due to the severe Georgian façades. Contrasting with these are Victorian edifices such as the Corn Hall and the Kings Head Hotel.

2 ST JOHN THE BAPTIST PARISH CHURCH

Gloucestershire's largest parish church seems all the more splendid because of its position at the heart of the town, where it dominates the busy streets. The first church to stand in the Market Place – about 80yds north-east of the present one – was Saxon, and here Guthrum, King of the Danes, was baptised in AD879. Later, in 1117, Henry I destroyed this church to make way for the building of a great abbey. However, the Normans replaced the Saxon church and over the centuries this has been rebuilt into the existing one. Inside the church, entered through a magnificent three-storey south porch, there is a feeling of great light and spaciousness. This is mainly created by the nave, which was widened between 1515 and 1530, and the tall clerestory windows above the six pairs of arches rising up to the panelled wooden ceiling. Five chapels in all lead off the aisles and, rich in

brasses and monuments, they are well worth exploring. Of all the church's treasures, however, the most famous is probably the Boleyn Cup. This, made for Anne Boleyn in 1535, 12in high and made of silver gilt, is set into the wall in a glass-fronted safe opposite the pulpit. The church tower, built in about 1400, affords a rewarding view of the town and is the best way to see Cirencester Park and its handsome house.

3 CORINIUM MUSEUM

Not surprisingly, a large part of the museum is devoted to Roman times and the most impressive exhibits are the large mosaics that have been found in the town. There are also reconstructions of a Roman living room, kitchen and a stonemason's workshop. A pleasant feature of the museum is a small courtyard complete with fishpond, fountain, seats and patches of herbs that were used in Roman cooking.

4 CECILY HILL

Until the early 19th century this wide, quiet street was the main route to Stroud, but now only visitors to Cirencester Park pass up and down it. The houses – those on the left set back behind gardens, those on the right with doorsteps on the pavement – represent styles from the 1600s to the 1900s and dates can be seen carved on many of the houses. All individually of merit, they are given unity by the consistent use of local limestone. At the top of the road the Victorians' love of romantic imitation can be seen in the towers and battlements of The Old Barracks, built in 1857 as an armoury but now used as a warehouse. Beyond the wrought iron gates at the end of the road stretches Broad Walk – a five-mile-long avenue open to the public for walking and riding by courtesy by the Earl of Bathhurst, owner of Cirencester Park. His family have owned the 3,000 acre park since the late 17th century. The mansion itself is private and made practically invisible, except from the top of the church tower, by the extraordinary 40ft-high yew hedge which surrounds it.

5 COXWELL STREET

This quiet back street with its mixture of old buildings leaning towards each other is one of Cirencester's most appealing. One of the houses is called 'Woolgathers' and was built for the owner of the adjoining warehouse in Thomas Street in the 17th century. On the left-hand side of its garden is the old counting house, still with its own steps leading up to the door. Further along, typical Cotswold cottages with steep gables contrast with the larger houses built by wealthy merchants. No. 10 is of interest, because the level of the pavement has risen since it was built over 350 years ago, giving the archway a somewhat stunted look. Most of the houses along here date from the 17th and 18th centuries, but the larger ones are later.

6 THE HOSPITAL AND CHANTRY OF ST JOHN THE EVANGELIST

Four pairs of large open arches facing each other with a roof over them are all that remain of the hospital founded by Henry I in 1133 to provide rest for passing travellers and a home for the destitute. The hospital became attached to the abbey when it was founded, and was consequently left to fall into ruins after the Dissolution. The row of cottages next to the arches was built during the 18th century to replace the ruined hospital and they have served as almshouses ever since.

Cirencester market is held on Fridays

Cirencester Park, a handsome mansion built at the beginning of the 18th century, is best seen from the tower of St John's Church.

7 ABBEY GROUNDS

All that is left of the enormous abbey church that was so prosperous at the height of the wool trade is Spital Gateway which, now incorporated into a private house, marks the northern end of the abbey precincts. The grounds have been turned into a delightful informal park that has the River Churn flowing through it.

EARLY CLOSING: *Thu.*

MARKET DAY: *Mon & Fri.*

PARKING: *Dugdale Rd (Abbey); Forum (Northway).*

OPENING TIMES:

Corinium Museum: *open all year. Closed Mon Oct–Apr, and Sun am all year.*

16 | COLCHESTER

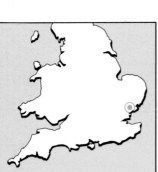

When the Roman legions invaded Britain in AD43 they made straight for the capital of the south east and built their first town within the great walls that can still be seen today. From then on the town grew both in size and importance as a trading centre. Its easy access to the Continent led to the arrival of Flemish refugees during the 16th century, and they revived the cloth trade that had flourished here in the Middle Ages. Today the town is a mixture of old and new – on the one hand maintaining its old traditions and customs, and on the other forging ahead with new industries and cultural facilities.

ROUTE DIRECTIONS

Start from the Balkerne Gate (1). Continue along Balkerne Passage (2), bear l. then r. and at the end cross North Hill to St Peter's Church (3). Continue down North Hill and turn r. into Nunn's Rd then r. again into West Stockwell St (4). Shortly, turn l. into Stockwell, then r. along East Stockwell St. Turn l. down St Helen's La. At the end cross Maidenburgh St, go through a narrow passageway between nos 15 and 16 and keep forward to enter the castle grounds for the castle (5). Leave the castle grounds by turning l. into Cowdray Cresc and shortly turn l. into the High St. Immediately on the l. is Hollytrees Museum (6). From here turn r. along the High St, passing All Saints Church (7) to the Town Hall (8). Turn l. along Pelham's La and at the end bear r. then l. along Trinity St, past Holy Trinity Church (9). At the end turn r. along Sir Isaac's Wk and keep forward into Church Wk. Bear r. at the end to reach St Mary-at-the-Walls Church (10). Turn l. past the church, go through a gap in the Roman wall, descend the steps and turn r. along Balkerne La alongside the Roman Wall (11) back to Balkerne Gate.

1 BALKERNE GATE

Measuring 107ft across, this is the largest surviving Roman gateway in Britain. It was originally built as a monumental arch. Later, when the town wall was constructed in about AD 125, it was converted into a gateway, and pedestrian passageways and two D-shaped bastions holding guard rooms were added. Today ruins of the two pedestrian archways and the wall remain, and one of the bastions, rising to a height of over 10ft, is still impressive.

2 BALKERNE PASSAGE

The Mercury Theatre was designed by Norman Downie and opened in 1972. It is an attractive building of concrete and glass with a green bronze statue of Mercury perched on the corner. Directly in front, and dwarfing all before it, is the extraordinary Victorian creation known as 'Jumbo'. This is a huge water tower, named after a great African circus elephant who was a national hero during the late 19th century.

3 ST PETER'S CHURCH

This interesting church has a red-brick tower dating from 1758, but the main body of the church, constructed of Roman brickwork, tiles and stones, was remodelled in 1550. Of particular interest are the late 17th-century pulpit and the communion table.

4 WEST STOCKWELL STREET

A plaque on the side of a house in West Stockwell Street indicates that this area is known as the Dutch Quarter, after the influx during the 16th century of 500 Flemish refugees who revived the cloth trade in the town. Houses with pointed gables and plaster fronts painted in a variety of colours line the street, making it one of the most attractive in Colchester.

5 COLCHESTER CASTLE

Far bigger than the White Tower of the Tower of London, the great keep of Colchester Castle retains an air of dark medieval menace. It was originally built in about 1080 on the stone masonry platform of the Roman Temple of Claudius. Once twice as high as it is now, it remained for many years a royal fortress. Now the interior of the castle houses a museum. Among the exhibits is a model of the Balkerne Gate in AD 120 showing a company of Roman soldiers marching underneath the monumental arch, and a large Roman mosaic pavement. On the first floor, glass cases contain Roman pottery of varying styles, including beautiful terracotta Samian ware. More glass cases contain many articles from Colchester's

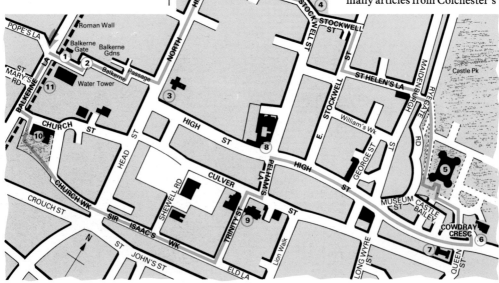

Colchester Castle was built in the 11th century by Eudo, a steward of William the Conqueror. The massive keep is built on the base of a Roman temple

ancient past, including finds from the Bronze and Iron Ages. Below the castle, the vaults of the original Roman temple can be seen.

6 HOLLYTREES MUSEUM

Colchester's most handsome 18th-century house, Hollytrees is a three-storeyed brick-built structure with a particularly beautiful carved doorcase. It has been a museum of costume and antiquities since 1929.

7 NATURAL HISTORY MUSEUM – ALL SAINTS CHURCH

A Norman foundation altered many times through the centuries and virtually rebuilt in the 19th century, All Saints now serves as a natural history museum and contains many beautiful dioramas depicting various species of wildlife found in the Colchester area.

Especially interesting is the diorama of the salt marshes at Fingringhoe Wick Nature Reserve, showing how land is naturally reclaimed from the sea.

8 TOWN HALL

Built between 1899 and 1902 in an elaborate style on the site of an earlier Town Hall, this white stone building is crowned by a tower that reaches 162ft above street level.

9 MUSEUM OF SOCIAL HISTORY – HOLY TRINITY CHURCH

The tower was built about AD 1000 and is the only Saxon building in the town, but the church was extensively restored during the 19th century and the north aisle and chapel were added in 1886. Particularly noteworthy is the Saxon triangular-headed doorway to the tower. As a place of worship the church was closed in 1952 and reopened as a Museum of Social History in 1974. It is mainly concerned with country

life and crafts, and there are displays and reconstructed scenes containing 19th- and early 20th-century objects and craft tools. Among the displays are a number of old bicycles.

10 ST MARY-AT-THE-WALLS

The medieval church was ruined during the great siege of 1648 when it was a Royalist stronghold. The lower stages of the 15th-century tower are all that remain of the original building. Most of the existing structure is 19th century. It was still in use as a church until 1979, when it became St Mary's Art Centre where works by local artists are displayed.

11 ROMAN WALLS

Colchester's town walls are unique in Britain as they largely date from Roman times, although they were repaired by the Saxons. The walls were also used to defend the medieval town that grew up, and they protected the town for 10 weeks during the Civil War siege of 1648. Eventually the town capitulated, and the wall's parapets were dismantled.

MARKET DAY: *Sat.*

EARLY CLOSING: *Thu.*

PARKING: *Crowhurst Rd, Shewell Rd, Culver St, Nunns Rd.*

OPENING TIMES:

Colchester Castle: open all year. Mon–Sat all day. Sun pm only. Closed on major public holidays and Sun Dec–Feb.

Hollytrees Museum: open all year. Mon–Sat all day. Closed Sun.

Natural History Museum: open as above.

Museum of Social History: open as above.

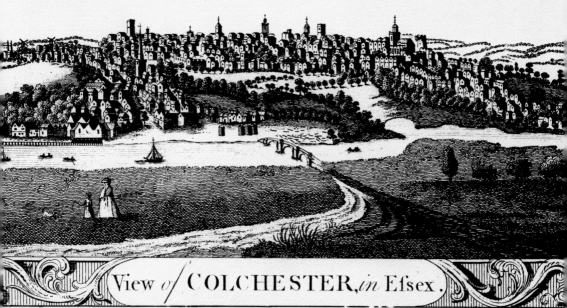

View of COLCHESTER, in Essex.

17 | CONWY

Set against a backdrop of wooded hills above the wide river are the great towers of Conwy Castle – one of the best preserved medieval fortresses in Britain. The main advantage of the site from a defensive point of view was its inaccessibility and this remained unchanged until the 19th century when Telford built the first of the three bridges now spanning the water.

ROUTE DIRECTIONS

Start in Castle Sq at the entrance to the castle (1). From the castle turn r. and before reaching the Conwy Road Br (2) bear r. down a path to Telford's Suspension Br (3), built alongside Stephenson's Tubular Railway Br (4). Return to the main road, cross and go down to The Quay (5). Continue into Lower Gate St, passing 'The Smallest House In Great Britain' (6) and go through the wall arch at the end. Continue up the steep slope to the l. to reach the A55. Here, either turn l. into Berry St through the arch and turn immediately l. up the steps for the Wall Walk (7), or for the less energetic, continue into Town Ditch Rd and Mount Pleasant, turn l. into Sychnant Pass Rd and keep l. for the arch at the top of Upper Gate St which is the end of the Wall Walk. Continue down Upper Gate St into Chapel St (8) and turn r. into Crown La past Plas Mawr (9). Turn r. into the High St to Lancaster Sq (10) and turn l. into Rose Hill St past the Conwy Visitor Centre (11). Here turn l. along Church St and r. by the Baptist Church to reach St Mary's Church (12). Leave the churchyard by the path leading to the High St and turn r., past the Castle Hotel (13). Turn r. into Castle St, past Aberconwy House (14) on the corner, for the return to Castle Sq.

1 CONWY CASTLE

Conwy Castle, the third of Edward I's great Welsh fortresses, was built on this strategic site offering river, sea and land defences when he had gained control of the Conwy Valley. The castle consists of an inner and outer ward surrounded by eight great battlemented drum towers which are all linked by a high curtain wall. Extra turrets were placed on the four eastern towers, as this was the residential half of the castle and required even greater protection. A walk around the castle takes in all the towers, and the far-reaching views they provide prove the strategic importance of the site. All the towers, apart from Chapel Tower, have lost their dividing floors, and here there is a room known as Queen Eleanor's Chapel, although in fact she died before it was completed. This is one of the best preserved parts of the inner ward.

2, 3 & 4 CONWY'S BRIDGES

Before Thomas Telford built his graceful suspension bridge here in 1826 the only way across the wide estuary was by ferry. For many years the bridge, which appears to swing away from the castle like a drawbridge, carried traffic, but in 1956 a new road bridge was built next to it and Telford's bridge is now for pedestrians only. The third bridge spanning the river at this point is Stephenson's Tubular Railway Bridge, which was completed in 1848.

5 THE QUAY

Set beneath the castle walls, the quay is one of Conwy's most attractive features. Trawlers unloading their catches, fishermen mending their nets, mussel-fishers putting out from the shore with their long-handled rakes, and pleasure cruisers setting off with holidaymakers, all contribute to the lively atmosphere. During the 19th century slate was exported from the quay, and when that industry declined, shipbuilding took over for a while.

6 THE SMALLEST HOUSE IN GREAT BRITAIN

Wedged against the town wall between other newer houses is a red-painted mid Victorian house which, measuring just 122ins high and 72ins wide is, literally, the smallest house in Britain: the cooking was done in a tiny fireplace, a settle doubled as a coal bunker and the water tap was situated behind the stairs. It was nearly demolished in 1900, but eventually left as a tourist attraction.

Britain's smallest house – dwarfed by the buildings around it

Edwards I's superb castle

The doorway of Plas Mawr

7 TOWN WALL WALK
For most of the year it is possible to walk along the north-west section of the town walls, which stretches for a quarter of a mile, gradually ascending from quay level to the highest point in the town. The views from the wall are tremendous and encompass the slate-grey roofs of the town, the castle, with the estuary beyond, and the wooded foothills and mountains of Snowdonia.

8 CHAPEL STREET
To the left of the street lie the stone ruins of the medieval house, Parlwr Mawr, which was the family home of John Williams, who became Archbishop of York during the Civil War. As a supporter of the king he took refuge in Conwy but later changed his allegiance and took part in the siege of the town. Standing beside the ruins is a slate tablet commemorating the coronation of King George VI. Towering over the other coloured terraced houses in the street is the large Carmel Methodist Church, which is a fine example of 19th-century Welsh architecture.

9 PLAS MAWR
An Elizabethan adventurer built this stately gabled mansion for himself in 1577 and today it is the town's finest building: the Royal Cambrian Academy of Art now maintain the house and use it as their headquarters. Features of note include fine decorative plasterwork, huge open fireplaces, dark oak panelling, an upper courtyard, a watchtower with fine rooftop views, and a room where art exhibitions are held. There is also supposed to be a haunted room here – a tale one can well believe having seen this fascinating old house.

10 LANCASTER SQUARE
A statue of Llewelyn the Great, founder of Conwy Abbey, has marked the centre of the square since 1898. It depicts the prince in a red and grey cloak and a golden crown with a sword in his hand. Standing in one corner of the square is the former Boot Inn, now called the Alfredo Restaurant, which is believed to have been where Charlotte Brontë spent her honeymoon.

11 CONWY VISITOR CENTRE
Here the past 800 years of Conwy's history is brought to life on film and through scenic displays representing the abbey, the castle, and everyday life. There is also a shop selling craft goods, books and guides.

12 ST MARY'S CHURCH
Eight hundred years ago a Cistercian abbey was founded in Conwy on the site now marked by St Mary's parish church, and parts of the walls and buttresses can be dated back to the original abbey church. During the 14th century the area north of the tower, now housing a parish museum, was sealed off and used as a charnel house. The tower, begun in the 1300s, was completed during the 15th century. There are many interesting monuments in the church, an early Tudor font,

and a fine screen representing 15th-century craftsmanship at its best.

13 CASTLE HOTEL
The hotel stands on the site of an ancient spital – a medieval monastic hospital or guesthouse – remains of which survive in the stable yard. The present building is a combination of two old inns, the King's Head and The Castle. The hotel is famous for its fine collection of old Welsh furniture and its collection of pictures, including a number by the little-known Victorian artist Dawson Watson.

14 ABERCONWY HOUSE
Aberconwy House, dating from the 14th century and now the property of the National Trust, is the oldest house in the town. It is an attractive, stone-fronted building with a black-and-white, timbered, overhanging upper storey and a slate roof. Built by a prosperous merchant, the house now contains an exhibition depicting Conwy through the centuries and includes a traditional 18th-century kitchen, and a display of mussel-fishing – an occupation dating back to Roman days.

EARLY CLOSING: *Wed.*

MARKET DAYS: *Tue & Sat in Summer, Sat in winter.*

PARKING: *Vicarage Gardens (Rose Hill St); Morfa Bach (Llanrwst Rd).*

OPENING TIMES:

Castle: open all year except Christmas & New Year. Also closed Sun pm Oct–Mar.

The Smallest House: open summer only. Mon–Sun all day.

Conwy Visitor Centre: open Easter to Christmas. Mon–Sat all day except Wed pm and Sun from Oct–Dec.

Plas Mawr: open all year except mid Dec to mid Jan.

Aberconwy House: open Apr–Oct. Closed Wed in Apr and May, and only open Sat & Sun in Oct.

18 | DUMFRIES

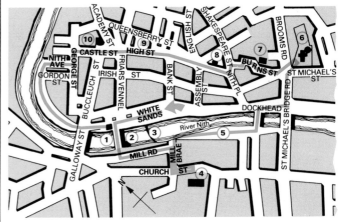

ROUTE DIRECTIONS

Start at the tourist information centre on the Whitesands. Go over the bridge (1), noticing the Old Bridge House (2) and turn l. onto Mill Rd. Turn l. to the viewpoint overlooking the Caul (3), go back to Mill Rd and then up pathway into Mill Brae. Cross Church St and turn l. up the footpath into the museum grounds to the museum (4). Return to the foot of Mill Brae and turn r. into the park (5). Cross the suspension bridge and turn r. to Brooms Rd. Turn l. to reach St Michael's Church (6). From the church cross the main road and take the first r. into Burns St for Burns House (7). Continue forward and cross Shakespeare St. Turn l. then r. into High St, passing, r., the Globe Inn (8). Keep the Midsteeple (9) on your r. and continue to Greyfriars Church (10). Go straight on along Castle St, l. into George St and r. down Nith Ave beside the old people's home. Turn l. and r. onto the riverside footpath to return to the Whitesands.

Dumfries, the 'Queen of the South', was created a royal burgh in 1186. For three full centuries, it bore the brunt of the incessant wars and border raids between Scotland and England. After the Union of 1707, trade developed. Milling and leatherwork flourished, and for a time this was the most important Scottish port in the tobacco trade with the American colonies. Dumfries has important literary connections, notably with Robert Burns; and it was here that Sir James Barrie first thought of the characters in Peter Pan.

1 THE OLD BRIDGE

Tradition says that the first wooden bridge across the Nith at this point was set up in the 13th century by the Lady Devorgilla, who was also responsible for the building of Sweetheart Abbey – a few miles south of the town – in memory of her husband John Balliol. The present stone bridge dates from around 1430.

2 OLD BRIDGE HOUSE

This is the oldest house in Dumfries, built by James Birkmyre in 1660. Some of the original woodwork is still to be seen, although the low window line is caused by the fact that the road level on the bridge has been raised several times. The last tenant of the house died in 1959, and it has now been restored as a museum. There are six furnished rooms of different periods, from a childhood room

full of toys to an old-style dentist's surgery.

3 THE CAUL

A weir set diagonally across the Nith, this once diverted water towards the riverside mills established from 1704 onwards. Small coasting vessels used to come to Dumfries, and at high tides even reached as far as the foot of the Caul.

4 DUMFRIES MUSEUM

In the 18th century a windmill was built on the summit of Corberry Hill. It went out of use, and in 1834 was taken over by the Dumfries and Maxwelltown Astronomical Society, who rebuilt it as an observatory, with a *camera obscura* as the main attraction. As well as this device, which still throws reflected pictures of the town and its surroundings on to a table, the museum also includes fine displays of wildlife, archaeology and social history.

Statue of Robert Burns

44

This ornate 19th-century fountain can be seen in the High Street

8 GLOBE INN

In a passageway to the right of the High Street is the Globe Inn, Robert Burn's howff – his 'local' – during the time he lived in Dumfries. Several mementoes of the poet are kept here, including his favourite chair.

9 MIDSTEEPLE

Built in 1707, this 'island' in the High Street housed the courtroom, prison and town offices. Across the High Street is the County Hotel, in which Prince Charlie's Room recalls the stay of the Young Pretender here for three days in 1745.

10 GREYFRIARS CHURCH

In the centre of the roundabout in front of Greyfriars Church is a statue of Robert Burns. The church dates from 1868, but the original Greyfriars monastery of Dumfries, now disappeared, was much older. It was at the altar of Greyfriars in 1306 that Robert the Bruce killed Sir John Comyn, representative in Scotland of the English King Edward I, and sparked off the War of Independence which put him on the Scottish throne.

EARLY CLOSING: *Thu.*

MARKET DAY: *Wed.*

PARKING: *Whitesands.*

OPENING TIMES:

Old Bridge House: open Easter to Sep. Mon–Sat all day, except Tue. Sun pm only.

Dumfries Museum: As above.

Burns House: open all year. Mon–Sat all day, Sun pm only. Oct–Easter, closed Sun.

5 FALLOW DEER PARK

This riverside parkland by the Nith has its footpath well away from the water's edge, in case of floods. On the slope of the hill is an enclosure of fallow deer right in the heart of the town.

6 ST MICHAEL'S CHURCH

The graveyard of this parish church is where Robert Burns was buried, with great ceremony, on 25 July 1796. His funeral was attended by something like 10,000 mourners, and included a military escort. In 1815 his coffin was moved from its original resting place to an unexpectedly ornate mausoleum, with dome pillars in blue and white, the colours of Scotland's national flag, the St Andrew's Cross. It stands in sharp contrast with the local red sandstone of the church itself and the other memorials round about. A brass tablet in the church indicates the pew at which Burns sat.

The six arches of Old Bridge have spanned the Nith for over 500 years. In the 18th century it had nine arches

7 BURNS HOUSE

Robert Burns spent the last five years of his life in Dumfries, after giving up his farm. He and his wife Jean moved to this house in 1793. Seriously ill in the summer of 1796, he was advised to take the sea-bathing cure at Brow on the Solway coast. But it did him far more harm than good, and he died back at his Dumfries home on 21 July. His wife survived him by many years, living here until 1834 in a house which is now a Burns museum, with many relics and original manuscripts.

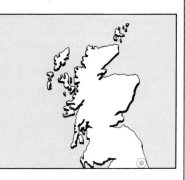

ROUTE DIRECTIONS

Start at the Market Pl by the Town Hall (1) and walk down Silver St towards Framwellgate Br. A few yards before the bridge, turn l. down the steps and follow signs to the riverside footpath leading to the Archaeology Museum (2). From the museum, keep forward then turn sharp l. up a steep path to the cathedral walls, and follow signs for the cathedral. Enter Palace Grn and turn r. to reach the cathedral (3). Leave by the cloisters to emerge (turning l. and l. again) into College Grn (4) and walk round to the arched gateway into South Bailey. Turn l. here, passing the Durham Heritage Centre (5), then cross to Duncow La and walk up into Palace Grn (6). Walk round the green past Bishop Cosin's Library and enter the castle (7) grounds. On leaving the castle, walk down to Owengate, turn l., then l. again into North Bailey (8) and Saddler St to return to the market place.

One of the most splendidly sited cities in Britain, Durham's rocky outcrop, washed on three sides by the River Wear, was from the earliest times a secure fortress against invading Scots and Danes. The town grew up in the shelter of the towering cathedral and castle, both built by the Norman Prince Bishops who ruled Durham as a city state. Their unique powers gradually diminished and finally ended in 1836, but they had done much over the centuries to enhance the great medieval city.

1 TOWN HALL

Like so many town halls, this one is Victorian, but it is less flamboyant than some. It is worth visiting for its collection of mementoes of 'King Tom Thumb', a midget who lived in Durham for the last 17 years of his life. Polish by birth, Joseph Boruwlaski was only 39 inches tall, but he lived for 98 years, achieving considerable fame and becoming a fine violinist.

2 ARCHAEOLOGY MUSEUM

This interesting little museum is housed in an old fulling mill where woollen cloth was once treated with fullers' earth to cleanse it of grease. On the opposite bank, across the weir that provided power for both, is an old corn mill.

3 DURHAM CATHEDRAL

Set on a great spur of rock and rising from a surrounding screen of trees, the group of buildings which forms the heart of Durham is one of the most lovely compositions in Britain. The great cathedral which dominates this scene is among the finest buildings in Europe, and is considered by many to be the supreme example of Norman architecture in the world. The foundation stone was laid on August 11, 1093,

and nearly all of the major work was completed by 1133 – a short span of time which gives the building a remarkable unity. Perhaps its greatest contribution to the history and progress of architecture is that at Durham rib-vaulting was used for the very first time. This technical breakthrough, the work of an inventive genius, enabled Gothic architecture to flower and develop. It is as a magnificent whole that the cathedral should be seen, but it does have a host of fascinating details. The north door bears the famous 12th-century sanctuary knocker, a grotesque head which, once they had seized hold of it, gave fugitives the right of sanctuary within the cathedral precincts. In the Galilee Chapel at the west end of the cathedral is the tomb of the Venerable Bede, the great early English historian whose remains were moved from Jarrow in 1020 to the old Saxon cathedral which once stood on this site. The original church here was built in the tenth century to house the shrine of St Cuthbert, whose body was brought here from Lindisfarne for safety from the marauding Danes. Although the shrine was destroyed at the Reformation, the oak coffin, re-discovered in the 19th century, is one of the

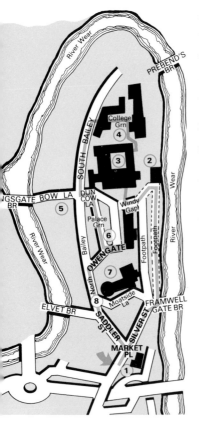

6 PALACE GREEN

Along the east side of the green are pretty, mock-Tudor almshouses, also an elegant 18th-century hall, and the Bishop's Hospital, dating from 1666. On the other side, the old Tudor Grammar School adjoins the university buildings, and next to the University Library stands Bishop Cosin's Library, founded in 1669.

7 THE CASTLE

When the powers of the Prince Bishops, who ruled Durham as Counts Palatine for 800 years, were finally ended in 1836, the castle became the seat of the University of Durham, which was the first new university to be founded in England after Oxford and Cambridge. The castle itself was built soon after the Norman Conquest as a defence against the Scots, and in the succeeding centuries was enlarged and strengthened by the bishops, who used it as their residence. A polygonal 14th-century keep dominates much of the complex, while the castle's most famous single feature is the lovely Black Staircase at the junction of the north and west ranges. There are two chapels; the first dating from the 11th century, and an outstanding example of early Norman architecture; the second being 16th-century with exquisitely carved choir stalls.

8 NORTH BAILEY

Perhaps the finest streets in Durham, North Bailey and its continuation, Saddler Street, are lined with well-preserved 18th-century houses. Winding down to the river from both streets are a number of quaint alleys known as vennels which have changed little since medieval times.

EARLY CLOSING: *Wed.*

MARKET DAY: *Sat.*

PARKING: *Milburngate, Leazes Bowl.*

OPENING TIMES:

Archaeology Museum: open Tue, Thu & Fri all day, Wed pm only.

Castle: open all year. 1st 3 wks of Apr & Jul–Sep, Mon–Sat all day. Rest of year, Mon, Wed, Sat, pm only.

Far left: Durham Castle's Black Staircase dates from 1662

Left: The cathedral is known for its exquisite stone carvings

Below: Durham has one of the most dramatically sited cathedrals in England

many rare treasures that can be seen in the monks' dormitory museum in the cloisters. Other items displayed are illuminated manuscripts, a 10th-century embroidered stole and maniple of exceptionally fine workmanship, Norman caryatid figures from the cathedral, and a collection of ancient crosses and Saxon hogs-back gravestones.

4 COLLEGE GREEN

This secluded open space is surrounded by pleasant houses of the 18th and early 19th centuries. One of the most interesting buildings is the Stables, close to the west end of the cathedral, which still has an original Norman north wall, where small windows high up in the loft point to the existence of the monks' latrine. Below the stables, a staircase leads 23ft down to the tunnel-like monks' prison, where monks were incarcerated for serious offences.

5 DURHAM HERITAGE CENTRE

The 17th-century church of St Mary-le-Bow has been transformed into a heritage centre with fascinating displays of the history and conservation of the city. The church itself contains beautiful woodwork.

20 EDINBURGH

As the capital city of Scotland, Edinburgh is rich in history of a most dramatic kind, centred first on the castle, and later, at the far end of the Royal Mile, on Holyroodhouse. In the 18th century Edinburgh became one of the most cultured and civilised cities in Europe and was known as 'the Athens of the north'. Writers, poets, painters, philosophers and scientists made it their home and it nourished them; they left behind a rich legacy for visitors, not the least of which is the New Town to the north of Princes Street, whose Georgian avenues and squares contrast sharply with the medieval jumble of the old city.

ROUTE DIRECTIONS
The walk starts from Waverley Br by Waverley Station. Cross over Market St and continue up Cockburn St. Meet High St (part of the Royal Mile) and turn r. Pass the Wax Museum (1) and continue up the High St to St Giles Cathedral (2). Behind the cathedral stands Parliament House (3). Carry on along Lawnmarket, passing Lady Stair's House (4) and entry to Gladstone's Land (5), then bear r. up Castle Hill, on which stands the Outlook Tower (6), to the castle (7). From the castle take the path through the gate on l. at the foot of the Esplanade, taking the first branch r. to zig-zag to the railway line. Cross the railway bridge into the gardens and turn l. on to the main path to emerge by St John's Church in Princes St at West End. Cross Lothian Rd and Rutland St to Shandwick Pl, passing the Scottish Experience (8). Then cross Queensferry St and walk up Hope St to Charlotte Sq to reach West Register House (9). Walk round the north side of the square passing the Georgian House (10) and turn l. into George St. Turn r. down Castle St and first l. into Rose St. Turn r. down Frederick St, cross over to the south side of Princes St and turn l. Cross the Mound, where the National Gallery (11) stands, and take the path along E. Princes St Gdns leading past the Scott Monument (12). Turn r. on to Waverley Br to return to the start. For a detour to Holyroodhouse, walk on up Cockburn St to High St again, and turn l. to the Museum of Childhood (13) and John Knox's House (14). Continue into Canongate with Canongate Tolbooth (15) and Canongate Church (16) on the l. and Huntly House (17) more or less opposite on the r. The Palace of Holyroodhouse (18) is at the end of the street. Return along Canongate, turn r. along Jeffrey St, go under North Br to meet Waverley Br, and turn r. for the return.

1 WAX MUSEUM
Housed in the fine Georgian New Assemblies Hall, the Wax Museum contains models of the famous people in Scottish history set in tableaux reflecting their lives.

2 ST GILES' CATHEDRAL
A beautiful 15th-century crown steeple adorns Edinburgh's most famous church. The Gothic nave is hung with the colours of the Scottish regiments and there are many historic memorials in the cathedral, including those of John Knox and R. L. Stevenson. John Knox was minister of St Giles in the 16th century, a very turbulent period in Edinburgh. The most spectacular part of the cathedral is Thistle Chapel, whose ornately-carved interior was built in 1911. Outside the cathedral a heart-shaped design in the cobblestones, known as the 'Heart of Midlothian', marks the site of the Old Tolbooth prison.

3 PARLIAMENT HOUSE
The home of the Scots Parliament from 1639 until 1707, this is now the High Court. Parliament Hall itself is famous for its magnificent hammerbeam roof.

4 LADY STAIR'S HOUSE
Set in a pleasing close (Wardrop's Court), just off Lawnmarket, Lady Stair's House dates from 1622. It is now devoted to exhibitions about Robert Burns, Sir Walter Scott and R. L. Stevenson.

5 GLADSTONE'S LAND
The preservation and restoration of this 17th-century merchant's house has resulted in a vivid recreation of that period of history. The rooms are filled with period furniture, and colourful ceiling and wall paintings have been uncovered.

6 OUTLOOK TOWER
Climb the 98 steps to the top of the Outlook Tower and you will be rewarded with wide views over Edinburgh's rooftops. The fascinating *camera obscura* at the top is still used, and showings are given of scenes from all round the city.

The castle's main gate and drawbridge

7 THE CASTLE
The focus of Edinburgh is, undoubtedly, the castle. Built so commandingly on a great volcanic rock, it can be seen from all parts of the city. The oldest part is the beautiful and simple little Norman chapel dedicated to Queen Margaret. The famous canon, Mons Meg, stands next to the Chapel. The history of the castle is almost a history of Scotland and this is reflected in many of the rooms to be seen, such as Queen Mary's Room and James IV's Great Hall, with its fine hammerbeam roof and displays of weaponry.

8 THE SCOTTISH EXPERIENCE
The history of Edinburgh is brought to life here by the use of exciting audio-visual devices.

9 WEST REGISTER HOUSE
An impressive collection of historic documents is displayed here in what used to be St George's Church. One of the oldest is the Charter of David I dating from 1137, and there are many others telling, at first hand, of great moments in Scottish history.

10 THE GEORGIAN HOUSE
The whole of Charlotte Square is a gem of Georgian architecture, and a close look at one facet of it can be made in the Georgian House at No. 7, which was designed by Robert Adam.

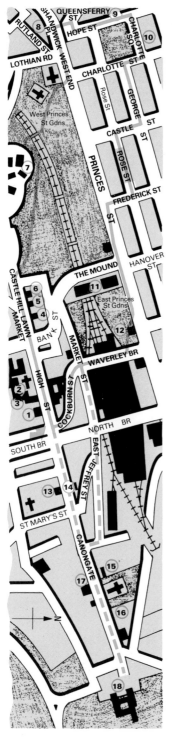

The 200ft-high Scott Monument in East Princes Street Gardens

14 MUSEUM OF CHILDHOOD

Children of all ages will be enthralled by the rich collection of toys, books, games, dolls and dolls' houses imaginatively displayed in this museum.

15 CANONGATE TOLBOOTH

The projecting clock and outside stairs mark this unusual building which was once used as a courthouse and prison. Now it houses exhibitions, a stone and brass rubbing centre and a collection of Highland dress.

16 CANONGATE CHURCH

Beautifully restored in recent years, this 17th-century church is a particularly good example of Scottish-style architecture.

17 HUNTLY HOUSE

The varied and fascinating history of everyday life in Edinburgh is most imaginatively displayed in this reconstructed 16th-century town house.

18 PALACE OF HOLYROODHOUSE

The palace is the official Scottish residence of the Queen. It has a history stretching back to 1128, when an abbey was built here, but most of what can be seen today dates from a rebuilding carried out for Charles II. Conducted tours of the palace include the extraordinary Picture Gallery where 111 portraits of Scottish kings adorn the walls. These were painted for Charles II but many of them have only the most tenuous links with

historical accuracy. The most macabre rooms are those associated with Mary Queen of Scots and the ignominious murder of her secretary Rizzio. All that remains of the Abbey of Holyrood is the ruined nave known as the Chapel Royal, which was founded in 1128.

EARLY CLOSING: *Tue, Wed, Sat in different areas of city.*

MARKET DAY: *Tue.*

PARKING: *Market St. Bank St.*

OPENING TIMES:

Canongate Tolbooth: open all year. Mon–Sat all day. Sun pm only during festival.

Castle: open all year. Sun pm only Nov–Apr.

Georgian House: open Apr–Dec. Apr–Oct Mon–Sat all day. Sun pm only. Nov–Dec Sat all day, Sun pm only.

Gladstone's Land: open Apr–Dec. Apr–Oct, Mon–Sat all day, Sun pm only. Nov–Dec, Sat all day, Sun pm only.

Huntly House: as Canongate Tolbooth.

John Knox's House: open all year. Mon–Sat.

Lady Stair's House: open all year except Jun, as Canongate Tolbooth.

Museum of Childhood: as Canongate Tolbooth.

National Gallery of Scotland: open all year. Mon–Sat all day. Sun pm only.

Outlook Tower: open all year.

Palace of Holyroodhouse: open all year.

Parliament House: open all year. Tue–Fri.

Scott Monument: open all year.

Scottish Experience: open all year.

Wax Museum: open all year.

11 NATIONAL GALLERY OF SCOTLAND

This is one of the most important small galleries in Europe. It has an excellent collection of paintings by Raphael, Titian, Gainsborough, Cézanne and many others.

12 SCOTT MONUMENT

Characters from Scott's work fill 64 niches in the monument, and it is possible to climb 287 steps almost to the top.

The following places of interest are to be seen on the detour to Holyroodhouse

13 JOHN KNOX'S HOUSE

This is probably the only surviving Scottish example of a 16th-century house complete with timbered galleries.

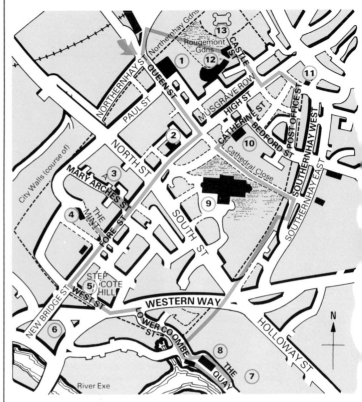

ROUTE DIRECTIONS

Begin in Queen St at the Northernhay St junction. Walk along Queen St past the Museum (1) and turn r. into High St. Pass the Guildhall (2) and at the traffic lights continue into Fore St. Turn r. along Mary Arches St to the church (3) and return to Fore St. Continue down to The Mint, turn r. and walk up to St Nicholas' Priory (4). Return to Fore St and go down to the crossroads, turning l. into West St and St Mary Steps Church (5). Before crossing the dual carriageway, look r. for the old Br. (6). Cross, turning l. and r. into Lower Coombe St. Bear r. to the quay (7) and the Maritime Museum (8). On the return, turn r. by the Custom House to follow the path beside the city walls. Cross Western Way at the top and pass another section of city walls. Cross South St to reach another path beside the walls. Cross the car park, then turn r. and l. into Southernhay West. Turn l. after about 150yds into the Cathedral Close for the Cathedral (9), continuing to St Martin's Church. Turn r. here and continue into Catherine St, past the almshouses (10), then turn r. into Bedford St and l. past the Post Office into Post Office St, following the city walls. Turn l. at the end of the wall, cross a paved area, passing the entrance to the Underground Passages (11), then turn l. into High St. After about 50yds turn r. into Castle St and just before the top of the hill, turn l. through the gates into Rougemont Gdns, where the Museum (12) and the Castle (13) ruins are. Bear r. where the path forks and turn l. through the arch into Northernhay Gdns. Turn l. and walk downhill to the Queen St gate, then turn l. into Queen St to complete the walk.

SEMPER FIDELIS

A *thriving city and excellent shopping centre, Exeter has a long and fascinating history and is packed with interesting things to see. The city suffered devastating bomb damage in World War II and as a result there is a lot of modern building. However, many gems of the medieval and Georgian city have survived, and in several places old and new stand companionably side by side. The new Guildhall shopping centre is built around the city's oldest church, whilst the historic quay and canal basin have been enhanced by the splendid Maritime Museum.*

The decorated bulkhead of a Portuguese boat in the Maritime Museum

1 ROYAL ALBERT MEMORIAL MUSEUM AND ART GALLERY

Opened in 1868, this large Victorian-style building has 14 exhibition rooms covering a wide range of subjects and periods. Natural history exhibits range from a stuffed Kilimanjaro giraffe and a tiger shot in Nepal by King George V, to the displays in the Devon Gallery, where many species of local wildlife are depicted in their various habitats. Other items of local interest include lacework from Honiton, an 18th-century wooden fire engine that belonged to the cathedral and a scale model of the old city of Exeter.

2 THE GUILDHALL

One of England's oldest municipal buildings, the Guildhall was rebuilt in 1330 on foundations that were Norman, or possibly even Saxon. Most of the outstanding features of the present building are later. The Tudor portico dates from 1593, as does the ornately carved inner doorway that leads into the hall. A striking feature of the interior is the medieval timbered roof.

3 ST MARY ARCHES CHURCH

This is the only church in Devon to retain its double Norman nave arcade. The interior is spacious and airy, and has interesting 16th- and 17th-century monuments to two mayors of Exeter.

4 ST NICHOLAS PRIORY

Founded soon after the Norman Conquest, the priory is one of Exeter's most fascinating buildings. The entire west range, consisting of the guest rooms, has survived. The Guest Hall, with its magnificent timbered roof, is where guests would have been entertained, with the sleeping quarters adjacent. After the Dissolution of the Monasteries by Henry VIII, the ecclesiastical buildings of St Nicholas were demolished whilst the domestic quarters eventually became the residence of a wealthy family.

5 ST MARY STEPS CHURCH

Originally adjoining the west gate of the city, this church is set in a delightful corner of Exeter, next to Stepcote Hill – a steep, cobbled medieval street – and near several lovely Tudor houses. On the tower wall is a lovely 17th-century clock with three figures – two quarter jacks and a central figure which strikes the hours. Features of the church's interior include the carved screen, with painted panels, and the Norman font.

St Mary Steps Church clock

6 MEDIEVAL EXE BRIDGE

The building of the new road system near the twin Exe bridges has made it possible to expose this substantial survival of the medieval city. Eight-and-a-half of the original arches have been revealed.

7 THE QUAY

Exeter has traded from here since Roman times, at first by river and, since 1566, by canal – the first canal with pound locks to be built in England. At the water's edge stands the fish market, whilst nearby is the Custom House, an elegant 17th-century brick building with a coat of arms on its pediment.

8 MARITIME MUSEUM

Over 100 craft from all over the world can be seen here. Some are afloat in the canal basin and may be boarded. These include a Hong Kong junk and the world's oldest working steam vessel, the dredger *Bertha*, designed by Brunel and built in 1844. Smaller craft are on display in two large warehouses. Here may be seen many kinds of primitive boat, from Welsh coracles to boats made from reeds and from dugouts to an ornately crafted small canoe from the Ellice Islands.

9 EXETER CATHEDRAL AND CLOSE

An almost miraculous survivor of the devastation that Exeter suffered during World War II, the Cathedral Church of St Peter is still the city's centrepiece 600 years after its completion. The west front is adorned with exquisitely carved figures, while, inside, the 14th-century rib-vaulting of the nave is breathtaking. It is the longest stretch of such vaulting in the world. Exeter is noted for its roof bosses, beautifully carved and recently repainted in their original brilliant colours. Exquisite medieval craftsmanship can be seen in the huge, pinnacled Bishop's Throne and in the misericords of the choir stalls. The north-eastern side of Cathedral Close retains many lovely old buildings; notice particularly No. 10, the residence of the Bishop of Crediton, which has a beautifully carved oak door leading into a little cobbled courtyard. At the corner is what was once Mol's Coffee House. It is said that Sir Francis Drake, Hawkins and others used to meet here.

10 RUINS OF ST CATHERINE'S ALMSHOUSES

Founded in 1450 as a charity to take care of 13 poor men, these almshouses suffered terrible bomb damage in 1942. The buildings comprised a refectory, rooms for the inmates, and a chapel, much of the shell of which still stands.

CITY WALLS

Early in the third century the Romans improved the original earthen rampart round the city by building a massive stone wall. Enclosing almost 100 acres, the wall was strengthened in medieval times and much of it still survives, though none of the original gates which once pierced it have survived.

Mol's Coffee House, in the Close

11 UNDERGROUND PASSAGES

Exeter was privileged among medieval cities in having a supply of fresh spring water piped into the middle of the city. The water ran through a network of vaulted underground conduits. Part of the system – now dry of course – has been restored and is a fascinating place to explore.

12 ROUGEMONT HOUSE MUSEUM

This is Exeter's main collection of archaeological material. Most of the exhibits were found locally, many of them as a result of excavations by the museum's own archaeological field unit.

13 ROUGEMONT CASTLE AND GARDENS

All that survives of Exeter's Norman castle today is the restored gatehouse – which also served as the keep – and what is known as Athelstan's Tower. A section of the walls also survives, and the moat and castle precincts have been landscaped to form pleasant, shady gardens around the ruins.

EARLY CLOSING: *Wed & Sat.*

MARKET DAYS: *Mon & Fri.*

PARKING: *Paul St, Mary Arches St, Queen St.*

OPENING TIMES:

Royal Albert Memorial Museum and Art Gallery: open all year. Tue–Sat.

Guildhall: open all year (except when in use). Mon–Sat.

St Nicholas' Priory: open all year. Tue–Sat.

Maritime Museum: open all year.

Underground Passages: open all year. Tue–Sat pm only.

Rougemont House Museum: open all year. Tue–Sat.

The largest city in Scotland, but never the capital, Glasgow grew up on the banks of the Molendinar Burn, a tributary of the Clyde, round a church established by the 6th-century Kentigern, otherwise known as Mungo and under that name the city's patron saint. By Victorian times, Glasgow had far outgrown its medieval boundaries and was beginning to expand relentlessly to the west, across the valley of the River Kelvin.

ROUTE DIRECTIONS

Start on the north side of the bridge on Kelvin Way, facing north. Take the path r. through the gates, turn r. over the footbridge, then l. along the riverside path, through Kelvingrove Pk (east) (1). At the next bridge turn r. around a war memorial, then take a path uphill to reach Earl Roberts Statue. Turn r. to leave park and immediately turn r. along Park Ter (2), turning l. into Park Gate and continuing forward to re-enter the park. Return to the war memorial, and bear right along path nearest river. Cross the river twice and go under four road bridges, including Belmont Br (3), with the Stevenson Memorial Church beside it, before turning l. over a footbridge and l. up the steps to the Botanic Gdns (4). At top of steps turn r. then l. to pass the entrance to Kibble Palace, then leave the gardens by the main exit gate. Turn r. to cross Gt Western Rd and continue l. then turn r. up steps into Hillhead St. At far end continue forward on short walkway passing the Hunterian Art Gallery (5) on the r. Cross University Ave to visit the university (6) and turn l., then at the foot of the hill turn r. into Kelvin Way. Take the first drive on the r. into Kelvingrove Pk (west) (7). Pass cottages (8), then turn l. over Partick Br (9), and l. again back into the park opposite Kelvin Hall. Bear r. beside the war memorial along the front of the Art Galleries and Museum (10) and at the far end turn l. then r. at the bowling greens back to Kelvin Way.

Elegant Kibble Palace in the Botanic Garden

1 KELVINGROVE PARK (EAST)
In 1854 Sir Joseph Paxton, the Berwickshire-born landscape architect who also designed the Crystal Palace in London, was commissioned to lay out what was originally known as the West End Park around the banks of the River Kelvin. Soon renamed Kelvingrove, it is one of more than 60 parks within the city boundaries.

2 PARK TERRACE
The curving terrace on the summit of Woodlands Hill, overlooking the park, is one of the most elegant architectural designs in Glasgow. It is the work of Charles Wilson, who completed the terrace and the broad staircase which leads to it from the south-east wing of the park in 1855.

3 BELMONT BRIDGE
This high-level bridge dates from 1870. Beside it, rising above the tree-lined riverbank, is Stevenson Memorial Church, built in 1902 and topped by a crown tower. When the site of the church was being prepared, workmen struck a seam of coal. It was dug out and used to fire the boiler of the steam crane which lifted the blocks of sandstone to the roof.

4 BOTANIC GARDENS
After passing under Queen Margaret Bridge, opened in 1929, the walk enters the Botanic Gardens, moved here from another site in 1842. At first the property of the Royal Botanic Institution, they were taken over by the city and opened to the public in 1891. The most notable feature of the gardens is the spectacular

Kibble Palace with its series of linked glass domes. Originally the conservatory of a mansion house at Coulport on Loch Long, and transported here pane by pane for its opening in 1873, it has 23,000 square feet of floor area and is one of the largest glasshouses in Britain.

5 HUNTERIAN ART GALLERY
Completed in 1981, the gallery contains Glasgow University's museum and art treasures, based on a collection bequeathed by William Hunter in 1783. There are prints, sculptures and a world-famous Whistler collection. But the centrepiece of the gallery is a reconstruction of the house at 78 Southpark Avenue, one street down the hill, where the architect and designer Charles Rennie Mackintosh lived for 8 years from 1906. On three floors, the reconstruction

includes his dining room, drawing room and studio, the main bedroom, hall and staircase, all with authentic furnishings.

6 GLASGOW UNIVERSITY

The University was founded in 1451 by Bishop William Turnbull. Classes were held at first in the crypt of the cathedral, and then a college was built in the High Street. In 1870 the move was made here to Gilmorehill, to a range of buildings designed by Sir George Gilbert Scott.

7 KELVINGROVE PARK (WEST)

From this hillside the main spire of the University is clearly seen. It was not part of Sir George Gilbert Scott's original design, but was added in 1887 by his son, John Oldrid Scott.

8 COTTAGES

Downhill from the University and beside the Western Infirmary, these buildings are the only ones left in Kelvingrove Park from the 1901 exhibition. They were built by Lever Brothers as replicas of the workers' cottages at their factory at Port Sunlight on Merseyside, and were presented to the City of Glasgow once the Exhibition had closed.

Kelvingrove Park

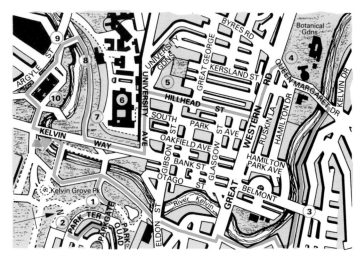

9 PARTICK BRIDGE

The walk crosses the River Kelvin by the bridge of 1800, which used to carry the main road between Glasgow on the east bank and Partick, then an independent burgh, on the west. Alongside it, the present main road goes over the second Partick Bridge, opened in 1878.

10 ART GALLERIES AND MUSEUM

Housing one of the finest art collections in Britain, this riotous design, with its hugely ornamented upper area, was the winner out of 62 entries in a competition held after the 1888 Exhibition. The collections include paintings by Dutch,

French, Italian and British masters, and there are also extensive collections of sculpture, pottery, porcelain, costumes and armour, as well as archaeology and natural history departments.

EARLY CLOSING: *Tue.*

PARKING: *Kelvin Way & neighbouring streets.*

OPENING TIMES:

Botanic Gardens: open all year.

Kibble Palace: open all year.

Hunterian Art Gallery: open all year, Mon – Fri all day. Sat am only.

Art Galleries and Museum: open all year. Mon – Sat all day, Sun pm only.

ROUTE DIRECTIONS

Start the walk in College St and walk up to the cathedral (1). Leave the Close (2) at the northeast corner and turn l. through St Mary's Gateway. Continue along the footpath through St Mary's Sq and turn r. into Archdeacon St to reach the remains of St Oswald's Priory (3). Return along Archdeacon St and turn l. into Westgate St passing Bishop Hooper's Lodging (4) and St Nicholas Church. Turn r. into Berkeley St (5) passing the Fountain Inn and the Transport Museum. Here turn l. into Longsmith St, r. into Ladybellegate St and shortly l. into Blackfriars to reach Blackfriars Abbey (6). Return to Ladybellegate St and turn l., to reach the Old Custom House (7) ahead. From here turn r. into Commercial Rd, fork l. and turn l. into Southgate St. Continue past St Mary de Crypt Church and School (8) to reach the Cross and St Michael's Church Tower (9). Here turn l. along Westgate St to return to College St.

Metal bellringers, made in 1904, above a shop in Southgate Street

Gloucester had its origins in a Roman fortress called Glevum, but it was not until late Saxon times, when it became an important seat of the Mercians, that its story became at all well documented. The city gradually increased in importance, reaching a position of great wealth and prestige as a port in the 13th century. However, Bristol took over the vital sea trade later in the Middle Ages, and Gloucester became something of a backwater until the arrival of the Industrial Revolution when new docks were built and a canal cut to the Severn. Since then it has expanded rapidly and both new housing and industry are much in evidence in and around the old city.

1 GLOUCESTER CATHEDRAL

One of the glories of British architecture, Gloucester Cathedral is built on the site of a monastery founded in 681. In 1072 William the Conqueror appointed a Norman chaplain called Serlo abbot of what had long been a spiritually exhausted community. By 1100 Serlo had transformed the old monastery into a thriving and increasingly powerful abbey with a magnificent new church

Half timbering in Southgate Street

that survives almost intact. The body of Edward II, refused burial at other foundations, was brought here and interred with great ceremony in 1327, and very shortly his tomb became a place of pilgrimage. Income obtained from gifts to the shrine enabled new building to take place, much of it done in the Perpendicular style, which was to dominate all ecclesiastical architecture for the next 150 years. The tower was built in the mid 15th century, and the lovely Lady Chapel redesigned at the end of the same century. Apart from the architecture, the chief treasures are perhaps the tomb of Edward II, the superb east window with its 14th-century glass, and the manuscripts preserved in the library. Many of the monastery buildings, for example the lavatorium and the chapter house, still stand intact within the abbey precincts.

2 CATHEDRAL CLOSE
Several fine houses dating from the 16th to 18th centuries flank the dignified Close, but of particular interest is the Parliament Room – a timber-framed hall set into a 13th-century stone building. It was here that Richard II held his Parliament in 1398. To the west of the Close is St Mary's Gateway. This dates from the 13th century and features elegant Norman vaulting.

3 ST OSWALD'S PRIORY
Ethelfleda, the Lady of the Mercians, founded this priory in 909 and turned it into a national shrine by moving the bones of St Oswald – king and martyr of Northumbria – to it. One of the remaining arches in the ruins is believed to date from the 10th century, but the others are probably two or three hundred years later.

4 BISHOP HOOPER'S LODGING
Traditionally painted in black and white, one of this attractive group of three buildings is held to be where a protestant bishop, John Hooper, spent his last night before being martyred in 1555. The house is now used by the Gloucester Folk Museum.

5 BERKELEY STREET
Standing on the right of the street is the 17th-century Fountain Inn. Decorating the exterior is a relief portrait of William III on horseback which is said to commemorate the king riding a white horse up the inn stairs. Further along the street is the old fire station, which has been converted into a transport museum. The exhibits include horse-drawn vehicles, pedal cycles and early motor vehicles.

6 BLACKFRIARS ABBEY
Blackfriars is one of only three Dominican friaries that have survived in Britain. It is situated just inside the walls that encircled both Roman and medieval Gloucester. Henry III donated large sums of money to the Dominican friars who were

established in Gloucester during the 13th century and the church and cloister buildings date mainly from this time.

7 THE OLD CUSTOM HOUSE
Built in the 19th century, when there was a bustling quayside here, the Old Custom House is now the headquarters of the Gloucestershire Regiment. The regiment has a museum here featuring a collection of uniforms, pictures, old weapons, models and personal relics recalling over 280 years of regimental history.

8 ST MARY DE CRYPT CHURCH AND SCHOOL
The cruciform plan of this church has remained unaltered since Norman times, but the only Norman work that has survived is to be found in the arches of the crypt: the style of the rest of the church is mostly 14th- and 15th-century. George Whitefield, the famous Gloucester preacher, delivered his first sermon here after his ordination in 1734. A grammar school was built into the north wall of the church in the 16th century.

9 THE CROSS AND ST MICHAEL'S CHURCH TOWER
The Cross has been the focal point of the city since Roman times and marked the entrance to the forum which extended beneath Southgate Street. At one time four churches were grouped near the Cross, but the only survivor of these is the tower of St Michael's Church.

MARKET DAY: *Sat.*

PARKING: *Longsmith St, Eastgate St.*

OPENING TIMES:

Bishop Hooper's Lodging: *open all year except BHs. Mon–Sat all day. Sun pm summer only.*

Blackfriars Abbey: *open all year. Mon–Sat all day, Sun pm only.*

Custom House: *open all year. Mon–Fri.*

Established around AD 700 as a cathedral city, Hereford soon assumed the role of watchdog – and often victim – in the turbulent Welsh border lands. Its first cathedral was burnt down by the Welsh, and the castle, also destroyed, was rebuilt to withstand a few more centuries of conflict before being captured during the Civil War and subsequently demolished. Today Hereford is better known as a thriving agricultural centre. The rich, red soil that surrounds it makes ideal pasture, and the world's most widely distributed breed of beef cattle takes its name from the city. Much of Hereford's charm for the modern visitor lies in the old streets of its compact centre, still laid out to their original medieval plan. The city has many fine Georgian houses, and though the magnificent cathedral is still its chief treasure, there are a host of lesser-known attractions – like the houses in St Owen's Street or All Saints' Church – that should not be overlooked.

ROUTE INSTRUCTIONS

Begin the walk in High Town (1) by the Old House. Walk westwards by the Old House past the Button Market into the High St and turn l. opposite All Saints Church (2) into Broad St. Take the first l. into East St and turn r. into Church St (3) to reach the cathedral (4). From the cathedral turn l. and go forward into King St (opposite west front) with the Museum and Art Gallery (5) opposite. Turn l. into Bridge St, cross the Wye Bridge (6) and immediately turn l. on to a riverside footpath beside the Saracen's Head Inn. Follow this path through Bishop's Meadow (7) to the Victoria Footbridge, recross the river, then go up the steps on the l., to reach Castle Green (8). Follow the path along the green's left-hand side, then at the Canoe Centre go forward passing Castle Cliff and on to Quay St with Redcliffe Gardens (9) on the r. Turn r. into Castle Hill, passing St Ethelbert's Well, then turn l. along the alleyway in front of The Fosse. At the end turn r. into Castle St. Turn l. by the Castle Pool Hotel into St Ethelbert St. At the end turn l. into St Owen's St (10), and fork l. by St Peter's Church, passing the Shire Hall to reach High Town again.

Wye Bridge and the cathedral

1 HIGH TOWN
This spacious pedestrianised area was the market place in Saxon times and is still the heart of Hereford's shopping centre. In the midst of all the modern stores stands the Old House, a fine black-and-white timbered building dating from 1621. It is all that remains of Butcher's Row, a range of similar Jacobean buildings that once stood here. The house contains 17th-century furniture, including four-poster beds. In summer it is used as a brass-rubbing centre. On the north side of High Town is the Butter Market, with an elaborate 19th-century façade topped by a clock-tower and a bell.

2 ALL SAINTS' CHURCH
The crooked spire of this fine medieval church is one of Hereford's principal landmarks. The church dates almost entirely from the 13th and 14th centuries, and contains some exquisite examples of the woodcarver's art. Among them are the canopied choir stalls with their carved misericords, the 15th-century roof beams and the ornate pulpit, which is of Flemish design and dates from 1621.

3 CHURCH STREET
This quaint, narrow shopping street is one of the city's most attractive. Most of its old shop-fronts have survived, and house a variety of small specialist businesses.

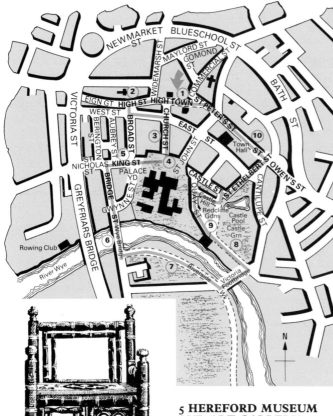

In the cathedral is St Stephen's Chair, said to be the oldest in England

4 CATHEDRAL

The present cathedral was probably begun in about 1080. Little Norman work is visible on the outside, but the majestic semicircular arches and massive round pillars of the nave betray the cathedral's origins. Later additions include the lovely Early English Lady Chapel, the fine 14th-century crossing tower and the present west front, completed in 1908. One of many outstanding treasures in the cathedral is the Mappa Mundi, made around 1290. The map is over four feet across and depicts a flat world with Jerusalem at its centre. Near the Mappa Mundi in the north choir aisle, 54 steps lead up to the room where the famous chained library is kept. Four large bookcases, made in 1611, house some 1,500 volumes which are attached by chains to rods on the bookcases. Many of the books are hundreds of years old, including the *Anglo-Saxon Gospels*, written around AD 800. The buildings that adjoin the cathedral on the south side are well worth visiting. From the south-east transept the Vicars' Cloister, which has an exquisitely carved roof, leads to the College of the Vicars Choral. Built in the late 15th century, this consists of a delightful quadrangle surrounded by cottages where the 27 vicars choral lived.

5 HEREFORD MUSEUM AND ART GALLERY

Opened in 1874, this distinctive building in the High Victorian style is lavishly embellished with all kinds of decorative carvings. The museum collection is based on local archaeology and natural history, with exhibitions devoted to rural life, including craft tools and farm implements. Works of art include English oils and watercolours as well as examples of the applied arts.

6 WYE BRIDGE

This handsome sandstone bridge over the Wye was built in 1490 and, although it was widened in 1826, four of its six arches are original.

7 BISHOP'S MEADOW

A riverside walk shaded by an avenue of majestic copper beeches skirts this grassy open space, offering fine views across the river to the cathedral and the Bishop's Palace.

8 CASTLE GREEN

Once the bailey of Hereford Castle, this area overlooking the river is now a well-kept garden with a bowling green. Its focal point is a tall column erected by the citizens of Hereford in 1809 in honour of Lord Nelson, who was a freeman of the city. On the western side of the Green is Castle Cliffe, the only medieval building in the bailey and once the castle's water-gate. The building later became the Bridewell, or city gaol.

9 REDCLIFFE GARDENS

Now a public garden with a modern bandstand and small pond, this was once the site of the Norman keep of Hereford Castle. The castle covered a large area, and was an important base for Henry III's campaigns in Wales. It was a Royalist stronghold in the Civil War, but fell to the Parliamentarians in 1646 and was demolished in 1660. On the north side of Redcliffe Gardens, a plaque and drinking fountain record the site of St Ethelbert's Well, whose water was said to have healing powers. Nearby stands an extraordinary 19th-century mock-Jacobean villa known as the Fosse. Its frontage, which has unusual octagonal-paned windows, overlooks Castle Pool, once part of the moat.

10 ST OWEN'S STREET

This is a wide street of handsome buildings, many of them Georgian or Queen Anne, with typically fine doorways and windows. At the north-western end is the town hall, a turn-of-the-century extravaganza in rich reddish-brown stone. Across the road stands St Peter's Church, the Civic Church of Hereford, which has a fine Early English chancel and beautiful 15th-century choir stalls. Opposite, in Union Street, is the Shire Hall, an impressive classical building with an eight-pillared portico.

EARLY CLOSING: *Thu.*

MARKET DAY: *Wed.*

PARKING: *Gaol St, Bath St, Commercial St.*

OPENING TIMES:

Hereford Museum and Art Gallery: open all year. Tue–Sat.

The Old House: open all year. Mon–Sat.

The College of the Vicars Choral

The traditional 'capital' of the Highlands, and its industrial and transport centre, Inverness has a history going well back into Pictish times. The town itself was created a royal burgh by David I in the 12th century. Later monarchs fortified it, and it developed strong trading links with Scandinavia, the Low Countries and the Mediterranean. Many violent incidents have occurred here over the years: Mary Queen of Scots had the Constable of Inverness Castle hanged from its walls; Cromwell's clock tower serves as a reminder of the part Inverness played in the Civil War; and the town was involved in the Jacobite Rebellions of 1715 and 1745.

ROUTE DIRECTIONS

Start at the Town House (1) in High St (2). Turn l. up Castle Wynd, passing Inverness Museum (3) on r. Continue straight on up the steps and pathway to the Castle (4). From the Flora Macdonald statue (5) bear l. downhill to exit and bear r. into View Place, then turn sharp r. on to Castle Rd and immediately l. round a church, then l. onto Ness Bank beside the River Ness (6). Follow the riverside pavement and then go straight on along a riverside footpath. Just before this joins a public road, turn r. over a footbridge and l. onto another riverside path. Turn r. across a footbridge onto the first of the Ness Islands (7), and at the southern end cross a curving footbridge onto the next main island. From it, take another footbridge onto the far bank of the river and turn r. onto a footpath alongside the river bank. Follow the Ness Walk footway past the Eden Court Theatre (8) and St Andrew's Cathedral (9) to reach Ness Bridge. Turn r. to cross it and return to the Town House.

1 TOWN HOUSE

Not the kind of municipal building that might be expected in the north of Scotland, this exercise in Victorian Gothic was opened in 1882. When Lloyd George was on holiday in Ross-shire in September 1921 he had to convene an unexpected Cabinet meeting, and it was held in the Town House. The signatures of all the Cabinet Ministers who attended are still on display. Beside the entrance to the Town House is the restored mercat cross of Inverness, standing on the *Clach-na-Cuddain* – the stone of the tubs – on which women used to rest their baskets of washing.

2 HIGH STREET AND BRIDGE STREET

This route has been the main street of Inverness since the 1680s, when a toll-bridge was built across the River Ness. It was washed away in the great floods of 1849 and replaced six years later by a suspension bridge. The latest Ness Bridge was opened in 1961. On the north-east corner of the Bridge Street-High Street junction is the old Tolbooth, built in 1791. Prisoners awaiting trial by the circuit courts used to be held here. The steeple was damaged during an earth tremor which hit the town in 1816, but it was later repaired.

3 MUSEUM AND ART GALLERY

The present building was opened in 1966, on the site of an earlier museum of 1881. It houses collections and displays of Highland wildlife, history, weaponry, music and crofting, and there is a fine selection of Highland silverware. This is the resting-place of Duncan Morrison's famous Punch and Judy show, which toured the Highlands for a century until 1976.

4 INVERNESS CASTLE

Inverness was a fortified town for many hundreds of years. On this hilltop site there was an 18th-century stronghold called Fort George, captured and blown up by the Jacobites in the Rebellion of 1745. The site was cleared in 1834 and the first part of the present pink sandstone castle was built for the Sheriff Court. A second part, now council offices, was added in 1847. Between the two is the old well, discovered during building work in 1909 and dating at least from the time of the original Fort George.

5 FLORA MACDONALD STATUE

From the statue set up in 1899 in memory of the famous Jacobite heroine there is a fine view of the River Ness and of two wooded crags on the western edge of the town. The one to the left is Tomnahurich, a bare heathery slope until it was planted with pines in 1753 and now one of the most beautifully situated cemeteries in the country. To its right is Craig Phadrig, with the remains of a vitrified fort on the summit. This is said to be the site of the capital of the ancient Pictish kings.

6 RIVER NESS

An undisclosed part of the River Ness was the scene of an incident in 565, reported in the biography of St Columba. When one of his men swam across the river to bring a boat from the far bank, he was attacked by an *aquatilis bestia* – a water beast. Columba rebuked it, and it promptly swam away. This was the first written account of a monster, if not in Loch Ness, at least in its river.

7 NESS ISLANDS

At one time the Town Council of Inverness are said to have entertained visiting judges at open-air meals on the islands, serving them with fresh-caught salmon from the river. Towards the end of the 18th century the decaying trees were cleared and new ones planted. In the 1830s Joseph Mitchell, the civil engineer who lived in the town and worked with Thomas Telford, arranged for the two main islands to be linked with each other and with both banks by a series of footbridges. These were swept away in the floods of 1849. But Mitchell had new suspension bridges set up, and they remain there still, connecting a series of wooded island walks.

The Tolbooth Steeple, restored after earth tremor damage in 1816

8 EDEN COURT THEATRE

Opened in 1976, this very modern theatre is the main centre for plays, concerts and conferences in Inverness. It takes its name from Robert Eden, Bishop in Victorian times of the Episcopalian Diocese of Moray, Ross and Caithness. The original Eden Court was the Bishop's Palace, and is now part of the theatre complex.

9 ST ANDREW'S CATHEDRAL

Robert Eden was at first Bishop of Moray and Ross, but when Caithness was added to his diocese in 1864 he decided that he should move from Elgin to Inverness, which was more central. The original plans of the architect, Dr Alexander Ross, who was Provost of the town for a term of six years after 1889, included spires – which had to be omitted – on top of the square towers. With an interior as impressive as its Gothic Revival exterior, St Andrew's was completed in 1869.

EARLY CLOSING: *Wed.*

MARKET DAY: *Tue.*

PARKING: *Castle St, Ardconnel St.*

OPENING TIMES:

Town House: on enquiry at the Town House, Mon–Fri.

Museum and Art Gallery: open all year. Mon–Sat.

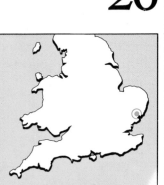

The county town of Suffolk stands on the estuary of the River Orwell, a position which led to its being an important port as early as the 10th century. The town was granted its first charter by King John in 1200 and for the next four centuries prospered thanks to the trade in Suffolk cloth to the Continent. Although greatly rebuilt during Victoria's reign, Ipswich retains part of its architectural heritage in the form of medieval churches and a few Tudor buildings. Present-day Ipswich is still prominent in shipping and remains one of the main commercial centres of East Anglia.

ROUTE DIRECTIONS

From Cornhill (1) walk along pedestrianised Lion St, then cross over the Arcade St – King St intersection into Elm St, passing the Chamber of Commerce. Continue along Elm St to St Mary's Elm Church (2). From here return, and turn r. into Museum St. Cross over Princes St into Friar St and take the path on the r., passing the Unitarian Meeting House (3). At the end of this walkway, across Franciscan Way, is St Nicholas Church (4). Facing the church, turn l. and then r. at the traffic lights into St Nicholas St. Pass Wolsey House and at the end of St Peter St, turn l. into College St (5). Just beyond Foundation St on the l., is the church of St Mary-at-the-Quay (6). Keep on past the Customs House (7). Continue into Salthouse St, then turn r. into Fore St where the Old Neptune Inn (8) is down on the r. From here, cross over and turn l. into Grimwade St, then l. again into St Clement's La via bollards. St Clement's Church (9) is on the r. Turn r. at the end of the path into Fore St, then l. into Orwell Pl. Beyond Tacket St and Dog's Head St, turn r. into St Stephen's La. Just before reaching Butter Market crossroads, the Ancient House (10) is on the r. From here go into Dial La, then r. into Tavern St where the Great White Horse Hotel (11) is at the end on the l. Return along Tavern St, and turn into Hatton Court, at the end of which is St Mary le Tower Church (12). From the church, walk along Oak La to Northgate St (13). Turn l. and cross St Margaret's Plain into Soane St, where an immediate l. leads into Christchurch Park, in which St Margaret's Church (14) is on the r. Further into the park straight ahead is Christchurch Mansion (15). From the mansion walk to the round pond, then bear l., following a path past the war memorial, to emerge in Fonnereau Rd. Turn l. then cross over into Neale St, then take a sharp r. into Charles St. At the end turn l. into the High St and pass the Ipswich Museum (16). Cross Crown St then Westgate St, into Museum St (17). Turn l. into Arcade St which leads via an archway into King St. Turn l. into Princes St to complete the walk at Cornhill.

1 CORNHILL

This was the borough's ancient market place, and it was the focal point of the Anglo-Saxon street plan whose shape can still be traced in Ipswich. Three buildings dominate the square today – the Post Office, Lloyds Bank and the Town Hall. The last of these is constructed in Italianate style with a French pavilion roof.

2 ST MARY'S ELM CHURCH

A handsome Tudor tower is the most striking external feature of this church. It has a Norman doorway, while most of the rest of the structure dates from the 15th century.

3 UNITARIAN MEETING HOUSE

Considered by many to be one of Ipswich's finest buildings, this lovely chapel was built by a local carpenter at the very end of the 17th century. Its simple interior achieves great dignity and spaciousness by the careful placing of the windows.

4 ST NICHOLAS CHURCH

Perhaps the most interesting items in this church are the carved stones in the chancel. They are thought to date from the 11th century, and show Scandinavian influence. One depicts St Michael and the dragon, while on another is a relief of a boar.

5 COLLEGE STREET

Wolsey's Gateway is all that remains of an unfinished college in honour of Cardinal Wolsey, who fell from favour before completion of the ambitious project. Opposite are various gloomy dockland buildings.

6 ST MARY-AT-THE-QUAY

A disused church which has a fine hammerbeam roof in the nave. The exterior is decorated with patterns of dressed flints; a type of ornamentation typical of East Anglia and usually called flushwork.

7 CUSTOMS HOUSE

At one time this striking Victorian building overlooked what was, in its heyday, the largest dock in Britain.

8 THE OLD NEPTUNE INN

Although dated 1639, interior evidence suggests that this inn is, in part, almost 700 years old. Originally the home of a merchant, the premises were enlarged and as such served as a tavern for two centuries. Nowadays, it is once again a private residence.

9 ST CLEMENT'S CHURCH

Its position close to the historic quayside is reflected in the number of monuments here to seamen and men connected with shipping. One is to Sir Thomas Slade, designer of HMS *Victory*.

10 THE ANCIENT HOUSE

Built over 400 years ago, Ancient House is an excellent example of 16th-century domestic architecture. It is locally claimed to have been the hiding place of Charles II following the Battle of Worcester in 1651, and has a royal coat of arms above its main doorway. The outstanding feature of the building is its ornate plasterwork, known as pargeting.

11 THE GREAT WHITE HORSE HOTEL

It was here, Dickens wrote in *Pickwick Papers*, that Samuel Pickwick was found entering the bedroom of Miss Witherfield, an already engaged young lady. Although the building has a Georgian façade, it actually dates back to the early 16th century.

The Ancient House – a fine example of the decorative plasterwork called pargeting

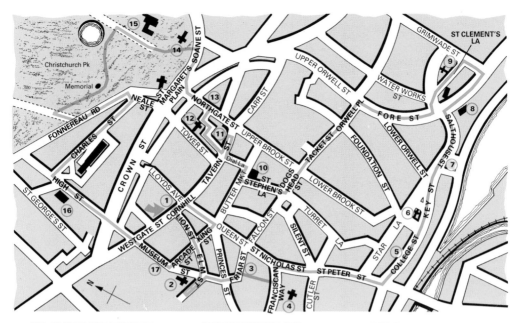

12 ST MARY LE TOWER CHURCH

Although mentioned in the Domesday Book, the major part of the present church dates from the 1850s and 1860s. Today, it is the civic church of Ipswich.

13 NORTHGATE STREET

Here can be seen a variety of early 19th-century buildings, the best of which is Northgate House. It was built in 1821 and has giant pilasters. Along on the left is the 15th-century Pykenham's Gateway, the fine entrance to a mansion named after William Pykenham, a one-time archdeacon of Suffolk.

14 ST MARGARET'S CHURCH

This superb example of ecclesiastical architecture has its origins in the 13th century, although the porch, tower and font are all 15th century.

15 CHRISTCHURCH MANSION

An outstanding Tudor house built on the site of an Augustinian priory that was founded in the 12th century. A fire in the 17th century necessitated the rebuilding of the upper storey. Nowadays, the mansion houses the Wolsey Collection, which includes paintings by Constable and Gainsborough. Also here is much of interest from old Ipswich – fragments of demolished buildings, pottery, and ancient furniture.

16 IPSWICH MUSEUM

This Victorian building houses a comprehensive collection of exhibits which monitor the history of Suffolk.

17 MUSEUM STREET

For centuries this was the town's business sector and as a result many interesting buildings line the thoroughfare, including a timbered house dating back to 1467 and the old museum, a stuccoed building with bizarre Tuscan columns.

MARKET DAY: *Tue, Fri & Sat.*

PARKING: *Tacket St, Cox La, Claude St.*

OPENING TIMES:

Christchurch Mansion: open all year. Mon - Sat; Sun pm only.

Ipswich Museum: open all year. Mon – Sat.

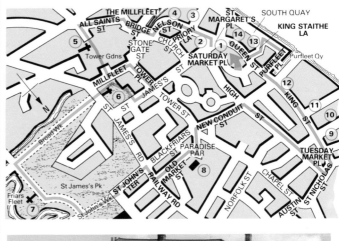

ROUTE DIRECTIONS

Start at Saturday Market Pl and the Guildhall of the Holy Trinity (1). From here, turn r. into St Margaret's Place where St Margaret's Church (2) is on the l. Continue, passing St Margaret's La (3), cross over Priory La and into Nelson St (4). At the next junction turn r. into Bridge St and straight along to All Saints' St, then turn l. along a path down which All Saints' Church (5) is on the r. At the end of the path pass under the arch, go across Millfleet and into Tower Pl. From here, turn r. into St James's St then turn r. again into the gardens of Greyfriars Tower (6). Leave the gardens by the steps, using the pedestrian crossing to reach The Walks. At an old archway turn l. for Red Mount Chapel (7). Beyond the tennis-courts turn l. into St John's Ter. Turn r. at the traffic-lights into Railway Rd. Turn l. into Old Market St where Lynn Museum (8) is situated. From here, walk along Paradise Rd, pass the post office, and turn r. into New Conduit St. Beyond the shopping precinct, turn r. into the High St and on to Tuesday Market Pl, in which is the Corn Hall (9). Enter King St with, on the r., the Fermoy Centre, contained in the Guildhall of St George (10). Further along King St, at No 27, is the Museum of Social History (11). Pass the Custom House (12). Turn r. into Purfleet Pl, then l. beside the River Great Ouse, and then l. again into King's Staith La. Turn r. into Queen St. Here along on the r. is Clifton House (13). Continue, keeping to the left-hand side (beware of the narrow pavement) until reaching Burkitt Court and Thoresby College (14). Return to Saturday Market Pl.

Wrought-ironwork in the town

Known locally simply as Lynn, the town is historically a market produce centre which, over the years, has developed into an important port and industrial hub. The town is located on the banks of the Great Ouse and is thus ideally placed to serve most of the Midlands via its many waterway connections. In the past there has been trade here in such diverse commodities as wine and furs. Lynn has retained much of its heritage, from 11th-century beginnings to present times, readily reflected in buildings spanning medieval to imposing Georgian.

1 GUILDHALL

Although forming one complex, the Guildhall in fact comprises four different parts built at differing times and in differing styles. The oldest part is the original Guildhall of the Holy Trinity. This was built in 1421, and with its façade of patterned flint and stone, is one of King's Lynn's finest buildings. Attached to it is an Elizabethan addition, also of brick and flint. Also in the group are the old gaol and the Assembly Rooms, both of the 18th century, and the town hall, built in 1895. The Guildhall houses a magnificent collection of civic regalia, including the famous King John's Cup, a superb 14th-century loving cup made of gold and enamel.

2 ST MARGARET'S CHURCH

The 12th-century towers of this lovely church form a prominent landmark in the tour. The interior was drastically remodelled in 1746, and further alterations were made in 1875. However, numerous internal

Top: ancient Tuesday Market Place

features remain, including two superb 14th-century brasses, among the best and largest to be seen in England.

3 ST MARGARET'S LANE

A glance to the right at the junction of this street with Priory Lane will reveal the Georgian façade of St Margaret's House. Next door is the Hanseatic Warehouse, built in the great days of Baltic trading during the 15th century. Ahead and to the right is the red-painted Hampton Court. This building dates from the 12th century and has seen many modifications and restorations over the years.

4 NELSON STREET

Many 17th- and 18th-century buildings can be seen in this street. One of the best is Hampton Court, a timber-framed merchant's house which still has its counting house, warehouses and apprentices' hall. The traceried doorway of No. 9 is particularly interesting

and No. 15 is a fine two-and-a-half storey Georgian house with a pedimented doorway and Tuscan columns. Further down this pleasant thoroughfare, just at the left-hand curve, is a handsome converted 18th-century granary.

5 ALL SAINTS' CHURCH
This church has a history stretching back to Norman times, but most of its present structure is of 14th-century date. It retains traces of a little Norman chapel that stood on the south side, while nearby are well-preserved remains of an anchorite's cell. Also of interest are the remains of a 14th-century wooden screen.

6 THE GARDENS OF GREYFRIARS TOWER
Here will be found the town's war memorial, under the shadow of a 14th-century octagonal tower which is the most substantial remnant of a monastery which once covered a considerable area.

7 RED MOUNT CHAPEL
A relic of the Virgin Mary was said to have been kept here, and the chapel was certainly a stopping place of early pilgrims on their way to Walsingham. The building was begun in 1485, and is an octagon of red brick, each side having an angled buttress. The upper floor chapel has an exceptional fan-vaulted roof.

8 LYNN MUSEUM
Formerly a chapel, this building now houses a wide range of local exhibits covering archaeology, geology and natural history. Of special interest is an unusual collection of medieval pilgrims' badges.

9 THE CORN HALL
Ionic columns, a statue of Ceres, the goddess of corn, sheaves, and the town's coat of arms all decorate this exuberant 19th-century structure.

10 GUILDHALL OF ST GEORGE
Constructed in the 15th century, this is the oldest and largest medieval guildhall in England. Its present function is as a theatre and occasional concert-hall.

11 MUSEUM OF SOCIAL HISTORY
The collections here give an insight into many local crafts and customs, and include an excellent toy collection.

12 THE CUSTOMS HOUSE
Standing proudly alone by the quay, this delicate-looking building is perhaps the most famous in the town. It was built in 1683 from stone shipped direct to the site along the navigations which contributed so much to Lynn's prosperity. A statue of Charles II graces the niche above the main doorway. The ground floor is partly

Designed by a local architect who was also an artist and scientist, the Custom House is a fine Renaissance building which embellishes the quayside

arched and at one time opened straight onto the street. A lantern tower crowns this prettiest of official buildings.

13 CLIFTON HOUSE
In some ways this merchant's house tells the whole story of King's Lynn. Its earliest parts date from the 12th century, and remains from virtually every succeeding century can be found somewhere in the structure. The most prominent part is the tall courtyard tower, added in Elizabethan times.

14 THORESBY COLLEGE
Originally this college was founded in 1500 for Trinity Guild priests. It was restored in the 1960s, and its fine hammerbeam roof was saved.

EARLY CLOSING: *Wed.*

MARKET DAY: *Tue & Sat.*

PARKING: *King St, Queen St, Tuesday Market Pl.*

OPENING TIMES:

Guildhall: open all year. Mon–Sat.

Lynn Museum: open all year. Mon–Sat.

Museum of Social History: open all year. Tue–Sat.

Clifton House: open all year.

OLD STREET SCENES

Sepia tints of streets in bygone days may suggest an air of unhurried elegance, strollers unassailed by noisy traffic and exhaust fumes or by the impact of others going urgently about their business. The picture is a false one, as many Edwardian photographs testify. As well as acting as a thoroughfare for a wide variety of horsedrawn vehicles, some both bulky and unstable, the narrow streets were the social and economic centres of the time.

Congestion in the narrow, cobbled streets of Victorian times, where pedestrians mingled with traffic and the various impedimenta of numerous pedlars, must have been acute. Houses opened straight onto the street without the benefit of a pavement, spilling their occupants into the centre of tumultous activity.

Above: City bustle in Fleet Street

Left: market day at Ripon, a familiar scene in most country towns

'Buy my hot pies!'

The cries of tinkers, rag-and-bone men, flower-sellers, knife-grinders, bakers, fishmen and piemen must have competed with the clatter of horses' hooves to create a considerable din.

Organ-grinders with their mischievous monkeys, jugglers and travelling players provided entertainment for the ordinary working people, who nevertheless probably preferred the amusement of gossiping together in groups on the street. Many traders left their shops and bargained vociferously in the thoroughfare. In 20th-century terms, the street must have been like a cross between a television studio and a supermarket. In place of today's newscaster, the town crier, in his official braided uniform, clanged his bell, intoning 'Oyez, Oyez' to gain attention, often with news of disease, fire or war.

No street was without signs of extreme poverty; pathetic beggars, clothed in filthy rags and often deformed or diseased, constantly accosted passing noblemen. Hordes of children from deprived homes were trained in the art of picking pockets, as Dickens portrayed in *Oliver Twist*.

Around the pump

Without piped water, most people relied on the street water pump for all their needs. With no means of preventing contamination of the pump water by sewage, these installations became the source of several terrible epidemics of cholera in the 19th century. Street cleaners were employed to keep the pumps, the horse troughs and the streets themselves clean, but, through ignorance of the causes of disease, it was a losing battle. The streets were filthy from the turmoil of people, horses and vehicles and the removal of horse excreta was an impossible task.

Modern streets are in sharp contrast with the narrow, cobbled alleys of yesteryear, being wider, smooth-surfaced and boasting wide pavements allowing pedestrians comparative safety from passing traffic. Though cleaner, free from obvious sources of disease and offering excellent facilities for shoppers, they somehow lack the magic and romantic atmosphere we still ascribe to Victorian and Edwardian street scenes.

Something for everyone

Happily, pockets of the past still linger on in our street markets. Almost every sizeable town still possesses one or more of these fascinating relics. The hotch-potch of stalls with their amazing variety of wares never ceases to attract, and even the busiest people are tempted to linger over the goods offered for sale – gaudy souvenirs, cheap clothes, hardware, haberdashery, jewellery, confectionery, flowers, fruit and vegetables and sometimes fish and meat. Markets are meeting places, where bartering is encouraged and cheerful, confident stall owners like to exchange more than a few words with their customers.

Some famous streets are the scene of renowned specialist markets. A prime example is the Portobello Road, a long, winding street on Notting Hill which attracts hundreds of stalls and street sellers every Saturday morning, whatever the weather. Antiques are the famed commodity of the market, though it is only since the 1950s that these wares have become dominant.

A feature of most street markets is that they are traffic-free. The aim of many town-planners has been to create traffic-free pedestrian precincts. Among the best-known (and one of the first) is the Pantiles at Tunbridge Wells, an elegant parade built in the 18th century when the town was at its height as a fashionable spa. Here, the use of a tasteful variety of building materials and an eye for colour have made a haven for shoppers. Sadly this is not true of a majority of more recently designed precincts. However, an encouraging sign is the Guildhall Precinct in Exeter. Existing features, instead of being demolished, have been integrated into the precinct, and the central attraction is the well-preserved, minute, 11th-century church around which the precinct shops cluster.

Many arcades, such as the Burlington Arcade in London, are, in effect, small pedestrian precincts. Here the shops are picturesque and inviting, recalling the leisurely atmosphere and pleasant surroundings of a bygone age.

Another encouraging touch today is the appearance of street traders and buskers in our precincts. The delicious aroma of baked potatoes, the playing of the Salvation Army band and the handkerchief-and-tie stall add the human touch which many shopping precincts lack, and can help restore our streets to something approaching their former colour and cheerfulness.

This old city has all the bustle of a busy shopping and commercial centre, combined with a long history that can still be recalled in many of its buildings. It is impossible to avoid the castle, built high on a rock, overlooking the town and the whole of the surrounding area. Somewhat surprisingly, Lancaster used to be a busy port with wealthy merchants filling the city, but its heyday has passed now and the riverside is once again quiet and peaceful. Some of the old mill buildings, dating from the heyday of the textile industry, remain beside the canal. These many aspects of Lancaster give it a fascination which may not be immediately apparent from its stern stone aspect.

ROUTE DIRECTIONS

Start from the City Museum (1) in Market Sq. Walk down Old Sir Simon's Arcade on the south side of the Market Sq and turn l. up King St, passing Penny's Hospital Almshouses (2) on the r. Continue up King St to reach the Lancaster Canal (3). Cross bridge then turn l. along towpath. At Quarry Road bridge change over from r. to l. of towpath. Go forward under Clayton Bridge to Moor Lane. Climb up steps to road level and turn l. then r. to walk down St Peter's Rd to visit St Peter's Cathedral (4). Walk west down Nelson St to reach Dalton Square (5), cross the square to north side, and continue down Great John St then Rosemary La. At St John's Church in North Rd, turn l. then r. into Damside St to reach St George's Quay (6). Turn l. at footpath (signposted) and ascend steps to walk up Vicarage La to Priory Church of St Mary (7) and the Castle (8). Then walk down Castle Steps to Judges Lodgings (9). Cross China St and walk down Church St. Turn r. into Sun St past the Music Room (10) and then reach Market St to turn l. and return to starting point.

1 CITY MUSEUM

The dignified building of the old town hall now houses the city's very interesting museum. Exhibits range from Bronze Age coffins and Roman finds, including some important inscribed stones, to the story of the city's former importance as a port and shipbuilding centre in the 18th century. Many other aspects of the city's history can be studied here, such as the fine-quality furniture-making that was carried on by the local firm of Waring and Gillow. The local regiment, the King's Own Royal (Lancaster) Regiment, also has its museum in the same building.

2 PENNY'S HOSPITAL ALMSHOUSES

A small gateway in King Street opens into a tranquil courtyard that belongs to Penny's Hospital Almshouses. These were built in 1720 for twelve old people, and a chapel was built at the end of the courtyard. In 1974 the buildings were restored and modernised, and are now once more used for housing old people.

3 LANCASTER CANAL

To the south of the town runs the Lancaster Canal, and along its banks are some of the many cotton mills that grew up in the town in the 19th century. They produced a huge population boom that led to thousands of workers having to live in the town in conditions of unbelievable squalor. Today, the mill buildings have been converted to other uses, but the tow-path beside the canal provides a very pleasant walk.

4 ST PETER'S CATHEDRAL

The tall spire of this Roman Catholic cathedral can be seen from all parts of the city. It was built in 1857–9 and is decorated in an elaborate Victorian style.

5 DALTON SQUARE

Queen Victoria presides over the respectable solidity of Dalton Square. The statue of her in the centre of the square was put up by Lord Ashton, and has figures of writers, public benefactors and scientists on the four sides. She faces the daunting bulk of the town hall which was erected in 1909.

6 ST GEORGE'S QUAY

One of the most peaceful areas in the city, St George's Quay used to be a hive of activity. In the 18th century, before the rise of Liverpool, Lancaster was England's chief port for trade with America. Much of this trade involved the triangular circuit via Africa in which the main cargo was usually slaves. As trade expanded, the facilities at St George's Quay were improved and the elegant Customs House, designed by Robert Gillow, was built. This can still be seen today, although it is not open to the public. As the port of Liverpool expanded, and as the River Lune silted up, so maritime trade declined in Lancaster. Another industry that used to thrive beside the river here was shipbuilding. One of the yards was located near Cable Street and many large ships were built there. That industry also declined and now the area is given over to boating and fishing.

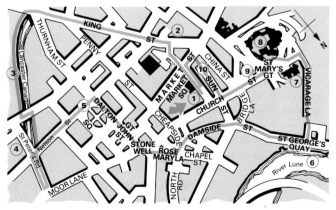

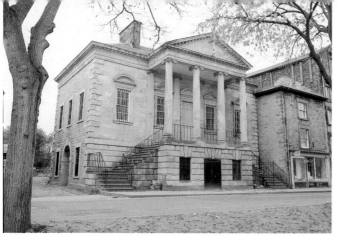

The town centre of yesteryear

Perpendicular style. Its outstanding treasure is the set of oak choir stalls, carved in the 14th century and brought here from Cockersand Abbey.

8 CASTLE

The Romans built a fort on the hill at Lancaster, and traces of this have been found in the area. It was followed by a wooden Saxon tower, and then, in 1102, the Normans built a huge, square stone keep. King John extended it by the addition of a curtain wall and gateway around the keep. The castle is most closely associated with John of Gaunt, however. He was the son of Edward III and was the 1st Duke of Lancaster. He built the gateway tower that bears his name, as well as banqueting halls, living apartments and also the dungeons. It is currently used as law courts. Inside the castle is the Victorian Shire Hall which features on its walls a collection of over 600 coats of arms, including those of all the sovereigns since Richard I.

7 PRIORY CHURCH OF ST MARY

Competing for attention with the castle on Castle Hill is the large and imposing Priory Church of St Mary. There has been a church on this site since Saxon times, and the doorway from this old church can be seen at the west end. A Saxon font has also been found recently and this too is on display. The present church was built in the 15th century in the

The Shire Hall ceiling in the castle

9 JUDGE'S LODGINGS

Just below Castle Hill is an elegant Georgian building that used to be the lodgings of visiting judges. It was originally built by one of Lancaster's wealthy merchants and has now been turned into a fascinating museum. The parlour, dining room, bedrooms and servant's hall have been faithfully reconstructed in 17th-century detail and with feature period furniture made by the Lancaster firm of Gillow's. The house also contains the Museum of Childhood, featuring the Barry Elder Doll Collection as well as historic children's games, toys and reconstructed nurseries and a school room.

10 MUSIC ROOM

Looking rather uncomfortably out of place in its present surroundings, the Music Room is a tall, narrow, dignified building. It has a remarkable carved plaster ceiling on the first floor which can be viewed at certain times. It dates from around 1730 and was cast by Italian craftsmen.

EARLY CLOSING: *Wed.*

MARKET DAY: *weekdays except Wed.*

PARKING: *Gt John St, Church St, Cable St.*

OPENING TIMES:

City Museum: open all year. Mon, Tue, Thu and Sat pm.

Judge's Lodgings: open daily Easter to Oct.

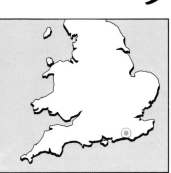

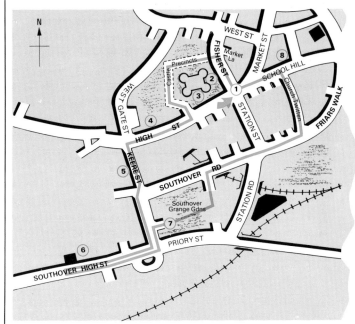

ROUTE DIRECTIONS

*Start outside the town hall (1).
Turn r. then r. again up Fisher St.
Turn l. along footpath opposite
Market Lane to reach Castle
Precincts and the castle (2).
Continue past Barbican House
Museum (3) to the High St and
turn r. Pass St Michael's Church
(4) then turn l. down Keere St (5).
At Southover High St turn r. and
continue to Anne of Cleves House
(6) then return to Southover
Grange Gardens (7). Walk
through these and leave by the top
left hand corner, turning r. into
Southover Rd. Cross Station Rd
and continue along Landsdoune
Pl. At All Saints Church turn l. up
Church Twitten. At School Hill
turn l., with the Military Heritage
Museum (8) on the r., to return to
the town hall.*

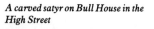
*A carved satyr on Bull House in the
High Street*

L*ewes was important enough during Saxon times to have two
mints and became even more powerful after the Norman
Conquest when its priory and castle were built by William
de Warenne. Throughout the Middle Ages the town prospered
further, and although its old town walls have virtually disappeared, Lewes has retained many medieval characteristics which
harmonise attractively with the Georgian architecture brought by
18th-century prosperity.*

1 TOWN HALL

During the 18th century this
red-brick building was the
town's principal inn – the Star.
Its oldest parts are the tunnel-
vaulted cellars and it was in
these that several Protestant
martyrs were imprisoned before
being burnt to death in the High
Street. By standing outside the
town hall and looking east, the
Martyrs Memorial can just be
seen on Cliffe Hill.

2 THE CASTLE

Shortly after the Norman
Conquest William de
Warenne built a castle here
consisting of two artificial
mounds at either end of a large
oval bailey. This was occupied
by the domestic buildings of the
castle and a tilting ground, now
occupied by a pleasant walled
bowling green. The castle
suffered considerable damage
after the de Warenne family
died out in 1347 because the
townsfolk used the stone for
building material. However,
parts of the flint keep on one of
the mounds remain and there
are still two of the semi-
octagonal towers which were
added in the 13th century.
There are tremendous views on
all sides from the top of the
keep. Diagrams set into the
parapet indicate the places of
interest which can be seen.
Apart from the rooftops of
Lewes, which show the true
medieval nature of the town,

these include Race Hill, where,
in 1264, Simon de Montfort's
army gathered before the Battle
of Lewes. The gatehouse, or
Barbican, at the bottom of
Castle Precincts, was built in the
early 14th century and has
survived more or less intact. An
earlier Norman gateway,
distinguishable by its rounded
arch, stands just inside the
Barbican.

3 BARBICAN HOUSE
MUSEUM

Like so many of Lewes's
houses, Barbican House is
Georgian fronted although the
interior is actually Tudor. The
Sussex Archaeological Society
now own the house and have
turned it into a museum.
Downstairs rooms are devoted
to the Bronze Age, the Iron Age
and the Romans, while upstairs
there is a Saxon room and the
Oak Room. The latter is
particularly attractive with its
carved oak panelling, and is
filled with period furniture.
There is a good view from this
room of Bartholomew House – a
tall, square house faced with
black mathematical tiles – very
popular as a façade during
Georgian times.

4 ST MICHAEL'S
CHURCH

A wall of knapped, squared
flints belonging to St Michael's
runs along the pavement of the
High Street to a tiny forecourt,

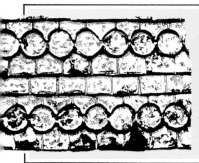

HUNG TILES

Tiles to protect walls as well as roofs are an important part of the townscape of Lewes. The most attractive are usually simple, homemade Georgian ones, but in Victorian times there was a vogue for tiles of many shapes to make patterned walls, as shown in the illustration.

behind iron railings, from where a small round tower rises up to its shingled spire. There are only two other towers like it in Sussex – both in the Ouse Valley – and the tiny round windows suggest they may have been designed as beacons. Looking down from the tower wall into the forecourt is a striking sculpture of St Michael the Archangel.

5 KEERE STREET

The lovely black and white timbered building, now a bookshop, marking the top corner of Keere Street gives some indication of how Lewes must have looked in the 15th century. Down either side of this steep, part-cobbled street is a mixture of tile, brick, flint and timber houses which make it one of the most picturesque in the town.

Keere Street bookshop

6 ANNE OF CLEVES HOUSE

The house, so named because it was part of the property Henry VIII gave Anne of Cleves when he divorced her, was originally part of the nearby Priory of St Pancras. All the large rambling rooms are heavily timbered and are packed with the museum's treasures which illustrate life in Sussex and the traditional crafts and industries of the area.

7 SOUTHOVER GRANGE AND GARDENS

Southover Grange was built in 1572 from the ruins of nearby St Pancras Priory by William Newton, whose family lived there until 1860. One of their most distinguished guests was George IV, then Prince Regent, who often stayed at the Grange on his frequent visits to Lewes. The lovely gardens (open to the public) consist of a formal area within the old walled part of the grounds. Running through the middle of the gardens is the small River Winterbourne – dry, as its name suggests, except in winter.

8 MILITARY HERITAGE MUSEUM

Dedicated to 'The British Soldier', this small museum represents one man's passion, and it took over forty years to amass. There are two main parts to the museum; the first one follows the theme of the British army from 1660 to 1914, and the second concentrates on cavalry and artillery. Head-dress, weapons and uniforms are all clearly labelled and there is much of interest to both the casual visitor and to the specialist.

EARLY CLOSING: *Wed.*

MARKET DAY: *Tue.*

PARKING: *West St, East St, North St.*

OPENING TIMES

Castle Keep: open daily Apr–Oct; Sun pm only.

Barbican House Museum: as Castle Keep.

Anne of Cleves House Museum: open daily Feb–Oct; Sun pm only.

Southover Grange Gardens: accessible 7.00am to 8.00pm.

Military Heritage Museum: open daily Tue–Sat.

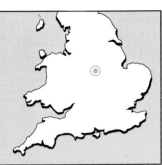

In the 'Ladies of the Vale' – the three tremendous spires of its cathedral – Lichfield possesses one of the most distinctive landmark groups in Britain. Below the spires is a little city that can trace its beginnings back to the 7th century, but which today has a markedly Georgian character. For many, however, it is Lichfield's distinguished sons that make it noteworthy. Among these are Samuel Johnson, Elias Ashmole and Erasmus Darwin.

ROUTE DIRECTIONS

Start the walk at the Cathedral (1) and walk round the north side of the Close (2). Leave the Close in the south-east corner and walk down Dam St (3). Turn r. into Market St and cross the Market Place (4), turning l. beside the Johnson Birthplace Museum (5) into Breadmarket St to reach Bore St. Turn r., and at the end of the street, l. into St John St (6). Walk down to St John's Hospital, then back up St John St, on into Bird St, and carry on past the cathedral to Gaia La. Turn r. here and follow the lane down to St Chad's Rd. Turn r. to St Chad's Church (7) and the saint's well. Cross the road and take the right-hand path along the north side of Stowe Pool (8). At Dam St, turn l. and r. to the footpath beside Minster Pool (8). At Bird St, turn r. to return to the cathedral.

1 ST CHAD'S CATHEDRAL

The Ladies of the Vale, as the three graceful spires of Lichfield cathedral are named, dominate the town and the surrounding countryside. The first cathedral church on this site was founded in AD 700 in honour of St Chad, first Bishop of Lichfield and the 'Apostle of the Midlands'. After the Conquest this was replaced by a Norman church, but the present building was begun in 1195, and work continued, with some interruptions, until 1338. The west front, with its elaborate carvings of saints and kings, is a spectacular sight, and the interior, ranging in style from Early English to Decorated, is very pleasing. The ancient windows of the Lady Chapel are one of the chief treasures of the cathedral.

2 THE CLOSE

Through an archway in the north-western corner of the close, lies Vicars' Close, the old lodgings of the vicars choral, a delightful little courtyard surrounded by half-timbered houses and one splendid 18th-century mansion. The cathedral close is surrounded by beautiful houses, many of them 17th- and 18th-century, especially on the north side, where the former Bishop's Palace stands. In fact, the bishop never lived here, and the residence has now become a school. In the 18th century it was the home of the 'Swan of Lichfield', the poetess Anna Seward, who was the daughter of one of the cathedral clerics. She was a friend of Wordsworth, Sir Walter Scott, and of Erasmus Darwin, the grandfather of Charles Darwin.

3 DAM STREET

Narrow Dam Street, leading from the cathedral to the Market Place, is one of the most charming Georgian streets in Lichfield. It was originally a medieval street, built on the dam separating Minster and Stowe Pools, by Bishop Clinton, who laid out the street pattern of the medieval town, which still survives in the grid pattern of Market, Bore and Wade Streets. During the Civil War, when Lichfield was besieged, Dam Street was reduced to rubble, and only a few of the old houses escaped destruction.

4 MARKET PLACE AREA

Dominating the market square, the old parish church of St Mary is now being converted into a multi-purpose building and contains a shop, restaurant and heritage centre devoted to local history. The two statues in the square are of Dr Johnson and his friend and biographer James Boswell. Further down Breadmarket Street, on the same side as the Johnson Museum, is the birthplace of Elias Ashmole, the 17th-century antiquarian scholar, whose collection of rarities was the foundation of the Ashmolean Museum at Oxford. Bore Street contains many fine buildings, including the picturesque Tudor Café, built in about 1510, and the imposing 18th-century Donegal House,

Dr Johnson's teapot is among the fascinating collection of his possessions in the Johnson Birthplace Museum

now part of the Guildhall. The Guildhall itself is a Victorian Gothic structure and contains the old Citizens' Prison.

5 JOHNSON BIRTHPLACE MUSEUM

The handsome three-storey house at the corner of Breadmarket Street was built in 1707 by Samuel Johnson's father, Michael Johnson, as a bookshop and family home. The great Dr Johnson was born here in 1709, and the house has survived virtually unchanged in appearance since then. It is now a fascinating museum, with eight rooms devoted to Johnson's life, work and friends, both in Lichfield and London. There are also two libraries of books and manuscripts including many which once belonged to Dr Johnson.

6 ST JOHN ST, BIRD ST AND BEACON ST

These three streets, leading into one another, run south to north through the centre of Lichfield to form the town's main thoroughfare. At the southern end of St John St, the eight massive Tudor chimneys of St

Boswell's statue in the Market Place

John's Hospital, founded by Bishop Smyth in 1495 on the site of an early Norman hospital, are a distinctive landmark. Opposite, set back from the road, is the Headmaster's House of the old Lichfield Grammar School. Among many distinguished pupils were the essayist Joseph Addison and, some 50 years later, Samuel Johnson and his friend, the actor David Garrick. Higher up St John Street, opposite the Friary School, the remains of the old Franciscan Friary church, dating from the 13th century, have been incorporated into a small garden. A little further up, on the right, stands the George Hotel, where the young Irish recruiting officer, George Farquhar, stayed in 1704. One of his best-known comedies,

The Beaux Stratagem, is set in Lichfield. On the other side of the bridge, opposite the Minster Pool, is the town library and museum, which stands on the site of the house where the Garrick family lived. Higher up, on the cathedral side, opposite the fine 18th-century Angel Croft Hotel, stands Erasmus Darwin's house, a lovely red-brick building, built in about 1760. Erasmus Darwin, a local doctor, was also a noted inventor and botanist. At the end of Bird Street is Dr Milley's Hospital a charming Tudor building.

7 ST CHAD'S CHURCH
The medieval church of St Chad, at the end of Stowe Pool, stands on what is thought to have been the site of the monastery founded by St Chad in 669 when he chose Lichfield as the site of his bishopric. The present church dates from the 12th and 13th centuries. St Chad's Well, in the churchyard, was the spring of water in which the saint baptised his converts.

The 'Ladies of the Vale'

8 MINSTER POOL AND STOWE POOL
These two pools were formed by damming the marshy valley where the town of Lichfield now stands. Domesday Book records two watermills, and cathedral records show that the mill at Stowe ground wheat for flour, and the one by the Minster Pool ground barley for malt: neither mill has survived. The walk along the north bank of Stowe Pool is known as Dr Johnson's favourite walk, and offers a superb view of the cathedral. Stowe House and Stowe Hill house, near St Chad's Church, were the homes of the two Aston sisters, friends of Dr Johnson.

EARLY CLOSING: *Wed.*

MARKET DAY: *Mon.*

PARKING: *off Bird St, The Friary.*

OPENING TIMES:

Johnson Birthplace Museum: open all year. Sun pm only; closed Sun Oct-Apr.

3I | LINCOLN

Rising spectacularly from the Lincolnshire plain, the hill on which the ancient city of Lincoln stands is a superb site for the majestic, triple-towered cathedral, the third largest in the country. Around it wind narrow medieval streets whose buildings include some of England's oldest houses. Older still are survivals of the city's Roman beginnings, such as the Newport Arch and the recently excavated Roman east gate. Fascinating museums and a splendid Norman castle complete the picture, making Lincoln one of our most remarkably preserved cities.

ROUTE DIRECTIONS

Start at the Stonebow (1) and walk up the High St. At the top, pass the Cardinal's Hat (2) and bear r. into the Strait (3). Continue up Steep Hill (4). At the top, the castle (5) lies to the l. whilst straight on is Bailgate (6), with the Newport Arch at its far end. Return from the arch and turn left into Eastgate (7). At the end, turn r. through the Priory Gate and then follow Minster Yard (8) round to the r. Follow the path round the cathedral (9). Go through the Exchequer Gate, then turn l. to retrace your steps down Steep Hill. Bear l. into Danesgate, then, opposite the Usher Gallery (10), turn r. into Danes Terrace and l. into Flaxengate. Follow it down to the end, crossing Grantham St and Clasketgate, then turn l. and r. to cross Silver St into Free School La. Turn l. beyond the library into Greyfriars Pathway, passing the City and County Museum (11) on the r. Then turn r. into Broadgate and r. again by the Green Dragon Inn along Waterside North with the High Bridge (12) spanning the river in front of you. At the end turn r. into High St to return to the Stonebow.

Quaint shopfront in Bailgate

1 THE STONEBOW AND GUILDHALL
This historic city gate stands on the site of the Roman and medieval south gates. The present gateway, with the Guildhall above, dates from the late 15th or early 16th century. It is topped by a clock and a bell, dated 1371, that is still rung to call council meetings.

2 THE CARDINAL'S HAT
This fine 15th-century timbered house, once an inn, is thought to have been named after Cardinal Wolsey, who was Bishop of Lincoln in 1514–15.

3 THE STRAIT
The 'feel' of the medieval city begins in this narrow, cobbled street of quaint little shops as the walk approaches the part of Lincoln known as 'above hill'. No. 14 has a rounded gable decorated with a figure of the Lincoln Imp, while next to it is one of Lincoln's two Norman houses, the Jew's House. Built about 1170–80, it has kept its original doorway, chimney stack and two first-floor windows. The stone building to its right, Jew's Court, may have been the synagogue.

4 STEEP HILL
This precipitous cobbled street was once the scene of a foolhardy exploit by a local MP, who drove a four-in-hand down it to win a bet. Many of the houses on the hill are Tudor or earlier, including Lincoln's second 12th-century house, Aaron the Jew's House.

5 LINCOLN CASTLE
Begun in 1068, Lincoln Castle has been repaired and added to in subsequent centuries but the basic plan remains unchanged. The walls are punctuated by three towers and two gateways. Only the 13th-century east gate is used today. The low tower in the north-east corner of the bailey, called Cobb Hall, was the castle dungeon. From its roof it is possible to walk along the battlements overlooking the medieval city to the Observatory Tower. Its circular turret was built on to the Norman base in the early 19th century, when a prison governor who was keen on astronomy used the tower to

A figure of the Lincoln Imp on a house in the Strait

observe the stars. The top can be reached by a steep spiral staircase, and offers a most spectacular view of the city, the cathedral and the Lincolnshire plain beyond. On the south side of the bailey, steep steps lead up to the Lucy Tower, or keep. Like the Observatory Tower, it stands on a motte or mound, making Lincoln one of only two Norman castles in England with two mounds. A fine example of a shell keep, the Lucy Tower was and is open to the sky. Two more recent public buildings stand in the castle bailey: the turreted stone Crown Court of 1826 and the stern red-brick prison, built in 1787 and now occupied by the County Archives and Magistrates' Court. The old prison chapel to the rear is open to the public. Its unique design, incorporating head-high cubicles for the prisoners, ensured that they could see the preacher but not each other.

6 BAILGATE AND THE NEWPORT ARCH
This unspoilt, village-like street of appealing old shop-fronts, inns and cottages leads to the Newport Arch. Built of huge stone blocks, this is part of the north gate of *Lindum Colonia*, the Roman town founded here in the 1st century AD. It is the only Roman gateway in the country that is still open to traffic.

The map shows numbered locations with streets including MINT ST, STONEBOW (1), HIGH ST, CORPORATION ST, ST MARTIN'S LA, STRAIT, (2) (3), Michaelgate, STEEP HILL (4), DRURY LA, (5), CASTLE HILL, WESTGATE, BAILGATE, To Newport Arch (6), EASTGATE (7), Waterside South, Waterside North, River Witham, SILVER ST, FREE SCHOOL LA, GREYFRIAR'S PATHWAY (11), CLASKETGATE, GRANTHAM ST, FLAXENGATE, DANES TER, DANESGATE, BROADGATE, (10), MINSTER YD, POTTERGATE (8), (9), (12).

The Jew's House in the Strait – one of the oldest houses in England

7 EASTGATE
In the forecourt of the modern Eastgate Hotel are displayed the excavated remains of part of the east gateway of *Lindum Colonia*. The stonework belongs mainly to a 3rd-century gateway, but post holes can also be seen which belonged to an earlier timber fortress.

8 MINSTER YARD
In medieval times the cathedral and clergy houses stood in a walled, fortified precinct. Pottergate and the Exchequer Gate are among the 14th-century gates that still stand, whereas Priory Gate, where the walk enters the precinct, is a 19th-century replacement. Nearby is a statue of Lord Tennyson, the Lincolnshire poet born at Somersby in 1809. The Old Bishops' Palace, the Precentory and the Chancery are among many interesting buildings in Minster Yard, some with architectural features dating back to the 14th century.

9 CATHEDRAL
No visitor to Lincoln can fail to be aware of the magnificent cathedral. Soaring majestically above the city on its hilltop site, its three towers dominate distant views of Lincoln from every direction. The beautiful Norman west front, where visitors enter the cathedral, dates in part from the 11th century. Fire and an earthquake a century later destroyed much of the Norman building, and St Hugh of Avalon, who became Bishop in 1186, began to rebuild the cathedral. The present transepts, nave, St Hugh's Choir and the Angel Choir date mostly from the 13th century. The Norman carvings of figures and animals on the west front are matched, at the opposite end of the cathedral, by the later craftsmanship of the Angel Choir, so called because of the 28 carved angels on the gallery. Other carvings here – best seen through binoculars – include fine roof bosses and corbels, one of which depicts the famous Lincoln Imp. To the north-east of the cathedral lie the cloisters and the chapter house. The north range of the cloisters was replaced in the late 17th century by the elegant Honywood Library, designed by Sir Christopher Wren. Part of the medieval library it replaced survives, and here can be seen one of the only four surviving original copies of Magna Carta.

10 USHER GALLERY
Opened in 1927, Lincoln's art gallery was financed by James Ward Usher, a local jeweller. A keen collector of watches, miniatures, porcelain and objets d'art, he died in 1921, bequeathing to the city both his collection and money to build a gallery for it, and the collection has grown considerably since. Paintings of many periods include works by well-known modern British artists such as L. S. Lowry and John Piper. One room of the gallery is devoted to memorabilia of Alfred, Lord Tennyson.

11 CITY AND COUNTY MUSEUM
Situated behind the domed, early 20th-century library building, the museum is housed in part of a former Franciscan friary. 'Greyfriars', as it is known, may well be the earliest surviving chapel of the Franciscan order in England. Visitors to the museum may now see both the fine vaulted undercroft and the upper storey, which has a magnificent barrel roof. The museum contains a good collection of local archaeological finds, including a 3,000-year-old dugout boat found near the River Witham. Upstairs is a natural history section, with an almost complete skeleton of a prehistoric plesiousaur, and the museum also possesses a fine collection of arms and armour.

12 HIGH BRIDGE
This stone bridge has spanned the River Witham here since Norman times. The original vaulting can still be seen underneath. It is the only medieval bridge in England that still carries a row of shops – housed in a 16th-century timber-framed building on the west side.

EARLY CLOSING: *Wed.*

MARKET DAY: *Fri and Sat.*

PARKING: *Saltergate, Flaxengate.*

OPENING TIMES:

Regional Craft Centre, Jew's Court: open Tue–Sat.

Lincoln Castle: open Mon–Sat all day, Sun pm only.

Usher Gallery: open as above.

City and County Museum: open as above.

Leicester Square to Jubilee Gardens

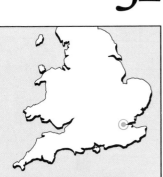

The Jubilee Walk – divided into four parts on the following eight pages – was inaugurated in 1977 to commemorate the silver jubilee of Her Majesty the Queen's accession to the throne. It is waymarked by special crown symbols, but the route is occasionally liable to change because of road improvements or building work. It can be joined or left at any point. Starting at Leicester Square, this part of the Jubilee Walk passes some of the capital's most famous places – Trafalgar Square, The Mall, St James's Park and the Houses of Parliament.

ROUTE DIRECTIONS

Follow west side of Leicester Sq (1) and cross into St Martin's St. At the end follow footpath alongside the National Gallery (2) to Trafalgar Sq (3). Cross Pall Mall East and continue along west side of sq. Cross Cockspur St into Spring Gdns, passing through the iron gates and descending the steps to The Mall, keeping Admiralty Arch on l. Turn r., passing Carlton House Terr (4), the Mall Galleries, and the Duke of York Steps and Column (5) on r. Cross The Mall (6), with a distant view of Buckingham Palace on r., and enter St James's Park (7). Bear l. to pass the lake then bear r. and shortly turn l. to leave the park. Turn r. along Horse Guards Rd, and at the end turn l. into Great George St passing Storey's Gate on r. At Parliament Sq (8) turn r. then l. along south side of sq and St Margaret's Church (9) with Westminster Abbey (10) to r. Turn r. into St Margaret St and continue into Abingdon St passing Houses of Parliament (11) on l. and the Jewel Tower (12) on r. Just beyond Great College St cross at pedestrian crossing and turn l. to return along Abingdon St. Shortly turn r. into Victoria Tower Gdns, and at the Burghers of Calais statue bear r. and follow the riverside pathway. At end ascend steps out of park and turn l. to cross Lambeth Bridge. On far side turn l. and descend steps onto Albert Embankment, with Lambeth Palace and St Mary's Church (13) to r. Walk along the Albert Embankment (14) with Westminster Bridge (15) ahead. Ascend steps and cross Westminster Bridge Rd by the South Bank Lion (16). Descend steps and continue along Embankment passing County Hall (17) on r. Keep on the South Bank (18) and then enter Jubilee Gdns, to finish the walk at the Silver Jubilee Pedestal in Jubilee Gdns (19).

1 LEICESTER SQUARE

This famous square takes its name from Leicester House, a mansion built here by the Earl of Leicester in the 17th century. The mansion has long since disappeared and in Victorian times the fields were laid out as a garden.

2 NATIONAL GALLERY AND NATIONAL PORTRAIT GALLERY

Housed in the National Gallery is one of the finest and most extensive collections of masterpieces in the world. All the great periods of European art are represented, although only a choice selection of British work is on display as the national collection of this is housed in the Tate Gallery. The adjoining National Portrait Gallery constitutes the world's most comprehensive survey of historical personalities. In addition to paintings the collection includes sculpture, miniatures, engravings and photographs.

3 TRAFALGAR SQUARE

Laid out in memory of Lord Nelson, Trafalgar Square was designed in 1829–41 by Sir Charles Barry. The 185ft Nelson's column is made of Devon granite, and is surmounted by an 18ft-high statue of Nelson.

4 CARLTON HOUSE TERRACE

John Nash designed this dignified group of buildings as part of his architectural scheme for Regent Street. No. 12 is now the Institute of Contemporary Arts, and houses an art gallery and a theatre.

5 DUKE OF YORK STEPS AND COLUMN

This 112ft granite pillar commemorating the second son of George III was designed by Bengamin Wyatt. The cost of its erection is supposed to have been largely defrayed by stopping a day's pay from every man in the army.

6 THE MALL

The Mall was originally laid out in 1660–2 as part of Charles II's scheme for St James's Park. It was transformed into a processional way in 1910.

Westminster Abbey's south transept

7 ST JAMES'S PARK

Although it is comparatively small, St James's is perhaps the most attractive of the royal parks. Pelicans, ducks and many other water birds inhabit the lake; there are open spaces of grass, and areas shaded by trees; and fine views across to Whitehall and the towers of the Houses of Parliament.

8 PARLIAMENT SQUARE

The square was originally laid out by Sir Charles Barry in 1850, and redesigned in 1951 for the Festival of Britain. There are many statues of British politicians in and around the square.

9 ST MARGARET'S CHURCH (WESTMINSTER)

Dating from the late 15th century, St Margaret's has been the official church of the House of Commons since 1614. It contains an exceptionally interesting collection of monuments.

10 WESTMINSTER ABBEY

A church has stood on this site since at least as early as Saxon times. The church later built here was enlarged by Edward the Confessor and made the crowning place of English sovereigns. Henry III rebuilt the cathedral (1216–72) in tribute to Edward. Henry VII added the chapel at the eastern end (1503–19). The 225ft-high towers were added in the mid 18th century by Nicholas Hawksmoor. Many generations of English sovereigns are buried here in beautifully carved tombs. Elsewhere are memorials to the nation's great statesmen, politicians, scientists, poets and others.

County Hall

11 THE HOUSES OF PARLIAMENT

The 'Mother of Parliaments' is often called the Palace of Westminster because from the time of Edward the Confessor to Henry VIII the site was the main London residence of the monarch. Almost all the palace was burned down in a fire during 1834. Westminster Hall (1097–9), with its gigantic hammerbeam roof, survived. The present building was designed by Sir Charles Barry and Augustus Pugin and built in 1836–60. The 320ft-high clock tower contains Big Ben, the hour bell, weighing 13½ tons. The Victoria Tower is 340ft high. The House of Lords contains the thrones of the Sovereign and Consort, facing which is the Woolsack, the traditional seat of the Lord Chancellor. At the north end is the Bar, where the Commons, led by the Speaker, attend when Parliament is opened.

12 THE JEWEL TOWER

This inconspicuous moated tower is in fact a survival of the medieval Palace of Westminster. It was built in 1365 to house the monarch's personal treasure, and this remained its function until the death of Henry VIII. It now houses a collection of pottery and other items found during excavations in the area, and is open to the public.

13 LAMBETH PALACE AND ST MARY'S CHURCH

Much of this historic structure, which has been the London residence of the archbishop of Canterbury for 700 years, was rebuilt during the 19th century. Extensive damage was caused by bombs during World War II. Of the old palace, the most interesting parts are the Lollards' Tower and the Gatehouse, both of the 15th century, and the 13th-century Chapel Crypt. Parts of the palace and its grounds are open to the public. Adjoining the south gateway of the palace is the former church of St Mary, now restored as a Museum of Garden History in memory of John Tradescant, Charles I's gardener. Captain Bligh, of *Bounty* fame, is buried here.

14 ALBERT EMBANKMENT

The earliest section of walkway (1868) was designed by Sir Joseph Bazalgette and built as a river defence for St Thomas's Hospital. Named after the Prince Consort, it stretches between Vauxhall Bridge and Westminster Bridge.

15 WESTMINSTER BRIDGE

The present bridge was designed by Thomas Page and completed in 1862. It replaced a stone bridge of 1750 on which Wordsworth composed his famous sonnet in 1802. At the western end stands a statue of Queen Boudicca.

16 SOUTH BANK LION

The lion standing on a plinth at the foot of Westminster Bridge previously surmounted the Lion Brewery, which was demolished to build the Royal Festival Hall. It was made from Coade's famous artificial stone which had superb weathering qualities. Unfortunately the formula – which was a closely guarded secret – was lost after the factory was demolished.

17 COUNTY HALL

Originally erected in 1912–32, County Hall has since been vastly expanded in size. The colonnaded front facing the River Thames is 750ft long.

18 SOUTH BANK

The walkway between County Hall and Hungerford Bridge is lined with London plane trees. They probably originated as a hybrid between Oriental and American planes in the 17th century, when cultivated together by the gardeners to the Stuart kings at Lambeth.

19 JUBILEE GARDENS

These gardens were laid out as London's tribute to celebrate Queen Elizabeth II's Silver Jubilee in 1977.

OPENING TIMES:
National Gallery: open all year. Mon–Sat all day; Sun pm only.

National Portrait Gallery: as above.

32 | LONDON
Jubilee Gardens to Tower Bridge

*S**ince the Festival of Britain in 1951, a great concourse of buildings – some of them greeted with howls of protest – have been built on the South Bank. Whatever their merits as architecture, they form one of the greatest cultural complexes in Europe. Further down the river the old network of warehouses and docks is being replaced by hotels, offices and blocks of flats, but the fairy-tale structure of Tower Bridge remains.*

HMS Belfast *and the new City skyline, with the National Westminster building and other giants*

ROUTE DIRECTIONS

Starting from the Silver Jubilee pedestal follow Queens Walk and Riverside Walk northwards passing beneath Hungerford Bridge then the South Bank Arts Complex (1). Shortly pass the National Theatre then turn r. and at the end turn l. along Upper Ground. In just over 200yds turn l. into Barge House St passing the Old Barge House Stairs (2) and at end turn l. to rejoin Upper Ground. By Doggets Coat and Badge public house keep forward and cross Blackfriars Bridge (3) then on far side descend steps, pass along a narrow alley then turn l. along Bankside (4). Reach the Founders Arms Public House. Bear r. then keep forward and pass beneath Southwark Bridge into Bankside to the Anchor public house (5). Keep forward beneath railway bridge into Clink St (6) and at end turn r. along Winchester Sq. Turn l. into Winchester Walk for Southwark Cathedral (7). Bear l. through a private car park to the Mudlark public house and keep forward into Montague Cl then pass beneath London Bridge (8) into Tooley St (9) passing London Dungeon (10) r. In approximately 200yds turn l. into Abbots La (signposted HMS Belfast) and at end bear r. then turn l. through gate to reach HMS Belfast (11) and immediately r. through another gate along Thames Walk to William Curtis Ecological Park (12). Shortly pass under Tower Bridge (13) then immediately turn r. and ascend steps then turn r. for Tower Bridge.

Southwark Cathedral: part of the memorial to John Trahearne

1 SOUTH BANK ARTS COMPLEX

This huge assembly of cultural centres was begun in 1951 when the Royal Festival Hall was built for the Festival of Britain. It is one of the most successful examples of modern architecture in London, providing comfortable seating for 3,000 people. The complex was enlarged when, in 1967, the Queen Elizabeth Hall and the Purcell Room were opened. Also here are the Hayward Gallery and the National Theatre.

2 OLD BARGE HOUSE STAIRS

This is one of many watermen's steps to survive and serves as a reminder of the days when the river was an important means of transport. Watermen carried passengers up and down and across the river between convenient landing places. Watermen gradually became redundant as more and more bridges were built and as other transport systems became established.

3 BLACKFRIARS BRIDGE

This bridge, designed by James Cubitt in 1899, replaced an 18th-century structure. Its name is derived from the Dominican Priory which once stood nearby. Beneath the bridge the Fleet River – which runs below the streets of London for almost its entire length – can be seen flowing from a culvert into the Thames.

4 BANKSIDE

Here in Tudor times were situated the Bear Garden and the Globe Theatre, places of riotous entertainment. The whole area had an evil reputation; being outside the jurisdiction of the City, it became the centre for the darker side of life. Sir Christopher Wren is reputed to have lived at 49 Bankside during the building of St Paul's Cathedral.

5 THE ANCHOR PUBLIC HOUSE (BANKSIDE)

This historic pub with its Clink Bar is a reminder that it stands close to the site of the Old Clink Prison. Instruments of torture are on display in the bar – a gruesome reminder of the days when prisons were places of extreme cruelty. The pub has known pirates, smugglers and the Press Gang, who hauled men off to serve in the Navy.

Tower Bridge

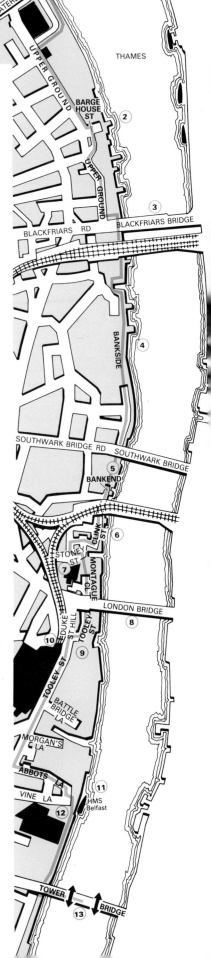

6 CLINK STREET

Gaunt 19th-century warehouses overshadow the cobbled alleyways and block the view of the Thames in this atmospheric part of South London. A plaque under the railway bridge tells the story of the 16th-century Clink Prison, from which the term 'in clink' is derived.

7 SOUTHWARK CATHEDRAL

A church has stood on this site since the 7th century, but it was not until 1905 that the basically 16th-century parish church of St Saviour was elevated to cathedral status. Despite rebuilding, particularly during the 19th century, its medieval Gothic style has remained largely intact, and parts of the church date back to at least the 13th century.

8 LONDON BRIDGE

The Romans built the first bridge across the Thames, and by doing so ensured the growth and future of London. In medieval times the bridge became almost a town on its own, having houses, shops, a chapel, fortified gates, and even water mills built upon it. All the buildings were pulled down in 1760, and the bridge itself was replaced in 1832 as it was rapidly being eroded away. The present structure dates from 1968, at which time its predecessor was dismantled stone by stone and reassembled in the USA.

9 TOOLEY STREET

In the 19th century this area was famous for its vast trade in food-stuffs and was known as the 'breakfast table of England'. In 1861 a fire raged in the warehouses along here, which it was said produced more flames and heat than the Great Fire of London.

10 THE LONDON DUNGEON

Appropriately set in slimy vaults, this exhibition recreates horrifying scenes from Britain's unsavoury past. There are galleries of medieval legend, the dark ages, the Reformation, the tortures of the Tower, demonology, astrology and witchcraft.

11 HMS *BELFAST*

Built by Harland and Wolff in Belfast and launched in March 1938, *Belfast* was one of the most powerful cruisers ever. After being damaged by a mine in November 1939, she was virtually rebuilt and did not rejoin the Home Fleet until November 1942. She saw active service in the convoys to Russia and played a key role in the battle of North Cape in December 1943, which ended in the sinking of the *Scharnhorst*. On D-Day she led the cruiser bombardment in supporting the Allied landing. She was saved from the breaker's yard by a trust fund set up by the Imperial War Museum and in September 1971 opened as a floating museum in full working order.

12 WILLIAM CURTIS ECOLOGICAL PARK

The park, created by the Jubilee Environmental Committee, was opened in 1977, on the 100th anniversary of the publication of Curtis's *Flora of London*. It is an interesting urban nature reserve where many species of plants are cultivated. Field study facilities are available on application to the warden.

13 TOWER BRIDGE

This fairy-tale structure, with its Gothic towers, steel lattice-work footbridge and road draw-bridge was designed by Sir John Barry and Isambard Kingdom Brunel in 1886–94. It was opened by the then Prince of Wales. The twin bascules, or drawbridges, weighing 1,100 tons each, were operated by four steam hydraulic engines until 1975, when these were replaced by electric motors as they had become uneconomical. The pedestrian walkway was re-opened to the public in 1982. It is reached by a lift at the North Tower. Descending via the South Tower there are exhibits illustrating the history of the bridge. A museum houses the great steam hydraulic engines previously used, together with other fascinating exhibits associated with the bridge.

OPENING TIMES:
The London Dungeon: *open all year.*

HMS Belfast: *open all year.*

Tower Bridge walkway: *open all year.*

32 | LONDON
Tower Bridge to St Paul's Cathedral

This part of the Jubilee Walk begins on Tower Bridge then leads through the converted warehouses and basins of St Katharine Dock before passing the walls of the Tower. It continues along some of the principal City thoroughfares before reaching the network of lanes and squares around St Paul's.

ROUTE DIRECTIONS

From the centre of Tower Bridge head northwards along Tower Bridge Approach. Shortly turn r., descend steps and keep forward, then bear l. passing Tower Hotel. Shortly cross a wooden bridge and follow signs 'Historic Ship Collection' for St Katharine Dock (1) and the Historic Ship Collection. Bear l. and cross bridge over the basin, then on far side turn l. then r. beneath a shopping arcade and keep forward. Shortly turn l. along East Smithfield, passing the World Trade Centre. At end turn l. and descend steps to subway following signs 'Tower of London'. On far side bear r. and ascend steps to Tower Hill, passing Tower of London (2) on l. and Trinity Sq (3) on r. Continue along Byward St to All Hallows-by-the Tower (4). Shortly turn r. and cross Byward St into Great Tower St and Eastcheap. At end descend subway signposted King William St. On far side keep forward along King William St to Bank underground station with the Manion House (5) on the l. Cross Threadneedle St, passing the Royal Exchange (6) and the Bank of England (7) on r. Bear r. and cross Gresham St into Moorgate. Shortly turn l. along London Wall (signposted Barbican Centre) and by second footbridge ascend steps (signposted Museum of London) and cross London Wall. On far side turn l. to Museum of London (8). Keep forward then descend steps into Aldersgate St and continue along St Martins Le Grand. At end cross Newgate St to St Paul's underground station; ascend steps into Panyer Alley for Cathedral Place (St Paul's Shopping Precinct) then bear l. and cross Paternoster Sq. Finally, descend Paternoster Steps to reach St Paul's Cathedral (9).

1 ST KATHARINE DOCK

Thomas Telford, one of the greatest engineers of the 19th century, designed this superb group of warehouses and basins. They were built in 1828 and the warehouses were used mostly for the storage of wool and wine. The docks were bombed during World War II and abandoned, until in 1968 the area was restored and adapted for a variety of uses. The dock basins have been transformed into yachting marinas, and there is also a floating museum of unusual water craft.

2 TOWER OF LONDON

Originally built by William the Conqueror to impress and dominate the population of London, the Tower soon became the symbol of ultimate power, the place where even the highest and mightiest in the land could be cast down. According to tradition 1078 marks the start of the building of the original tower (now known as the White Tower). The stronghold was enlarged in later years. Other places of particular interest are the Bloody Tower (15th-century), in which the little princes are said to have been smothered in 1483; St Peter Vincula's Chapel Royal in which Anne Boleyn, Lady Jane Grey and the Duke of Monmouth are buried; the

Norman St John's Chapel, the oldest in London; and Traitors' Gate, the old water-gate. Adjoining the Beauchamp Tower, near which was the site of the scaffold, is the Yeoman Gaoler's House in which Lady Jane Grey and latterly Rudolf Hess were imprisoned. The magnificent Crown Jewels are kept underground in the new Jewel House, entered from the Waterloo Barracks.

3 TRINITY SQUARE

In 1465, during the reign of Edward IV, the first permanent scaffold was set up on Tower Hill. It was situated in what is now Trinity Square, and the site, with its blood-drenched memories, is marked by a rectangle of bricked paving. Public executions were held here until the 18th century; more than 125 people were put to death, including Sir Thomas Moore (1535) and the Duke of Monmouth (1685).

4 ALL HALLOWS-BY-THE-TOWER

Preserved in the crypt here is part of the wall of a church which stood on this site in the 7th century. Also in the crypt are fragments of Roman paving, and the remains of two Saxon

The Historic Ships Collection, St Katharine Dock

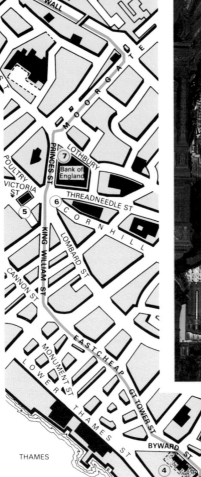

crosses. The shell of the church dates from the 12th to 15th centuries, but the interior, which was gutted during the Blitz, was rebuilt in the 1950s.

5 MANSION HOUSE

The principal rooms of this imposing mansion – the residence of the lord mayor – are the Egyptian Hall, or dining room, and the Salon, which contains 19th-century tapestries and an enormous Waterford glass chandelier. The Corporation plate and insignia are kept in the building and include the 15th-century mayoral chain of office, the 17th-century Sword of State, and the 18th-century Great Mace, which is over five feet long. The Mansion House also contains the Lord Mayor's Court of Justice, which is the only court in the country to be held in a private residence and has its own underground cells. Visits can be arranged by prior application.

6 ROYAL EXCHANGE

Founded by Sir Thomas Gresham, the Royal Exchange was opened in 1568 as a meeting place for City merchants. Queen Victoria opened the present building in 1844. No business has been transacted here for over 40 years, but important announcements such as the proclamation of new sovereigns and declarations of war are traditionally made from the broad flight of steps at its entrance.

7 BANK OF ENGLAND

The world's most famous bank operated from Grocers' Hall until 1734 when the new building was opened in Threadneedle Street. The building was greatly expanded by Sir John Soane at the turn of the 18th century, and was extensively modernised between 1925 and 1939. The Bank was nationalised in 1946 and has special responsibilities for printing and issuing notes, administering the National Debt and exchange control.

8 MUSEUM OF LONDON

This museum is devoted entirely to London and its people, presenting by way of exhibitions and tableaux the story of its development and

The choir and high altar of St Paul's Cathedral

life. Open-plan and arranged in chronological order, the museum affords a continuous view from prehistoric times to the 20th century. The exhibits include an audio-visual reconstruction of the Great Fire of 1666, an 18th-century prison cell, shop fronts, and a music hall. Behind the museum is the Barbican, an ambitious scheme to promote the city as a residential area. It contains high-rise flats, shops, offices, pubs and schools. Other features include an ornamental lake, an arts centre and the Guildhall School of Music and Drama.

9 ST PAUL'S CATHEDRAL

This is Wren's masterpiece. It was built of Portland stone in 1675–1710 to replace the former Gothic cathedral of the 13th century, which was altered early in the 17th century by Inigo Jones and finally destroyed in 1666 by the Great Fire of London. The cathedral rises to a hight of 365ft and in the south-west tower is 'Great Paul', a bell weighing some 17 tons. The west façade of the cathedral is 180ft wide and the

famous dome, 112ft in diameter, is buttressed by twelve massive supports. Carved woodwork by Grinling Gibbons and ironwork by Jean Tijou are features of the cathedral interior. The crypt contains the tombs of Wren, Nelson, Wellington, Reynolds and Turner. The Whispering Gallery and Golden Gallery may be visited for a small charge.

OPENING TIMES:

Historic Ships Collection: St Katharine Dock: open all year.

Tower of London: open all year. Mon–Sat all day; Sun pm only.

Museum of London: open all year. Tue–Sat all day; Sun pm only.

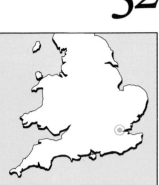

From St Paul's Cathedral, one of Britain's great religious foundations, this part of the Jubilee Walk leads to Fleet Street, heart of the newspaper industry. It then passes some of London's most venerable old buildings, before reaching Covent Garden and the shops and theatres of the West End.

ROUTE DIRECTIONS

Follow Ludgate Hill to Ludgate Circus, passing the Central Criminal Court (1) on r. (down Old Bailey). Keep forward along Fleet Street (2) passing the Inner Temple gateway and the Inns of Court (3) on the l. Turn r. into Chancery La and at the Public Record Office (4) turn l. into Carey St then r. into Serle St for Lincoln's Inn Fields (5). Pass Lincoln's Inn Old Buildings (6) on r. and turn l. along the top of the sq, passing Sir John Soane's Museum (7) on r. Keep forward into Remnant St and cross Kingsway into Great Queen St. Pass Freemason's Hall on l. and take second turning l. into Drury La. In 20yds turn r. into Broad Ct and at end turn l. into Bow St passing the Royal Opera House (8) on r. Turn r. into Russell St for Covent Gdn (9). At the market building turn r. then l. alongside it. Keep forward into King St, and at end cross Garrick St into New Row, then turn l. into Bedfordbury. Almost immediately turn r. into Goodwin's Ct (10), and at end turn l. into St Martin's La then r. into Cecil Ct. At Charing Cross Rd turn l. and cross at pedestrian crossing into Irving St for Leicester Sq. Turn r. along the sq then l. to complete the walk at the north-west corner of Leicester Sq.

Inner Temple Garden is a haven of peace surrounded by buildings of many periods

1 CENTRAL CRIMINAL COURT (THE OLD BAILEY)

The notorious Newgate Prison, which stood on this site, was the scene of public executions between 1783 and 1868 (sentence was subsequently carried out in private until 1901). It was demolished in 1902 and replaced by the Central Criminal Court, which takes its popular name from the street in which it stands. On the first two days of each session the judges carry posies of flowers, and the courts are strewn with herbs, a custom dating from the time when it was necessary to do so to disguise the stench of the prison. Most of the major trials of this century have been heard here, including those of Crippen, Christie, Haig and the Kray brothers. The public may view the proceedings in No. 1 Court by queueing for a seat in the Visitor's Gallery (entrance in Newgate Street).

2 FLEET STREET

Nearly every national and provincial newspaper or periodical has an office in or near Fleet Street. It is one of the most ancient thoroughfares in London, and has had links with the printing trade since about 1500. The present buildings are mostly modern.

3 THE INNER TEMPLE GATEWAY

This picturesque half-timbered building of 1610–11 has on its first floor 'Prince Henry's Room' (open to the public) supposed to have been the council chamber of the Duchy of Cornwall under Prince Henry, the son of James I. The room retains its original plasterwork ceiling. The gateway adjoins The Temple,

which was originally the English headquarters of the Knights Templar. The order was dissolved in 1312, and the Temple eventually passed to the Knights Hospitallers of St John, who leased it to a number of lawyers. From this point on, the Inner and Middle Temples began to develop into Inns of Court. The oldest building in the complex is the Temple Church, which is one of only four round churches surviving in England. The nave and porch date from the 12th century. The magnificent Middle Temple Hall dates from 1562 (it is open to the public).

4 THE PUBLIC RECORD OFFICE

This is the chief repository for the national archives. The search rooms, containing records from the Norman Conquest onwards, are open to the public, and there is a small museum in which may be seen famous documents such as Domesday Book. Also on display are letters from Cardinal Wolsey and Guy Fawkes.

5 LINCOLN'S INN FIELD

This large square is an essential part of Lincoln's Inn, and echoes the tranquillity of that ancient establishment. The central garden covers a surprising 12 acres and are well laid out with paths and lawns. Laid out in the 17th century, it was a famous haunt of duellists. A tablet marks the spot where Lord William Russell was executed in 1638. Handsome buildings, including Sir John Soanes Museum and the Royal College of Surgeons, surround the fields.

6 LINCOLN'S INN OLD BUILDINGS

These date mainly from the 16th and early 17th centuries. The Gatehouse, still with its original oak doors, was built in 1518 by Sir Thomas Lovell, whose arms appear above it. Lincoln's Inn was established in the 14th century when the Earl of Lincoln built himself a large mansion which he bequeathed as a residential college, or inn, for young lawyers. Dominating the Inn is the Victoria New Hall and Library, dating from 1843. The Old Hall dates from 1506, and was extensively restored in 1928. The chapel was rebuilt in the 17th century and is often said to have been designed by Inigo Jones.

7 SIR JOHN SOANE'S MUSEUM

This fine house of 1813 houses the private collection of pictures, sculptures and antiquities founded by Sir John Soane. A distinguished architect, he was Surveyor to the Bank of England (1788–1833) and was responsible for the design of the present building, which incorporates an earlier one.

8 ROYAL OPERA HOUSE

The present building had two predecessors, the second one being the scene of the famous Old Price Riots – the public's protestation against the sharp increase in the costs of seats. The theatre officially opened as an opera house in 1847 and opera has flourished here ever since, achieving its greatest peaks between 1859 and 1939 when it was the leading entertainment of 'society'.

The restored buildings of Covent Garden Market

Productions today are lavish and still attract a following who come to see and hear the best names in the world of opera.

9 COVENT GARDEN

Until 1974, when the famous fruit and vegetable market was moved to Nine Elms, near Vauxhall, there had been a market on this site for over 300 years. The original Covent Garden owed its name to the fact that the monks of Westminster Abbey had a 40-acre walled garden here. In 1631, Inigo Jones was commissioned to lay out the square. This grandly conceived estate, modelled on those he had seen in Italy, included a great Piazza, a church, and, on three sides, arcaded blocks of houses. The square and covered walks in front of buildings attracted market traders, and by 1670 the market had received official recognition. By the middle of the 20th century it had rapidly outgrown its site. After the market had moved, strenuous efforts were made to preserve the attractive old market building and these have been renovated and contain many small craft shops, business premises and restaurants.

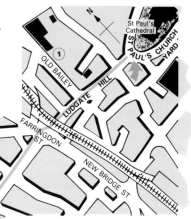

10 GOODWIN'S COURT

This narrow alley is entirely lined with the bow-fronted windows of former shops.

OPENING TIMES:

Middle Temple Hall: open all year; Mon–Sat.

Public Record Office: open all year; Mon–Fri.

Sir John Soane's Museum: open all year; Tue–Sat.

33 | LUDLOW

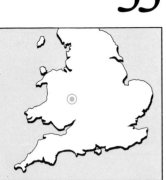

Set in the beautiful and unspoilt countryside of the Welsh Marches, Ludlow is a delightful blend of ancient border stronghold, medieval planned town and present-day country market centre. The street plan is still much as it was 800 years ago, but each street within it has developed its own distinctive character. In some, the feeling is of Georgian elegance, whilst elsewhere there is plenty of beautifully preserved Tudor half-timbering with bulging walls and steep, higgledy-piggledy roofs. All in all, Ludlow amply justifies the reputation it has gained as one of the best country towns in England.

ROUTE DIRECTIONS

From Castle Sq walk west towards the castle (1), then turn r. down the path that leads round the castle's perimeter. Bear l. where the path forks to return through a walled-off section of the castle bailey, and then go through Castle Gardens (2), bordering Dinham, to Castle Sq (3). Turn r. beyond Castle Lodge and go down Mill St (4). Turn l. at the bottom into Silk Mill La and r. at the end, through the Broad Gate, along Lower Broad St (5) to Ludford Bridge. Retrace your steps through the gate and go up Broad St (6). At the top turn r. into King St, then l. into Bull Ring (7). Turn l. through the coaching yard of the Bull Hotel, go up the steps and through the passageway into the churchyard (8). Turn l. to follow the path round the south side of the church (9), then turn l. and r. into Church St (10) and pass the market hall to reach Castle Sq again.

The massive castle, set in a loop of the rivers Teme and Corve, was first built shortly after the Norman Conquest

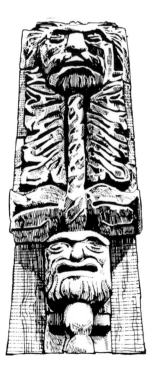

Detail on the Feathers Hotel

1 LUDLOW CASTLE

Being an ideal site for fortification, Ludlow has enjoyed the protection of its castle for almost 900 years. On two sides of the castle – now a dramatic ruin – the land falls steeply away to the rivers Teme and Corve. The breathtaking views from the top of the keep are a reminder that the medieval castle was for a long time a commanding watchtower in the turbulent Welsh border lands. Ludlow Castle has many times played a role in the lives of famous historical characters. From 1461 to 1552 it was a royal castle, used as a provincial retreat by the offspring of various monarchs. They included Edward IV's two sons, Edward and Richard – the ill-fated 'Princes in the Tower', who set out from here on their last, doomed journey. Prince Arthur, elder son of Henry VII, also spent several months here with his bride, Catherine of Aragon, shortly before his premature death, without which Henry VIII may never have become king. Perhaps the chief architectural treasure of the castle is the ruined round chapel in the inner bailey. One of only five round chapels remaining in the country, it retains its fine Norman west doorway, chancel arch and interior wall arcade. The castle's cultural associations begin with Milton, whose masque 'Comus' had its first performance here in 1634, and continue with the internationally famous Ludlow Festival, which is held every summer and always includes a Shakespeare play staged in the grounds of the castle.

2 CASTLE GARDENS AND DINHAM

Bright flower beds and a tree-lined promenade stand between the castle and Dinham, a winding medieval street named after Dinam, a 7th-century settlement on the site. Near the castle stands Dinham House, an elegant early 18th-century building that was briefly the home of Lucien Bonaparte, captured brother of Napoleon. The house is now a craft centre.

3 CASTLE SQUARE

Once the western end of the medieval high street, Castle Square is now dominated by the bright red-brick market hall, a Victorian monstrosity set in its midst. On the south side of the square is its oldest building, Castle Lodge, a 14th-century stone house with an overhanging first storey that was added later.

4 MILL STREET

Ludlow was laid out as a medieval planned town in the 12th century. Mill Street is a typical example of the straight streets that formed part of the original 'grid-iron' arrangement. The broad, sloping street lent itself perfectly to the elegant architecture of the Georgian era, and retains an air of great dignity. At the foot of the street is the site of Mill Gate, one of seven gates in the medieval town walls. Nearby stand some of the buildings of Ludlow College, including a 14th-century hall.

5 LOWER BROAD STREET

Perhaps Ludlow's first 'suburb', this street below the Broad Gate is lined with modest cottages that once housed workers in the cloth and glove-making industries. Spanning the River Teme at the foot of the hill is Ludford Bridge, a narrow 15th-century stone bridge with massive cutwaters, still coping manfully with modern traffic.

6 BROAD STREET

Claimed by some to be Britain's most attractive street, Broad Street, like Mill Street, owes its beauty largely to medieval street planners and Georgian builders. An added delight, at the top of the street, is a range of timber-framed houses with projecting upper storeys supported by slender columns on the pavement. Flanked by cobbled inclines, the street runs from the Butter Cross down to the Broad Gate, Ludlow's only surviving medieval town gate. It incorporates a handsome 18th-century house.

7 BULL RING

This area is so called because bulls used to be stockaded here before sales. Its namesake, the Bull Ring Tavern, is an impressive black-and-white building, whilst at the northern end is the Feathers Hotel, one of the most famous timber-framed buildings in the country. Built in 1603, the beautifully kept exterior is lavishly decorated with many different carvings. Opposite is the Bull Hotel, older than the Feathers, though the front was rebuilt in 1795 after damage by fire.

The Reader's House, overlooking the churchyard

8 CHURCHYARD AND COLLEGE STREET

The pleasant grassy area that surrounds the church is now a peaceful backwater and 'garden of rest'. An inscription on the north wall of the church records the burial nearby of the ashes of A. E. Housman (1859–1936), the 'Shropshire Lad' poet. Overlooking the churchyard from the east is the Reader's House, a 13th-century stone building with a lovely Jacobean timbered porch.

9 CHURCH OF ST LAURENCE

Largest and stateliest of Shropshire parish churches, St Laurence's is tucked away from Ludlow's main streets, yet still dominates the whole town and surrounding countryside with its great crossing tower, 135 feet high. The tower and much of the rest of the church date from the 15th century. Earlier features include the hexagonal porch – one of only two in England – and the south doorway, north aisle and transepts. Do not miss the chancel, with its lovely medieval carvings including the fine rood screen and the unusual poppy heads on the choir stalls. The misericords depict, among other things, a fox in bishop's robes preaching to geese, and a dishonest ale-wife being carried off by a demon.

10 CHURCH STREET

This is one of four parallel streets that grew up during the early Middle Ages in an area which had originally formed one wide high street or market place. The area is well worth exploring, and glimpses down small alleyways and yards leading off Church Street and its neighbours will often reveal an unsuspected half-timbered wall, a quaint cobbled passageway or a medieval roof-line. At one end of Church Street stands the classical stone Butter Cross, built in 1746. The first floor was once a school and is now Ludlow Museum. The collection concentrates on local history from prehistoric times, with items arranged in chronological order and including relics from Ludlow Castle and the town's old whipping post.

EARLY CLOSING: *Thu.*

MARKET DAY: *Fri.*

PARKING: *Castle Sq, Broad St, Corve St.*

OPENING TIMES:

Castle: open daily, but closed Sun Oct–Apr.

Craft Centre, Dinham House: open daily except Christmas.

Museum: open Easter–end Sep, Mon–Sat. Also open Sun in June, July and Aug.

Marlborough's exceptionally wide and handsome main street must be remembered by many thousands of holidaymakers who passed through the town before the M4 became the great artery to the West Country. The old A4, which forms the main street, brought trade and prosperity to the town, especially in the 18th and 19th centuries, accounting for the grand array of shops and hotels that line it. Leading away from the High Street are numerous lanes and alleys that reveal intimate little corners and something of Marlborough's more distant past.

ROUTE DIRECTIONS

Start the walk in the High St by St Peter's Church (1). Head westwards, turning r. into Bridewell St, and walk under the college bridge then turn l. into the college (2). Walk through the college courtyard and leave via the Masters' Lodge at far left-hand corner of the courtyard. Take the path to the l, then continue along the High St and turn r. down Figgins La then l. into the Priory Garden (3). Walk through the garden and out into the High St again. Turn r. and continue to the Town Hall (4). Turn l. up the steps (known as Perrin's La) behind the hall then r. into Patten Alley to St Mary's Church (5). Continue through the churchyard to The Green (6). Turn l. here then l. again along Silverless St and at the end turn l. back to the High St (7). Return to St Peter's Church.

1 ST PETER'S CHURCH

St Peter's, partly hidden by trees at the southern end of the High Street, forms an attractive part of the townscape, although it has not been used as a place of worship for many years and was eventually declared redundant in 1974. Today, concerts and other community events are held here and it is also the home of the tourist information centre. The church has narrowly escaped destruction several times since it was built in the 15th century – for it was threatened with demolition at the Reformation, survived the fierce fighting which took place here during the Civil War and was unscathed by the fire that devastated the town in 1653.

2 MARLBOROUGH COLLEGE

Marlborough is well known for its boys' public school which was founded in 1843 primarily for clergymen's sons. Now, not only do the pupils' fathers represent every sort of profession, but there are also about 70 girls at the college. Geographically the red brick college is set completely apart from the town. The oldest of the college buildings predates the foundation of the college and lies at the far end of College Court. This, known as C-House, is a red brick mansion built by the 6th Duke of Somerset at the end of the 17th century. In 1750, however, the house was sold and turned into the Castle Inn. Sited on the busy Bath road, it became a popular coaching inn until 1843, when it was sold to the college. Over the next century many extensions and alterations were carried out as the school grew. Of the college buildings only the

chapel is open. A chapel was one of the first things built after the college was founded. However, by 1884 it had become too small to accommodate all the boys and a larger building was erected on the same site. It is made partly of stone from the local downs.

3 THE PRIORY GARDEN

The name of priory is all that remains of the Carmelite friary built here in the 14th century. A handsome ivy-covered house stands on the actual site and the grounds are a pleasantly informal public garden leading down to the river which runs parallel to the High Street.

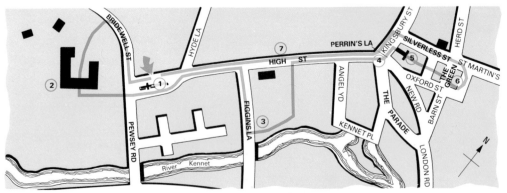

4 TOWN HALL
Set boldly at the northern end of the High Street, the Town Hall is one of the town's most prominent buildings. Although 17th-century in style, it was actually built between 1901 and 1902 by C. E. Ponting and is notable for the wealth of brick and stone decoration. It is also distinguished as one of the last buildings in England to have a traditionally constructed roof of massive timbers.

5 ST MARY'S PARISH CHURCH
The covered passageway leading from the High Street to the church is called Patten Alley because there used to be a shelf here where ladies could leave their pattens (raised wooden overshoes) before entering the church. All that remains of the Norman church which originally stood on this site is the west door. Much of the present structure dates from the 15th century, but during the great fires that swept through Marlborough in 1653 the entire building was practically gutted. Evidence of the fire can be seen by the reddish colouring of the stone on the west door and on the Norman pillar standing inside the church. The interior of the church, rebuilt with the help of funds raised by Cromwell because the town had supported Parliament during the Civil War, still has the austerity favoured by the Puritans. Its flat ceiling, plain arches and lack of decorations still have something of the appearance of a preaching house.

6 THE GREEN
On leaving St Mary's churchyard a path through two rows of lime trees leads out onto the Green. During Saxon times this was the centre of Marlborough, and throughout the 18th and 19th centuries it was the working class area with industries and ale houses: now the Green is a peaceful residential part of town that comes as a delightful surprise after leaving the busy High Street. Some of the houses are red brick Georgian and some are timbered cottages, but all styles blend happily.

Part of Marlborough College

7 HIGH STREET
This especially wide, slightly sloping street has been a through route from London to the West for centuries and travellers have always been tempted to stop and explore. At first sight the street seems to be a continuous sweep of attractive buildings – tile-hung, brick, whitewashed or timbered – but on a closer examination there are also numerous alleyways and yards leading off it where the work of the town is carried out. The northern side of the street is the most impressive. Many of the buildings here seem to be 18th-century but in fact are façades covering mid 17th-century properties, and some of the parapets disguise steeply pitched roofs that became unfashionable in Georgian times. All in all, this is one of the best streets in England. A market is held down the middle of the street twice a week.

EARLY CLOSING: *Wed.*

MARKET DAY: *Wed and Sat.*

PARKING: *High St, The Parade, George La.*

ST MARY'S CHURCH
The fine west doorway is all that remains of the Norman church, which stood here until 1653, when it was gutted by fire. The round archway and decorative zig-zag carving are typical of Norman architecture. Such work was usually done by schools of highly-skilled local masons. The doorway was built around 1150, at a time when Marlborough also had a castle, only the mound of which remains.

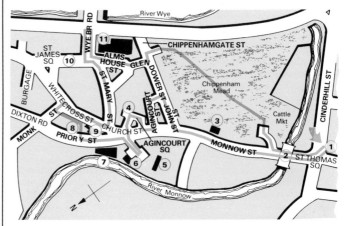

ROUTE DIRECTIONS

Start from St Thomas's Church (1) and walk north, crossing Monnow Bridge (2). Continue up Monnow St passing the Robin Hood Inn. Further along on the r. is Cornwall House (3). Once beyond Lloyds Bank, turn r. into St John St, then l. into Agincourt St. At the end turn r. into Agincourt Sq (4). Leave the square on the l., up a narrow alley called Castle Hill. Great Castle House (5) is on the r., while the castle (6) itself is straight ahead. Return down Castle Hill and turn l. into Priory St. On the l. is the combined Post Office, Nelson Museum and Local History Centre (7). Further along Priory St are the remains of Monmouth Priory (8). Facing back towards Monnow St, cross over to a pathway and keep l. through St Mary's churchyard which leads out into Monk St. Turn r., then r. again into Whitecross St. The entrance to St Mary's Church (9) is at the end on the r. From the church cross into St Mary St. At the end turn l. again into St James St (10). Go over the staggered crossroads into Wye Bridge Rd where Monmouth Grammar School (11) is on the r. From here return and turn l. into St James St, to where the thoroughfare becomes Almshouse St. Follow the road into Glendower St, then turn sharp l. into Chippenhamgate St. The next r. leads on to Chippenham Mead. Bear diagonally r. across this open space along a tree-lined path. Reach a cattle market, turn l. and return to the River Monnow.

M onmouth dates back to Roman times when it was a military station known as Blestium. Then in the 11th century a Norman castle was built, only to be virtually destroyed during the Civil War. The town received its charter in 1550 and slowly changed from military garrison to market town. Although modern-day Monmouth still has market days for both produce and livestock, it is as a focal point for visits to the Wye Valley and Welsh border regions that the town now thrives. Famous names connected with the borough are Lord Nelson, and Charles Rolls of the famous Rolls-Royce partnership.

1 ST THOMAS'S CHURCH

Dating from the late 12th century, this church has an original Norman chancel. Features of special interest are the early 19th-century timbered galleries and an unusual font.

2 MONNOW BRIDGE

Both the bridge and the fortified gateway which straddles it date from the 13th century. The gateway once formed part of the town's defences, and would have been closed every night. There are no other surviving gateways of this kind left in Britain.

3 CORNWALL HOUSE

Positioned slightly back from the road in a small courtyard, this elegant Georgian property has an arresting mustard-coloured exterior with white window frames.

4 AGINCOURT SQUARE

In this picturesque old square a country-style market is held every Friday and Saturday. Shire Hall was erected in 1724 on the site of an earlier Elizabethan market hall. In 1840, as a consequence of the Newport Riots, John Frost and some fellow Chartists were tried here. The tall windows above the six-arched colonnade are surmounted by a portico which incorporates a clock. A statue of Henry V was added to a recess at the centre of the frontage in 1792, commemorating Monmouth as the monarch's birthplace in 1387. In contrast,

Contrasting statues in Agincourt Square – Charles Rolls and Henry V

the statue in front of the hall is that of Charles Rolls, one half of the world-renowned Rolls-Royce partnership. The Beaufort Arms Hotel, in common with other buildings in Agincourt Square, is adorned with many hanging plants. It is an excellent example of a black-and-white building and in its days as an old coaching inn counted Lord Nelson as one of its overnight guests.

5 GREAT CASTLE HOUSE

This handsome mansion was built in 1673 by the 3rd Marquis of Worcester on the site of a round tower that had once formed an integral part of the castle. Inside, the ceilings are finely decorated. Nowadays the house serves as HQ for the Royal Monmouthshire Engineers.

6 THE CASTLE

Founded in 1068, the castle was one of many built by the Normans to subjugate the Welsh. It was here, in 1387, that the future Henry V was born. By Tudor times the castle was in a bad state of disrepair and it was finally reduced to ruins by Parliamentary artillery in the Civil War. The most substantial remains are those of the 12th-century hall-keep.

7 NELSON MUSEUM & LOCAL HISTORY CENTRE

These two foundations are housed, along with the Post Office, in purpose-built accommodation that blends quite well with nearby buildings. In the museum is the collection of Nelson memorabilia amassed by Lady Llangattock, mother of Charles Rolls. It includes model ships, documents, silver and the admiral's fighting sword. The Local History Centre provides detailed information on all buildings of note in the area and has displays of many interesting maps, papers and prints. There are also displays concerned with the Rolls-Royce company.

Monnow Bridge and its fortified gateway

8 MONMOUTH PRIORY

Virtually all that remains of the priory is what is popularly referred to as 'Geoffrey's Window'. The Geoffrey is Geoffrey of Monmouth, a 12th-century cleric who wrote one of the most influential of all medieval books. His *History of the Kings of Britain* collected many legends about Dark Age Britain, and inspired later authors to weave the stories of King Arthur from a few tenuous threads. The window is in fact 15th-century.

9 ST MARY'S CHURCH

Apart from the tower, this church was rebuilt in 1881. However, its history dates back to a medieval church built here soon after Monmouth Castle.

10 ST JAMES STREET

One of the most outstanding buildings in this street is The Grange, an imposing preparatory school with cream walls and white window-frames. Inside, there is a fine 18th-century staircase. Immediately opposite is the Queen's Head, a good example of a black-and-white timbered inn.

11 MONMOUTH GRAMMAR SCHOOL

Most of the present buildings were constructed in the late Victorian era with financial backing from the Haberdashers Company. There has been, though, a school on this site since 1614.

EARLY CLOSING: *Thu.*

MARKET DAY: *Fri & Sat.*

PARKING: *off Monnow St.*

OPENING TIMES:

Nelson Museum: open all year. Mon–Sat all day; Sun pm only.

36 | NORWICH

The capital city of Norfolk, and the market centre for a large part of East Anglia, Norwich can trace its existence back 1,000 years to the time when it was a Saxon settlement, the name of which appeared on the coins of King Athelstan. Today, as well as a Norman cathedral, and 33 other ancient churches, Norwich has an extremely attractive and varied range of secular buildings, dominated by the massive keep of the restored castle.

ROUTE DIRECTIONS

Start at St Peter Mancroft Church (1). Walk along St Peter's St, passing the Market Pl on the r. and the City Hall (2) on the l. Reach the Guildhall (3), cross St Giles St and enter Lower Goat La. Turn r. into Pottergate, then l. along the pathway under the tower of St John Maddermarket Church (4). Pass the Maddermarket Theatre (5). Turn l. into Charing Cross to reach Strangers' Hall (6). Return to St John Maddermarket, keeping left into Lobster La, and cross Exchange St into Bedford St. Turn l. into Bridewell Alley, passing the Mustard Shop (7) and then Bridewell Museum (8). At the end of the alley turn r. into St Andrew's St, passing St Andrew's Church (9). Across the next lane is Suckling House (10). Cross St Andrew's St to reach St George's St and St Andrew's and Blackfriars Halls (11). Continue into Prince's St and reach St Peter Hungate Church (12). Turn l. into Elm Hill (13) and at the bottom turn r. into Wensum St and reach Tombland (14). Cross Tombland and go through the Erpingham Gate (15) to reach the cathedral (16). From the cathedral walk south along Upper Close, turn l. and then l. again before Lower Close to reach the east end of the cathedral and the grave of Nurse Edith Cavell. Follow the path round and emerge into Bishopgate. Keep right to Bishop's Bridge, and turn r. along Riverside Walk to Pull's Ferry (17). Walk up the path to the cathedral, and leave the Cathedral Close by the Ethelbert Gate (18). Cross Tombland into Queen St and keep forward across Redwell St into London St. Bear left up Castle St, then l. into Davey Pl. Cross Castle Meadow and turn r., then l, to climb steps to reach the Castle (19). Return to Castle Meadow, cross it by the pedestrian crossing, and turn l. then r. into Arcade St. Walk through Royal Arcade (20) and at the end turn l. into Gentleman's Walk, with the market place opposite. Cross into Hay Hill and return to St Peter Mancroft Church.

1 ST PETER MANCROFT CHURCH

Largest of the city's churches, St Peter Mancroft was begun in 1430 and has kept a remarkable unity of style. Its spacious interior – with a fine hammerbeam roof and walls covered in fascinating memorials – is lit by 15th-century glass.

2 CITY HALL

George VI opened this monumental example of civic architecture in 1938. Opinions were mixed then as to its appearance, and it still draws comments today. Inside is the city's superb civic regalia.

3 THE GUILDHALL

Built in 1407, with walls of chequered flint, the Guildhall was the seat of government until 1938. Today it houses the Magistrates Courts, and when these are not sitting, the Council Chamber, with its carved Tudor ceiling and 15th-century stained glass, can be viewed.

4 ST JOHN MADDERMARKET CHURCH

The name maddermarket comes from an area near by where madder roots – used to prepare a red dye – was sold to Norwich weavers. The church itself is primarily of note for its collection of 15th- and 16th-century brasses.

5 MADDERMARKET THEATRE

This little Elizabethan-style theatre has been the home of the Norwich Players since 1921.

A fitting shop sign in Bridewell Alley

6 STRANGERS' HALL

This is a marvellously rambling old building, with a history stretching back more than 600 years. Its twisting stairways lead to a multitude of rooms, each of which sheds some light on six centuries of life in Norwich. It is a folk museum, with exhibits which range from shop signs to toys, and costumes to vehicles.

7 THE MUSTARD SHOP

Norwich and mustard go together – the city has been a centre for the production of that hot yellow condiment for several centuries, and in the Mustard Shop there is a small museum which tells the story of the industry. The shop itself is a museum-piece – still equipped like a Victorian grocer's.

8 BRIDEWELL MUSEUM

Originally a merchant's house, this 14th-century flint-faced building was used as a prison from 1583 to 1828, principally to hold beggars and tramps. It is now a museum of local crafts and industries.

Picturesque houses in Elm Hill

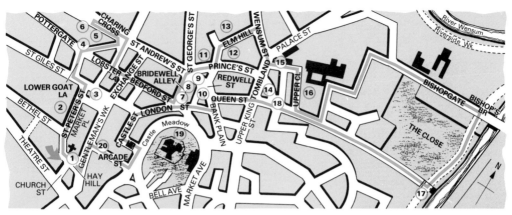

9 ST ANDREW'S CHURCH
The main parts of this church were built between 1478 and 1506. It contains a rich variety of monuments, including an ornate 17th-century one to Sir John Suckling and his wife.

10 SUCKLING HOUSE
Members of the Suckling family are buried in the Church of St Andrew, and this is where several generations of them lived. The banqueting hall is the best feature that survives from the original 14th-century house. The adjoining Stuart Hall was the scene of the first meeting of the now famous Round Table movement in 1927.

11 ST ANDREW'S AND BLACKFRIARS HALLS
Since the Reformation these adjoining halls have belonged to Norwich corporation and have been used for a great variety of civic and cultural occasions. Originally they formed the nave and chancel of a church of the Dominican friars. The church was completed in 1470, and its contemporary cloisters, and the crypt, can still be seen.

12 ST PETER HUNGATE CHURCH
This church now serves as a museum of church antiquities, with exhibits dating from the 9th to the 20th centuries. These include vestments, brasses, musical instruments and illuminated books, as well as a 14th-century coffin with a skeleton in it.

A tranquil scene at Pull's Ferry

13 ELM HILL
This is a charming, cobbled street, lined on both sides with ancient houses that are now mostly occupied by antique or craft shops. The oldest is the Briton's Arms, once a pub, which escaped a fire in 1507.

14 TOMBLAND
A wide thoroughfare just outside the cathedral precincts, Tombland has been a public open space since Saxon times, and was once the scene of busy markets, and sometimes riots between townspeople and monks. Among the best buildings around it are the Maid's Head Hotel, dating from the 15th century and later, Samson and Hercules House, with its namesake figures supporting the pediment above the door, and half-timbered Augustine Steward House, now the tourist information centre.

15 ERPINGHAM GATE
Elaborately decorated, this gateway into the cathedral precincts was erected in 1420. Just beyond it, on the left, are the buildings of Norwich School, established in 1553.

16 CATHEDRAL
Herbert de Losinga, the first Bishop of Norwich, founded the cathedral in 1096. It is a superb building, full of interest and beauty, and would repay many hours attention. Among its most notable features are the nave, with its huge round pillars, the bishop's throne (a Saxon survival unique in Europe), and the cloisters with their matchless collection of roof bosses.

17 PULL'S FERRY
This picturesque group of buildings was once a fortified water gate into the walled city; later it became the point from which a ferry plied across the River Wensum, and the name of an early ferryman became attached to it.

18 ETHELBERT GATE
This gateway was erected at the cost of the townspeople after a great riot in 1772, during which some of the monastery buildings were destroyed.

19 NORWICH CASTLE
The great stone keep of the castle stands on a mound high above the city and dominates all around it. Originally built in Norman times, the exterior was re-faced by the architect Anthony Salvin in 1834, giving it its present appearance. The keep now forms part of Norwich Castle Museum, whose collections span natural history, geology, archaeology and, most outstandingly, paintings by the Norwich School of artists.

20 CASTLE ARCADE
From the market place end, Castle Arcade is unremarkable, but the Arcade Street end is a riot of *art nouveau* decoration.

EARLY CLOSING: *Thu.*

MARKET DAY: *Mon–Sat.*

PARKING: *Bethel St, Meadow, Old Cattle Market.*

OPENING TIMES:

City Hall: open all year. Mon–Fri.

Strangers' Hall Museum: open all year. Mon–Sat.

The Mustard Shop: open all year. Mon–Sat (closed all day Thu).

Bridewell Museum: open all year. Mon–Sat.

St Peter Hungate Church Museum: open all year. Mon–Sat.

Cathedral: open all year.

Norwich Castle: open all year. Mon–Sat all day. Sun pm only.

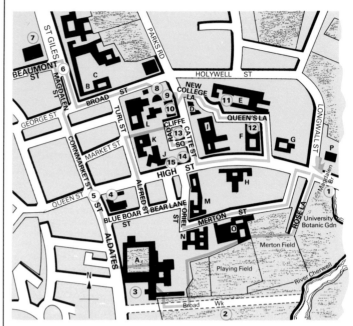

ROUTE DIRECTIONS

Start at Magdalen Bridge and pass the University Botanic Garden (1). Turn l. into Rose Lane. Follow the path through Christ Church Meadow (2) to Christ Church Cathedral (3). Walk through Christ Church College and leave by Tom Gate and turn r. along St Aldate's past Museum of Oxford (4) to Carfax (5). Continue along Cornmarket St into Magdalen St past Martyrs' Memorial (6) and turn l. into Beaumont St to the Ashmolean Museum (7). Return to Magdalen St, cross over and turn r. then l. into Broad St to the Museum of the History of Science (8). From the Sheldonian (9), turn r. into Catte St for the Bodleian Library (10), then pass under arch into New College Lane, passing New College (11). Continue into Queen's La with St Edmund's Hall (12) on r. On reaching the High St turn r. then r. again up Catte St to Radcliffe Sq and Camera (13). Opposite is St Mary's Church (14), with Brasenose College (15) nearby. Turn l. out of the sq to Turl St and turn l. Cross the High St into Alfred St and turn l. into Bear La to reach Oriel St. Continue l. along Merton St and turn r. at High St to return to Magdalen Bridge.

College key:
A *Christ Church* **B** *Balliol*
C *Trinity* **D** *Hertford* **E** *New*
F *Queen's* **G** *St Edmund's Hall*
H *University* **I** *All Souls*
J *Brasenose* **K** *Lincoln* **L** *Exeter*
M *Oriel* **N** *Corpus Christi*
O *Merton* **P** *Magdalen*

FORTIS EST VERITAS

For centuries Oxford has been famous as a seat of learning, and the scholarly atmosphere of the magnificent university buildings, the colleges with their high walls hiding peaceful courtyards and gardens, and the time-honoured traditions unique to Oxford student life, are an intrinsic part of the city's charm. Yet Oxford is not just a university town and architectural showpiece, it is also a commercial and industrial city providing work and entertainment for thousands of people. It is this combination of roles that makes Oxford one of the most fascinating cities in Europe.

Among the extensive collections of pottery and ceramics in the Ashmolean Museum is this Chinese figure

1 UNIVERSITY BOTANIC GARDEN

During 1621 this garden, the oldest of its kind in Britain, was laid out as a Physic Garden and the peaceful formality of those days still characterises it. To one side of the garden, near the river, there are greenhouses where more delicate and exotic plants are grown.

2 CHRIST CHURCH MEADOW

Keepers still watch the gates into the Meadow to prevent, according to the notice board, undesirables entering, and to lock the gates at dusk.

3 CHRIST CHURCH AND CATHEDRAL

Christ Church was founded as Cardinal College by Cardinal Wolsey in 1525. However, by 1546 Wolsey had fallen from grace and Henry VIII refounded it as Christ Church. The present cathedral, the smallest in Britain, dates mainly from the 12th and 13th centuries. Of all the stained glass in the cathedral the most precious piece is the window in St Lucy's Chapel, made in 1340 to commemorate the murder of Thomas Becket in Canterbury Cathedral. The huge quadrangle of the college is one of the most awe-inspiring in Oxford. Its main gateway has a tall dome on the top – added by Christopher Wren in 1682 – and called Tom Tower after the great bell, Great Tom, inside which strikes every hour.

4 MUSEUM OF OXFORD

The museum, housed in the old city library, is a branch of the Oxfordshire County Museum at Woodstock and has only been open a few years. Its exhibits illustrate the history of Oxford from Neolithic times to the present day. Different spheres of the city's life, including the University and the motor industry, have their own exhibits and displays. There are also reconstructions of such things as shops and college rooms.

Choirboys on their way to chapel at Magdalene College

A window in St Mary's Church, Magdalene Street

5 CARFAX
Carfax, the name a derivation of the Old French word *carrefour,* meaning four forks, is the crossroads at the centre of the old city. It is marked by a sturdy stone tower – all that survives of St Martin's Church.

6 MARTYRS' MEMORIAL
Three bishops were burnt at the stake here in the 16th century for their Protestant beliefs during Queen Mary's reinstatement of the Catholic faith. Three hundred years later this memorial was built to commemorate them.

7 THE ASHMOLEAN MUSEUM
The rare and exotic treasures that fill the Ashmolean's galleries – based on a collection begun in the 17th century – come from all corners of the world and include Egyptian furnishings, bronzes and sculptures, Chinese ceramics, Tibetan silverware, and Minoan seals, swords and jewellery. One of the museum's most famous possessions is the Alfred Jewel – a brooch of gold, rock crystal and enamel made for King Alfred in the 9th century. A very important part of the museum is its art collection, best known for its British paintings, including notable Pre-Raphaelite pictures.

8 MUSEUM OF THE HISTORY OF SCIENCE
Designed by Thomas Wood, this is one of the best examples in Oxford of 17th-century architecture. The entire building is now devoted to the Museum of the History of Science, which consists mainly of an amalgamation of private collections.

9 SHELDONIAN THEATRE
With the sculpted heads of Roman emperors ranged on pillars around its semicircular front, the Sheldonian Theatre is one of the city's most distinctive buildings. It was named after Archbishop Sheldon, who commissioned his friend, Christopher Wren, to build it in 1664 as a ceremonial assembly hall for the University. Concerts are also held in these elegant surroundings, and the acoustics are said to be perfect.

10 THE BODLEIAN LIBRARY
The Bodleian collection of today was really begun by Sir Thomas Bodley in 1598. Now it contains over 2½ million books and 50,000 manuscripts and is one of the six libraries in Britain entitled to a copy of every book published in the UK. The oldest building here is the 15th-century Divinity School with its collection of rare and priceless books. This and the Duke Humphrey's Library above it are the only parts of the Bodleian open to the public.

11 NEW COLLEGE
New College Lane seems remote from the rest of the city as it leads through high walls to New College. This, despite its name, was founded in 1379.

12 ST EDMUND HALL
St Edmund, only survivor of the medieval halls, is now a college. Founded in about 1220, its cottagey buildings contrast sharply with the other colleges' much grander architecture.

13 RADCLIFFE CAMERA
This huge domed building at the very heart of the university dominates Radcliffe Square – which is considered to be one of the finest in Europe. It was officially opened in 1757 as a library. However, in 1857 it was taken over by the Bodleian as a reading room.

14 ST MARY THE VIRGIN
Oxford's parish church, St Mary's was the scene of all university gatherings for nearly 400 years, and to this day its bells still ring out for all official functions. The most striking features of this large church are the tower and spire and the south porch. The latter has great barley sugar pillars and is an unusual example of baroque architecture. There are excellent views from the tower.

15 BRASENOSE COLLEGE
The curious name of this college is thought to be a derivation of bronze nose – the nickname given to the old door knocker of the 13th-century hall that formerly occupied the site. The present buildings date from the 14th century and later.

EARLY CLOSING: *Thu.*

MARKET DAY: *Wed.*

PARKING: *Thames St, Norfolk St.*

OPENING TIMES: *University Botanic Garden: open all year.*

Museum of Oxford: open all year, Tue – Sat.

Ashmolean Museum: open all year, Tue – Sat; Sun pm only.

Museum of the History of Science: open all year, Mon – Fri.

ROUTE DIRECTIONS

From the harbour (1) turn l. out of the car park along Wharf Rd. Turn r. up Abbey Slip and keep forward into Abbey St then go r. into Chapel St (2), passing the Egyptian House (3). Turn r. into Market Pl (4) and Market Jew St; cross over and turn l. along The Terrace, and then cross Causeway Hd to reach Alverton St (5). Cross by mini roundabout and turn l. into Wellington Pl. Turn l. at the foot of the car park (signposted 'Pedestrian exit to Morrab Rd') and then turn r. at Morrab Rd. At this point a detour can be made by turning r. into Penlee Gardens (6). Return, cross the road and go ahead down an unsigned alley. At the end turn r. to enter Morrab Gardens (7). Bear r. to pass Morrab Library, turn downhill and bear l. to exit from Gardens into Coulson's Pl. Immediately turn l. and then go forward into Coulson's Bldngs. Turn l. to go uphill, and then turn r. into Regent Sq (8). Turn r. into Chapel St. Turn r. into St Mary's Churchyard (9) and cross seawards into South Pl. Go left and continue through St Anthony's Gardens (10). Cross the Promenade to Battery Rocks (11) and return to the Harbour along the Quay.

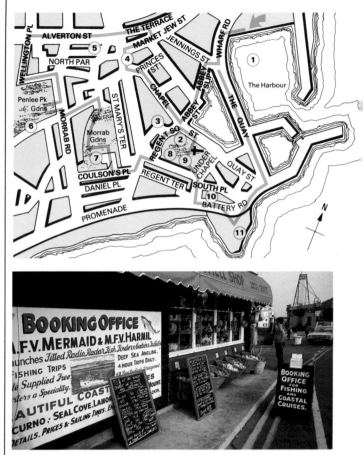

The 10th-century cross of King Ricatus in Penlee Gardens

B*almy Penzance takes its name and existence from the one time chapel-crowned headland which thrusts into Mount's Bay. In its lee, Pen sans (Cornish for holy headland) has grown from a humble fishing cove to the capital of Penwith despite being burnt to ashes by the Spaniards in 1595. No buildings survive from before that date but to compensate the town has a rich legacy from the Georgian era. Pilchards and tin supplied prosperity, but with the coming of the railway, the town's livelihood shifted from trade to a stylish tourism.*

1 THE HARBOUR
Stacked high on the wharves in the heyday of sail were tin blocks and fish barrels. Today, although those ancient trades and a 300-strong fishing fleet have gone, the harbour is still full of life and colour. Colossal red buoys identify the Trinity House building; the Barbican Craft Centre and Aquarium was formerly an old warehouse; and from the South Pier the MV *Scillonian* makes a daily forty-mile voyage to the Scilly Isles. In the dock there is usually a coaster or two and in the outer harbour a cheerful fleet of leisure craft. Behind the road and swing bridge is the inner harbour and the old granite-flagged Abbey Slip.

2 CHAPEL STREET
Memories of an older Penzance – of smuggling and dark lanterns – seem to linger in this ancient way that leads from the harbour. Its 17th- and 18th-century buildings now find a variety of pleasing uses. The

Top: boat trips, fishing and shells are among the harbour's attractions

400-year-old Admiral Benbow Inn with its rooftop pirate, and Roland Morris's Maritime Museum opposite, are run by Roland Morris, diver and finder of the wreck of the *Association*. The Turk's Head Inn with its fine signboard is the oldest in town, dating back to the 13th century. No. 18 boasts a ghost – a board outside tells the story. Tradition has it that in autumn 1805 the Assembly Rooms, now the Union Hotel, were the scene of the first announcement in England of triumph and tragedy at Trafalgar.

3 THE EGYPTIAN HOUSE
The most remarkable building in Penzance is Nos 6 & 7 Chapel Street, the Egyptian House. Built in 1835/6 and reflecting the then popular interest in Egyptology, it housed the collection of John Lanvin, a local mineralogist. It is now in the care of the National Trust.

4 MARKET PLACE

The shopping centre of the town is Market Place, Market Jew Street (actually derived from the Cornish words *Marghas Yow*, or Thursday Market) and Alverton Street. These are dominated by the high domed Market House, which was completed on the day of Queen Victoria's coronation. In front of the massive portico is a statue of Sir Humphry Davy, Penzance's most famous son, a brilliant chemist, inventor of the miner's safety lamp and President of the Royal Society. The Olive Branch Restaurant – on the right as you face the statue – carries a special plaque to mark the site and year of his birth, 1778.

5 ALVERTON STREET

Alverton Street has a fine example of a mid 18th-century cornish granite house, now the Camelot Restaurant. Further along, in the old Municipal Buildings, is the Geological Museum, where local examples of tin and copper ores and other specimens of Penwith's fascinating geology can be seen.

6 PENLEE GARDENS

Once the lush 15-acre surround of Penlee House (1866), the gardens are now a public park. By the house stands an 8ft 10th-century cross (formerly the town's market cross) and one of only two to bear the name of a Cornish king. A just legible inscription at the base reads *Regis Ricati Crux* (the cross of King Ricatus). Ricatus is thought to have been the father of King Howal, Cornwall's last recorded king.

7 MORRAB GARDENS

Morrab Place is probably the finest example of the early 19th-century granite or stucco terraces which elegantly line the way to Morrab Gardens. With their bamboo and tree ferns, the gardens offer a few acres of sub-tropical greenery in the heart of Penzance. Embellishing them are a large fountain and a traditional ironwork bandstand. At the top stands Morrab House, a cream Georgian-style villa, actually built in 1841, which once had the Gardens as its grounds. The house is now a private library.

8 REGENT SQUARE

The Square is a delightful little enclave of relaxed Regency style houses built in the 1830s. The road twists through the centre and offers a close view of these charming homes with their columned porches and pleasing colours.

9 ST MARY'S CHURCH

The church stands on the site of an earlier St Mary's Chapel destroyed by the Spaniards, though later rebuilt. Consecrated in 1836, it has a spacious blue-ceilinged interior and a font of Lizard serpentine. Wall tablets serve as reminders that Cornishmen travelled and died far from home.

10 ST ANTHONY'S GARDENS

The site of 12th-century St Anthony's Chapel (patron saint of fishermen) – the earliest place of worship in Penzance – is marked by these Gardens. Although containing an archway believed to have come

The Market House

from the chapel, a more certain relic is a 4ft piece of granite depicting Christ in a loincloth which stands in St Mary's Churchyard. The gardens also feature a huge 12ft fountain bowl carved from a single block of granite.

11 BATTERY ROCKS

This, the wave-washed tip of the 'Holy Headland' is almost covered by the war memorial and swimming pool. Its name comes from a small fortlet built in 1740 to defend the harbour. From the rocks, which mark the end of the walk, there is a sparkling sea-level view of St Michael's Mount, the Western Promenade, Newlyn and distant Penlee Point.

EARLY CLOSING: *Wed.*

MARKET DAY: *Thu & Sat.*

PARKING: *Harbour, Guildhall, Green Market, Wellington Place.*

OPENING TIMES:

Roland Morris's Maritime Museum: open May–Sep.

Barbican Craft Workshop: open all year.

Geological Museum: open May–Sep. Mon–Fri, pm only.

Elegant Morrab Place

39 | PERTH

Although the Romans were active in the area around Perth, the town itself is not mentioned in any document earlier than 1127. Previously, it was overshadowed by Scone, the first capital, under Kenneth I in the 9th century, of a united Scotland. In medieval times Perth was an important trading port, since the Tay is easily navigable as far as the town. Kings and queens of Scotland were often in Perth, and several parliaments were held here, the last in 1606. It is the Georgian town, however, which is the heart of Perth even today, as the suburbs spread well beyond the riverside.

ROUTE DIRECTIONS

Start at the Round House (1) and go north along Tay Street (2), passing under a bridge. Turn l. into South St and second r. into St John St. Go round St John's Kirk (3) and back into St John St. Turn r. into High St and l. into George St. Bear r. to pass Art Gallery (4) then cross Charlotte St and turn l. along far pavement. Bear r. on to path along west side of North Inch (5), keeping to l. of Albert Statue. Follow path along west side of playing fields. Immediately after Sports Centre and children's play area, turn l. onto path for Balhousie Castle (6) and Douglas Garden (7), then rejoin path, turn l. to go round playing fields and follow it to r. to go along the River Tay (8). At memorial take path to l., go under bridge then sharp r. onto Tay St and r. again over bridge. At far side turn r. at traffic lights, immediately r. again down steps past Riverside Inn and straight on past houses on r. Where this road begins to climb, turn r. down path and steps to turn l. along riverside. Keep as close to river as possible, into Norie-Miller Park (9), then up ramp to turn l. at main road. At traffic lights, cross over and turn r. along east-side pavement of Dundee Rd. Pass Hillside Hospital. Bear l. up driveway at sign to Branklyn Gardens (10). Return from Branklyn, cross Dundee Rd, turn r. along far pavement, and in about 80 yards turn l. down steps and footpath signposted to Moncreiffe Island (11) and Tay St. Follow path onto walkway beside railway bridge, turning down steps at far end. Turn l. from steps to pass under bridge and return to the Round House.

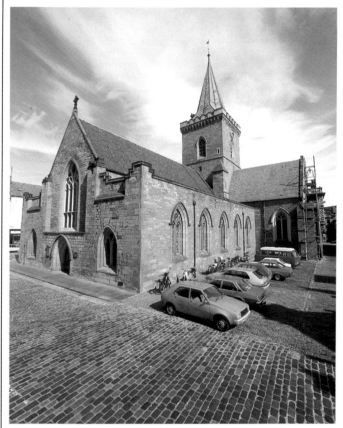

St John's Kirk dates from the 15th century

1 THE ROUND HOUSE
This was the original waterworks of Perth, designed in 1832 by Dr Adam Anderson, rector of Perth Academy. The cast iron dome housed the water tanks, and the pumping machinery was in the building underneath. In use till 1965, it was transformed into a tourist information centre and re-opened in 1974. The tall pillar behind it used to be the chimney of the furnace of the steam-engine which worked the pumps. It is now topped by a Grecian urn in disguised glass-fibre. Facing the South Inch, a publicly-owned open space since 1377, the Round House is in Marshall Place, which contains several of Perth's Georgian buildings. But the church of St Leonard's-in-the-Fields, with its graceful crown steeple, dates from 1885.

2 TAY STREET
A feature of this riverside street are the Doric columns at the entrance to the Sheriff Court, built in 1819. Tay Street is an entirely 19th-century creation, on ground previously occupied by the gardens of the houses in the Speygate and the Watergate, where kings and queens of Scotland used to lodge on their visits to the town.

3 ST JOHN'S KIRK
Perth was originally St John's Town of Perth, and St John's Kirk is almost the only reminder of the medieval town. The earliest church on this site was built in the name of John the Baptist in the early 12th century. The present building dates from the 15th century. It was here, on 11 May 1559, that John Knox preached the aggressive sermon which sparked off the Reformation in Scotland. In the years that followed, St John's Kirk was used at different times as a weapons store, a courthouse and a prison. But it remained the parish church – and was restored in the 1920s.

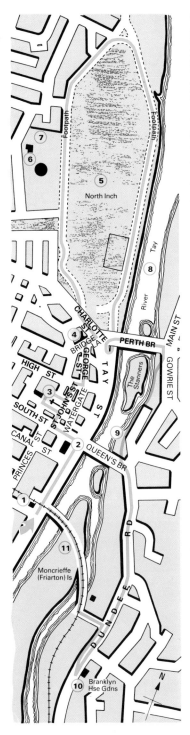

6 BALHOUSIE CASTLE
After the ultra-modern Bell's Sports Centre, opened in 1968, is the entrance to Balhousie Castle. The present castle is based on a 16th-century tower. Balhousie estate was owned by the Eviot, Mercer and – from 1626 – Hay families. The Hays became the earls of Kinnoull. It is now the Regimental Museum of the Black Watch, raised at Aberfeldy in 1739 but from a few years after that closely connected with Perth. The regimental depot was in the barracks, now demolished, which stood beside the North Inch. Part of the castle garden is laid out as a memorial to Field-Marshal Earl Wavell, Colonel of the Regiment from 1946 to 1950.

7 DOUGLAS GARDEN
This informal garden was set out in 1962 in memory of the botanical collector David Douglas, born in the nearby village of Scone, who brought the first seeds of the Douglas fir to Britain in 1827. He did not, however, discover the tree, which had been noted on Vancouver Island 36 years before by another Scottish botanist, Alexander Menzies. This explains why the Latin name of the Douglas fir is *Pseudotsuga menziesii*.

8 RIVER TAY
At almost 120 miles, the Tay is the longest river in Scotland, and one of the fastest-flowing. Pearl-bearing mussels are found near Perth, but this is above all a salmon river. Downstream from the town there is commercial salmon-netting. Upriver are the finest sporting beats, including the one where the British record salmon of 64 pounds was caught on an October day in 1922 by a 22-year-old girl, Georgina Ballantyne.

The pleasant green spaces of North Inch, which have belonged to the town since 1377

9 NORIE-MILLER PARK
Directly across the Tay from the General Accident Fire and Life Assurance Company's first office of 1885, this garden and riverside walk are named after the founding family. Known locally as the 'G.A.', this world-wide organisation still has its head office in Perth. The park was gifted to the town in 1971, and all the company's home and foreign branches are represented by individual features.

10 BRANKLYN GARDEN
Often described as the best two acres of private garden in Britain, this was nothing more than an overgrown orchard in 1922, when Mr and Mrs John Renton began the long work of creating a famous collection of dwarf rhododendrons and alpine plants. Ownership was transferred to the National Trust for Scotland in 1967.

11 MONCREIFFE ISLAND
Reached from the mainland on both banks of the Tay only by the footpath on the bridge which takes the railway from Perth to Dundee, Moncreiffe is nevertheless a useful amenity area of the town. There are allotments at the north end and, at the south, the King James VI Golf Course. Laid out in its present form in 1858, the 18-hole course is the most curiously situated in Scotland.

EARLY CLOSING: *Wed.*

MARKET DAY: *Fri.*

PARKING: *opposite Round House (enter from Shore Rd), Tay St.*

OPENING TIMES:

St John's Kirk: open all year. Mon – Sat. Services on Sunday.

Perth Art Gallery: open all year. Mon – Sat.

Balhousie Castle: open all year. Mon – Fri.

Branklyn Garden: open all year.

4 ART GALLERY AND MUSEUM
Designed by a local amateur architect, David Morison, this building, fronted by Ionic columns, was erected in 1824 as a monument to Thomas Hay Marshall, the progressive Provost of Perth who was responsible for most of the Georgian rebuilding of the town. George Street, where the Art Gallery stands, was opened in 1773.

5 NORTH INCH
Like the South Inch, this park has been town land since 1377. In 1396 it was the scene of the rather shadowy Battle of the Clans, which was, in effect, a tournament held in the presence of Robert III, but a bloody and deliberate fight all the same.

40 | PLYMOUTH

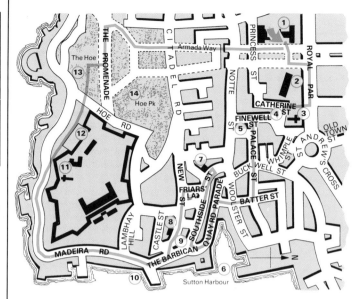

ROUTE DIRECTIONS

From the Civic Centre (1), turn r. into Royal Par. The Guildhall (2) is down on the r. St Andrew's Church (3) is the next building on the same side. Take the path between the Guildhall and St Andrew's Church through to the end of Catherine St, where Prysten House (4) is immediately on the l. With St Andrew's to the l. follow the pathway down steps and into a cobbled area bordering St Andrew's St. Turn r. and pass into Finewell St, then go l. into Palace St where the Merchant's House (5) is on the corner. Cross over Buckwell St and turn r. into Batter St. From here, cross over Woolster St, into an unnamed cobbled lane opposite, which leads into The Parade. Turn l. and walk along Quay Rd round to Sutton Harbour (6). Where the road becomes the Barbican, double back r. into Southside St. Coates & Co (7) is down on the l. just past the Blackfriars La turning. Return along Southside St, taking the second r. into Friars La. At the end turn l. into narrow New St. The Elizabethan House (8) is down on the r. At the end of New St, Island House (9) stands alone in the small square. Turn r. here into the Barbican, a quayside way. Once past the Mayflower Memorial (10), walk on into Madeira Rd and follow the water's edge round to the Royal Citadel (11) on the r. From here, follow the steps along the Citadel Wall to the Aquarium (12). At the pathway's end, cross over Hoe Rd into Plymouth Hoe where Smeaton's Tower (13) is situated. Beyond the broad walkway called the Promenade, Hoe Park (14) is straight ahead. From this point take the path leading away from the sea and cross over Citadel Rd into Armada Way, which leads back to the Civic Centre via the intersection of Notte St and Princess St.

P lymouth has grown out of all proportion since the days of its being a small medieval fishing port called Sutton. The modern-day naval base and commercial centre includes the towns of Devonport and Stonehouse, swelling the overall population to over a quarter of a million. The city is indeed fortunate that Plymouth Sound is one of the finest natural harbours in the world. As a result, industries such as shipbuilding and fish-canning became, and have remained, mainstays. Although given a radical face-lift following extensive damage inflicted by bombing in World War II, Plymouth still retains many of its older buildings and maritime connections.

1 CIVIC CENTRE

This large modern office block has a tourist information centre on the ground floor, while an exhibition hall featuring art and local history is above. At the top of the building a roof deck affords panoramic views of the city. A large grassy area at the front of the main entrance gives the centre an open-plan effect.

2 GUILDHALL

Originally constructed in 1874, this edifice had to be virtually rebuilt in 1959. Its main feature is a tall square tower. High up on one side are fourteen stained-glass windows which record the history of Plymouth in picture form from 1355 to 1953.

3 ST ANDREW'S CHURCH

Due largely to World War II damage, this building has had to be much restored. However, the modern stained-glass windows – in vivid red, green, blue and purple – blend cleverly with the older parts such as the 15th-century tower.

4 PRYSTEN HOUSE

At 500 years old, this is the oldest dwelling in the city. It is a smallish stone building, recently discovered to have been initially a merchant's house but, as its appearance testifies, was for many years a chapel believed to have housed priests from Plympton Priory. Nowadays,

John Piper was commissioned to undertake new stained glass for St Andrew's after it was virtually destroyed in the war

though not exactly a museum, the building's many chambers (such as the Bishop's Room and the Chapter Room) serve as a living history for all to study. The tree outside the house is a symbol of lasting friendship between Plymouth UK and Plymouth USA.

Sutton Harbour's fishing fleet

For 123 years Smeaton's Tower was lashed by storms on the Eddystone Rock. Replaced by a new lighthouse, it was given an honourable retirement on the Hoe

5 MERCHANT'S HOUSE
The building dates from 1601 and was originally the home of William Parker. It is the city's finest example of the period. A clever restoration was carried out in 1978 and the Palace Street façade is now impressive. On the second floor there is an interesting exhibition of the Siege of Plymouth (1642–46), with displays of nautical costumes of the day.

6 SUTTON HARBOUR
This is an area that exudes maritime atmosphere. Masted fishing boats bob about in the water while old bollards and netting line the quay. The Customs House and several stone warehouses are nearby. The attractive quayside inns make the harbour a popular place to take refreshment.

7 COATES & CO
This distillery is housed in a 15th-century protected building. Originally part of a Dominican monastery, it is now the home of Plymouth Gin. Visitors are welcome from June to September.

8 ELIZABETHAN HOUSE
The building is typical of its period in that the exterior is painted white with black window-frames, and has overhanging cottage-style windows. Inside there is much period furniture, including a small four-poster bed and several carved oak chests.

9 ISLAND HOUSE
This stone building is thought to be where the Pilgrim Fathers entertained on the night prior to sailing across the Atlantic.

10 MAYFLOWER MEMORIAL
Erected in 1891, this stone monument commemorates the sailing of the *Mayflower* in 1620. It takes the form of a square with an arched top.

11 ROYAL CITADEL
This impressive stronghold was built in 1666 by order of Charles II. Its imposingly high stone walls flank the Madeira Road all the way to the Hoe. Currently, the fortress is the home of the 29th Commando Regiment Royal Artillery. Although there are tours during the summer, the citadel is occasionally closed for security reasons.

12 AQUARIUM
Known grandly as the Plymouth Laboratory of the Marine Biological Association of the UK, this newish stone building houses a large collection of sea creatures with particular emphasis on crustacea.

13 SMEATON'S TOWER
This red-and-white structure once formed the upper part of the third Eddystone Lighthouse, which was named after its designer John Smeaton. It was moved to the Hoe when the present lighthouse was built in 1882.

14 HOE PARK
This pleasant stretch of open grassland is close to the sea-front and is the location of three notable statues. The National Armada Memorial is built of stone and has a bronze figure of Britannia atop, while the Naval War Memorial consists of a tall column surmounted by a green globe. The Sir Francis Drake Statue, erected in 1884, depicts the famous Elizabethan looking out to sea contemplating his momentous circumnavigation of the globe.

EARLY CLOSING: *Wed.*

MARKET DAYS: *Mon–Sat.*

PARKING: *Lockyer St, Guildhall, off Cornwall St.*

OPENING TIMES:

City Museum & Art Gallery: open all year. Mon–Sat.

Merchant's House: open all year. Mon–Sat all day, Sun pm only.

Elizabethan House: open all year. Mon–Sat all day, and Sun pm Easter–Sep.

Prysten House: open all year. Mon–Sat.

Smeaton's Tower: open Apr–Oct.

Royal Citadel: open Apr–Sep pm (may be closed at short notice).

ROUTE DIRECTIONS

*Start from Clarence Pier. Walk
away from the sea along Pier Rd,
Bellevue Ter, Jubilee Ter and
King's Ter. Turn l. along
Museum Rd to the Museum (1)
and to meet High St. ★ Turn l. to
pass Buckingham House (2) and
visit the Cathedral (3). Continue
along High St to Square Tower
(4) and turn r. along Broad St (5)
to Portsmouth Point (6). Turn l.
past the Lively Lady pub and at
the Still and West pub keep
forward into Bath Sq, passing
Quebec House (7), and continue
into West St. Keep forward into
Tower St to reach Round Tower
(8). Turn l. and at the Seagull pub
turn r. into Broad St. Ascend steps
on r. onto defensive walls to Sally
Port Battery and descend steps to
Sally Port Gate (9). Pass Square
Tower and turn l. up High St and
down Grand Parade to Garrison
Church (10). Walk round south
side of church and turn r. through
tunnel beneath King's Bastion
(11), turn l. and return to start
point. From here, it is possible to
walk along Clarence Esplanade to
visit Southsea Castle (1m).*

*★ To visit HMS Victory (1m),
keep straight on along St George's
Rd into The Hard to reach the
main gate, HM Dockyard.*

The home of the British Navy, Portsmouth is filled with the
sounds and smells of the sea, and Naval establishments
still dominate many corners of the city. The centre, badly
bombed in the war, has arisen again as a modern shopping area.
Old Portsmouth – the central feature of this walk – is a fascinating area of old houses, pubs and stone fortifications that create an
almost village-like atmosphere.

1 CITY MUSEUM AND ART GALLERY

Temporary exhibitions are held
in the ground-floor galleries
here and the permanent
collection is housed upstairs.
One gallery is devoted to 20th-
century art and furniture
(including pieces by Frank
Lloyd Wright), another has
19th-century collections, while
yet another is full of splendid
17th-century furniture. On the
second floor is an exhibition
telling the story of Portsmouth,
and also well-displayed
collections of domestic items
ranging from candlesticks to
mangles.

2 BUCKINGHAM HOUSE

Just south of the Grammar
School on the left is the house
where George Villiers, Duke of
Buckingham, was murdered in
1628. He was a very powerful
but unpopular man and was
killed by a former army officer.
The house itself is rendered, but
behind this there is a 17th-
century façade over an even
older timber-framed structure.

3 CATHEDRAL

A Jacobean tower presides over
the mixture of architectural
styles which make up the

Top: Round Tower and Tower House

cathedral. The earliest parts are
the 12th-century chancel and
choir, while at the centre are the
tower and the nave that was
built at the same time. The
cathedral was greatly enlarged
during the 20th century by the
addition of a new nave at the
west end. Among the special
treasures here is a plaque made
in Florence in 1500.

4 SQUARE TOWER

Charles I's bust can be seen on
the north face of the Square
Tower which stands right at the
foot of the High Street. This
tower has seen many different
uses – it was originally the
residence of the Military
Governor of the town; then it
was used as a magazine; it was
subsequently a meat store, a
semaphore signalling station
and an armed defence post.

5 BROAD STREET

A jumbled mixture of many
different styles of houses and
shops makes up this colourful
street. At one time it was a most
unsalubrious area outside the
town's jurisdiction, filled with
pubs and brothels. It earned the
nickname 'Spice Island'.

SOUTHSEA CASTLE

Fears of invasion led Henry VIII to build Southsea Castle as one of many new defences round the coast of Britain. In 1545 Henry watched from the castle while the English fleet engaged the French. To everyone's astonishment, and in calm, clear conditions, the English flagship, the *Mary Rose*, keeled over and sank with almost all hands. The wreck was recently raised amid worldwide publicity. A fascinating exhibition about the excavation and about the ship can be seen in Southsea Castle. The *Mary Rose* herself is now being preserved and can be seen near HMS *Victory*.

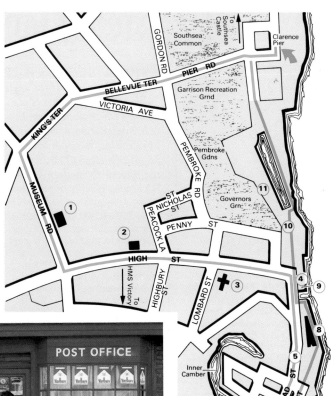

Broad Street Post Office

6 PORTSMOUTH POINT

From the tip of the Point it is possible to look across Portsmouth Harbour and see the ferries, the huge navy ships and the stately masts of HMS *Victory* in the distance.

7 QUEBEC HOUSE

Originally built by public subscription as a sea-bathing establishment in 1754, this is now a private house. White weatherboarding was once common in Portsmouth, but this house is now the only example left in the city.

8 ROUND TOWER

Henry VIII ordered the building of this tower to help defend the King's ships, and it was one of a pair of towers at the harbour entrance. A huge chain boom was hung between them across the harbour mouth as protection. Today the tower is the headquarters of the Fort Cumberland Guard, who regularly re-enact military ceremonies of the 1840s.

9 SALLY PORT

Naval officers came ashore, or embarked, through this gate, once known as the 'King's Stairs'. The fortifications along here are the longest remaining section of the walls that defended the town.

10 GARRISON CHURCH

Bomb damage ruined part of this church, but the oldest part, the 13th-century chancel, remains intact and is still used for services. Charles II married Catherine of Braganza here. Before that it was part of a hospital, founded in 1212.

11 KING'S BASTION

The old town of Portsmouth was originally protected by a formidable series of ramparts and a moat. The only part of this system remaining today is the King's Bastion and the Long Curtain Battery.

PARKING: *Clarence Pier, King's Terrace.*

OPENING TIMES:

City Museum and Art Gallery: open all year.

Garrison Church: Apr–Sep (exc 1 May), Mon–Thu all day, Sun pm only.

Southsea Castle: open all year.

HMS Victory and Royal Naval Museum: open all year Mon–Sat all day, Sun pm only.

HMS *VICTORY*

Nelson's name is forever linked to his flagship at the Battle of Trafalgar in 1805. The restoration of HMS *Victory* to its original condition is probably the best example of such work in the world. It is possible to walk through the ship and see the conditions in which the men lived and fought, and the spot where Nelson was fatally wounded. The Admiral's cabin has also been excellently restored. Although many relics of Nelson and Trafalgar are displayed on the ship, several more can be seen in the Royal Naval Museum in one of the 18th-century dockyard buildings nearby.

42 | RICHMOND

This ancient market town is delightfully situated in Swaledale at the eastern foot of the Pennines. The huge cobbled market place is dominated, as is the whole town, by the 11th-century Norman castle with its 100ft keep. Richmond is a combination of old buildings and alleyways, and attractive open spaces, incorporating a river, rocky hillocks and woodland. All of this was captured on canvas by the artist Turner. Despite the advent of modern industry, and the influences of tourism, Richmond retains its bluff northern character.

ROUTE DIRECTIONS

Start at Greyfriars Priory (1) on the corner of Queen's Rd and Victoria Rd. Walk across to Ryder's Wynd. Turn l. into the Channel which leads into Frenchgate. Turn r. at the junction into Lombard's Wynd. St Mary's Church (2) is on the r. Turn r., cross Station Rd and take the footpath alongside the River Swale. Eventually, past Park Wynd, turn r. into Castle Terrace. Go up the hill, then turn r. along a cobbled street. Then turn l. up steps and across cobbles to Richmond Castle (3). Walk due north to the Market Pl (4), in which is the Chapel of the Holy Trinity (5). Walk over into Friar's Wynd where the Georgian Theatre (6) is directly r. on the corner of Victoria Rd. Turn r. then cross over and return to Greyfriars Gardens.

1 GREYFRIARS PRIORY

The original Franciscan priory was built in 1288 but the tower, erected in 1500, is now all that remains. The gardens at the front contain a memorial to the sons of Richmond who lost their lives during the 1914–18 war.

2 ST MARY'S CHURCH

This, the parish church of Richmond, dates back to at least 1135 and there is inconclusive evidence that an early Saxon church was once on this site. Very little of the original structure remains, the majority dating from Sir George Gilbert Scott's extensive restoration of 1859–60. The finely carved canopied stalls in the chancel are from nearby Easby, while also inside is the memorial chapel of the Green Howards, a regiment closely linked with Richmond.

A plan of the castle, drawn in 1776, showing that much of it was totally ruined even then

3 RICHMOND CASTLE

Work on the original fortress was instigated by Alan Rufus in 1071, when newly conquered England had its north-west border just a few miles away. Its purpose was to provide sanctuary for Count Alan's

4 MARKET PLACE

Richmond is full of buildings and vistas which are not individually outstanding, but which add up to make one of the best townscapes in Britain. It is in the market place that the town's qualities are most easily appreciated. Here buildings of many ages and styles face an open, cobbled area which is dominated by the 18th-century market cross and the tower of Holy Trinity (see below). Of particular note are the Town Hall, built in 1756, the handsome Georgian King's Head Hotel and the Market Hall.

5 CHAPEL OF THE HOLY TRINITY

This early 12th-century building is the centrepiece of Richmond's large sloping market place. The many functions of the premises include being an assize court, prison, school, warehouse and

soldiers during the stormy years of early Norman settlement. Two of the original towers survive and Scollard's Hall, built in 1080, is possibly Britain's oldest domestic building. The castle's present form was reached in the mid-14th century, from which point it gradually fell into disrepair and decay. Despite this, it still remains the focal point of Richmond.

Scale of Yards.

RICHMOND TOWN

N.B. Where the foundation is shaded lighter, its level with the Surface.

Section at the Line A.B.

Wall *Wall* *Grafsy Plain* *Founders Hall* *Foot Path*

Foundation of a Wall

KEEP

Door

This part appears to have been Buildings

Abutments

Tower

THE COURT at present a Pasture.

Intrenchment

Footway

Gate way

Apartments

This part is at present A GARDEN.

River Swale

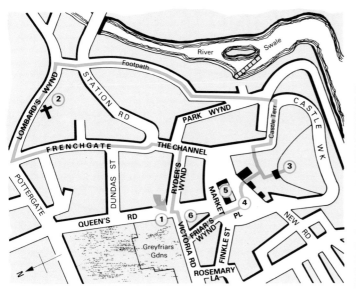

granary. Today it serves both ecclesiastical and secular needs by incorporating the old church and the Green Howards Museum. The latter includes uniforms, weapons and medals spanning nearly 300 years.

6 GEORGIAN THEATRE

The building, founded in 1788, is of no great significance externally. However, the inside décor and ornamentation have been faithfully kept exactly as they were nearly 200 years ago. It is one of Richmond's outstanding buildings.

EARLY CLOSING: *Wed.*

MARKET DAY: *Sat.*

PARKING: *Queen's Road, Victoria Road.*

OPENING TIMES:

Richmond Castle: open all year.

Georgian Theatre: open May–Sep. Mon–Fri all day, Sat am.

Green Howards Museum: open Feb–Nov. Mon–Sat. Also Sun pm Apr–Oct.

Below: the market place and St Mary's from the castle

Greyfriars Tower is all that survives of the priory

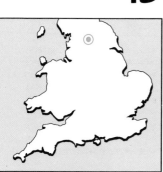

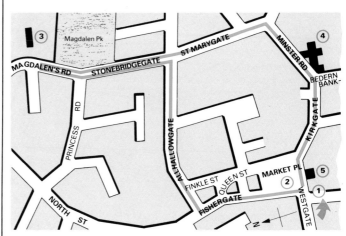

ROUTE DIRECTIONS
*From the Market Pl, site of
Wakeman's House (1) and the
Obelisk (2), walk into Fishergate
then r. into Allhallowgate. Next,
turn l. at The Fleece public house
into Stonebridgegate. Keeping to
the left-hand side, walk on into
Magdalen's Rd where, a little
way up on the r., Leper's Chapel
(3) is situated. From here, turn
back and through Stonebridgegate
once more and into Saint
Marygate. At the eventual fork in
the road, turn r. into Minster Rd
where Ripon Cathedral (4) is on
the l. On from this point the road
becomes Kirkgate, which leads
back to the Market Pl where the
Town Hall (5) is to be found
on the l.*

*Samson carrying off the gates of Gaza,
one of many outstanding carvings on
the misericords in the cathedral*

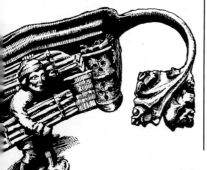

The towers of one of England's oldest cathedrals watch over the ancient streets and buildings of Ripon. The basic street plan has remained substantially unchanged since the 13th century and any visitor roaming the medieval thoroughfares will see a living reflection of Ripon's history written in the very stones of the surrounding buildings.

1 WAKEMAN'S HOUSE

The Wakeman's House was originally built in the 14th century and stands at the corner of the Market Place. It is open to the public as a museum and houses items of local history. Nowadays there is no longer a wakeman in Ripon, but a mayor instead. Despite this, the age-old tradition of the Hornblower 'setting the watch' is still continued today. Each night at 9pm a figure wearing a tricorn hat sounds a horn at every corner of the market cross and in front of the mayor's house. Residents are proud to say: 'It's been going on for a thousand years without a break. Earliest form of burglar insurance in the world.' Householders used to pay a premium of twopence per door per year and, if after the setting of the watch their houses were robbed, the wakeman had to compensate them.

2 THE OBELISK

Dominating the Market Square, the 90ft-high Obelisk was erected by William Aislabie at his own expense in 1781 to commemorate his Diamond Jubilee as the borough's Member of Parliament.

3 LEPER'S CHAPEL

This is the local name for the Chapel of the Hospital of St Mary Magdalene, a building which dates back to the 12th century, although it was considerably altered in medieval times. As its local name testifies, the hospital was founded for the care of lepers.

4 RIPON CATHEDRAL

Scottish monks founded a monastery in Ripon in about AD 657, but not very long afterwards St Wilfrid arrived,

The cathedral seen through a gate on the south side of the close. It is one of Britain's most venerable churches

establishing Benedictine disciplines and moving the foundation to the site occupied by the present cathedral. Of the original 7th-century building only the remarkable crypt survives, the rest of the cathedral having been destroyed in 950. Much of the existing structure is 13th-century, but there were many later alterations and extensive restoration in the 19th century. Externally, the cathedral has that look of austerity associated with the North Country, but once inside the first impression received is one of colour. The choir-screen has niches filled with brightly-painted statues of Ripon worthies spanning 1,200 years. They were donated by friends of the cathedral in 1947 to replace those lost at the time of the Reformation. The canon seats have intricately carved, pinnacled canopies and there are some fine bench-ends. It is the crypt which is Ripon's special treasure. It remains little changed since St Wilfrid's day, when it was built as a relic chamber. Today it contains well-displayed church treasures. Also inside, there is a narrow hole called St Wilfrid's needle, the ability to crawl through which, from the crypt

Although altered many times, the Wakeman's House still retains some medieval features

into the passage behind, was inexplicably regarded as a proof of chastity in medieval times.

5 THE TOWN HALL

Many of Ripon's treasures are housed here, however viewing is by arrangement only. The building itself dates from the early part of the 19th century and was designed by James Wyatt. In April 1974 Queen Elizabeth II granted to Ripon (and certain other 'old cities') a charter allowing it to retain traditional privileges. This charter is kept in the hall along with other civic regalia. On the front of the building, marked in glittering letters, are the words: 'Except ye Lord keep ye cittie, ye Wakeman waketh in vain.'

MARKET DAY: *Thu.*

EARLY CLOSING: *Wed.*

PARKING: *Market Place.*

OPENING TIMES:

Wakeman's House Museum: open May–Sep. Weekdays am and pm, Sat pm only.

44 | RYE

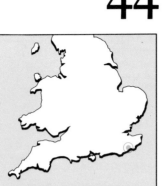

During the Middle Ages the small hill on which Rye is built rose out of the sea rather than the fenland which surrounds it now. At that time Rye was an important Cinque Port and as such suffered badly from raids by the French. However, despite these attacks and the loss of trade in the 16th century when the harbour silted up and the sea receded, Rye remained a prosperous market town and later profited from the lucrative smuggling trade. Now, with its compact medieval layout and mixture of cobbled streets and fascinating houses spanning the 15th to the 19th centuries, Rye is preserved as one of England's most perfect hill towns.

ROUTE DIRECTIONS

Start at Landgate (1). Walk up East Cliff and into the High St. Turn l. up East St (2) and turn r. into Market St (3), then turn l. to the church (4). Walk round Church Sq (5) to Ypres Tower (6) then return to Church Sq and keep l. along Watchbell St. At the Hope and Anchor Hotel take Traders' Passage on the l. of the hotel. On reaching Mermaid St (7) turn r., passing the Mermaid Inn, up to West St. Here turn r. to visit Lamb House (8), return down West St and turn r. into High St (9). Turn l. down Conduit Hill (10) then r. along Turkey Cock La back to Landgate.

A 'Sussex pig' from the town's fascinating museum

1 LANDGATE
During the Middle Ages there were four gateways in the defensive walls surrounding Rye, but Landgate is the only one that has survived.

2 EAST STREET
The distinctively-painted red and black shop-front on the corner belongs to The Apothecary's Shop, which has been in business here since 1787. Further up the hill on the left is Ockman Lane, a tiny part-cobbled alley between pretty cottages leading to Rye Art Gallery, where loan exhibitions supplement the permanent collection.

3 MARKET STREET
Dominating this short, wide street is the brick-built Town Hall crowned with a cupola: the Jurats' bell used to hang here to summon Jurats to the Quarter Sessions. This is still the town magistrates' court and can be visited by arrangement with the Town Hall Keeper. Many treasures are kept in the courtroom, but probably the most popular is the gruesome iron gibbet cage containing a human skull. Among Market Street's other attractive buildings is the black-and-white, timbered Flushing Inn. This has only been used as an inn since the 18th century, but the fresco in the dining room proves that the building is at least 400 years old. The building opposite with uneven roofs and

dormer windows is the town's old bakery, now called Ye Olde Shoppe, and is thought to date from the late 1300s. Bread and cakes are, to this day, baked in an oven that was built in 1750.

4 ST MARY'S CHURCH
In the tower is a famous clock, made by a Winchelsea man in 1560. This is one of the oldest turret clocks still functioning with its original works in England. It is worth waiting for a quarter-hour to see the two gilded cherubs above the clock face swing out and strike the bells between them. These figures, appropriately named quarter boys, were added in 1761, and in fact the originals now stand inside the church. The tower is open during the summer and is well worth a visit – but only by the fit and agile. A series of ladders leads up to the belfry with its peal of eight bells, dating from 1775, and out on to the tower parapet.

5 CHURCH SQUARE
This consists of cobbled lanes surrounding the churchyard and they are among the most enchanting in Rye: cottages – tile-hung, timbered and white-washed – mingle with more elegant Georgian houses and all are covered with flowers and shaded by the churchyard's trees. Notice in the churchyard the Water House. This domed structure covers the cistern which was installed in 1785 as a public water pump.

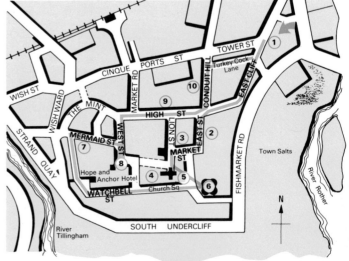

The quarter boys on St Mary's Church

6 YPRES TOWER
After the loss of Normandy in the 14th century, Rye was laid wide open to French attack and the Ypres Tower was built as a castle to defend it. During its history it has been a private dwelling, a prison and now houses Rye Museum.

7 MERMAID STREET
Mermaid Street – steep, curved, cobbled and adorned with window boxes and tubs of flowers – is probably the most famous of all Rye's picturesque streets. All the houses on either side are worth looking at, but of particular note is the tall, gabled black and white timbered Old Hospital, or Hartshorne House, which was used during the Napoleonic Wars as a hospital, and of course the famous Mermaid Inn. This was the favourite haunt of smugglers on their way up from the Strand to the many cellars and passages beneath Rye's houses.

8 LAMB HOUSE
Novelist Henry James moved to Lamb House in 1898. He lived here until 1914, and was inspired to write some of his best work here. The 18th-century red-brick house is charmingly informal and has a lovely walled garden. Only three of the rooms are open: the study, the dining room and the oak parlour. James called the study the telephone room (he was one of its earliest devotees) and here his personal effects are on show, including some letters belonging to his friend E. F. Benson, and first editions of most of his books. Both the other rooms have French windows to the garden and are simply but elegantly furnished.

9 HIGH STREET
Although this is the main shopping thoroughfare of the town, it is no less interesting or attractive than any other part of

Rye's most famous building – the Mermaid Inn

Rye. Opposite the imposing three-storey George Hotel is the Old Grammar School, which was one of the first brick buildings in Rye. It was built by Thomas Peacocke, who left it to the town as a free school, and it was used as such until 1908.

10 CONDUIT HILL
Standing on the corner of this steep cobbled side street – named because of the wooden pipes which used to run up from the pumping machinery in Cinque Ports Street to the water pump in the churchyard – is Adam's Stationers. On close inspection the building is actually hung with tiles and not made of brick as it first appears to be. These 'mathematical' tiles were often used in Sussex and Kent when bricks were in short supply, and at one time became more fashionable than red bricks. Further down the hill on the right are two of Rye's six potteries – an important trade in the town since the 13th century. Iden Pottery makes all the pretty handpainted house nameplates to be seen throughout the town, and the Cinque Ports Pottery is housed in the old Augustinian friary.

MARKET DAY: *Thu.*

EARLY CLOSING: *Tue.*

PARKING: *Fishmarket Road, Cinque Ports St, Bedford Place, Cattle Market.*

Rye Art Gallery: open all year. Tue – Sat all day. Sun pm only.

Ypres Tower: open Easter – Oct.

Lamb House: open Apr – Oct, Wed and Sat, pm only.

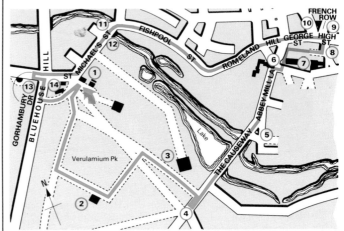

ROUTE DIRECTIONS

Start at the entrance to the Verulamium Museum (1). Bear r. then l., following signs for Hypocaust Bungalow (2) and Roman Wall, through the car park and take footpath to reach Verulamium Park. A short way from here, pass a stretch of Roman Wall (3) on the l. At the end of the pathway turn r. for London Gate (4). From here return along The Causeway, with the lake on the l. Continue along a gravel path where Ye Old Fighting Cocks Public House (5) is on the r. Keep forward into Abbey Mill La which leads to the Abbey Gateway (6). Turn r. here then sharp l. for St Albans Cathedral (7). From the west door keep forward, turn r. and walk through the churchyard, up three steps and turn l. along an alleyway to Wax House Gate (8). Keep forward, cross High St into the Market Pl for the Clock Tower (9). Bear l. into French Row for the Fleur-de-Lys Inn (10). Return to the High St and turn r. then keep forward into George St and Romeland Hill. Pass along Fishpool St for Kingsbury Water Mill Museum (11). Cross St Michael's Bridge (12) into St Michael's St. Shortly bear r. and cross Bluehouse Hill to reach the Roman Theatre (13). Return to Bluehouse Hill and turn r. then l. through the gateway to St Michael's Church (14), which leads to Verulamium Museum, to complete the walk.

There is a reminder of a sad royal procession on the clock tower

NEAR THIS SITE STOOD
THE ELEANOR CROSS
WHERE THE BODY OF
QUEEN ELEANOR
RESTED ONE NIGHT ON ITS
PROGRESS FROM
HARBY TO WESTMINSTER
13 DECEMBER 1290.

The Romans first established a community here around AD 43. Known as Verulamium and consisting mainly of timber buildings, the first town was devastated by Boudicca in AD 61. The phoenix that rose from the ashes was to last 300 years, covered 200 acres and was the third largest Roman town in Britain. Alban, after whom the town was named, was martyred in AD 209 on a green hill nearby. Following the decline of the Roman Empire, Verulamium became a ghost town. However, the shrine that had been erected to commemorate the heroic death of Alban became a magnet for pilgrims and over the years a medieval town developed with the abbey as its focal point.

1 VERULAMIUM MUSEUM

This modern, red-brick museum records every facet of the Roman occupation of St Albans. An outstanding display is a large-scale model of the town as it was 1,800 years ago. A clever diorama brings to life the town during the Iceni revolt of AD 61, while splendid examples of giant Roman mosaics are to be found at the rear.

2 HYPOCAUST BUNGALOW

The 'bungalow', with its hypocaust (an underfloor heating system with spaces for warming by hot air), was originally the bath wing of a large Roman town house. A feature of the building is a colourful geometric mosaic framed by a parapet flint wall. Norman monks damaged the mosaic when using the Roman ruins as a quarry.

3 ROMAN WALL

This section of the old town wall consists of flint and mortar bonded by layers of red tiles, and has undergone recent restoration. It was built in the early 3rd century to mark the north-east perimeter of *Verulamium*.

4 LONDON GATE

Watling Street once entered the town through this now disused gateway. Vestiges of the previous grandeur are now only discernible as broken flints protruding from the grass. Running alongside is a stretch of

late 2nd-century Roman wall. It is 10ft high in places and has giant circular bastions, once the strategic supports for ancient artillery. Though much overgrown, a deep V-shaped ditch dating from the same period is traceable across the pathway.

5 YE OLDE FIGHTING COCKS PUBLIC HOUSE

A 400-year-old timber-framed house which was originally, it is believed, a fishing lodge belonging to the abbey. Since 1600 it has been an inn, known subsequently as the Round House, and by 1855 it was called The Fisherman. The date of the cockpit installation, after which it is now named, is unknown.

6 ABBEY GATEWAY

This massive three-storeyed structure is built mainly of flint with sandstone windows and has had a chequered history. Constructed around 1363, it was firstly the gateway to a Benedictine monastery. In 1470 it is said to have housed only the third printing press in England. From 1553 to 1869 it served as the local gaol and the dungeons still exist today. After 1871 it became part of St Albans School.

7 ST ALBANS CATHEDRAL

This magnificent building is named after Alban, the Roman citizen of *Verulamium* who became the first Christian martyr in Britain. The dimensions are awesome – 550ft

St Albans townscape

Right: medieval wall paintings are an outstanding feature of the cathedral's interior

long; 177ft from north to south transepts; an overall floor area of 40,000 square ft. The nave, with its massive Norman piers is, at 285ft, the longest in the world. Its superb centrepiece is the Shrine of St Alban, built in 1320 of Purbeck stone. It was carefully reconstructed in 1872, after having been demolished in 1539. Behind the shrine is a watching chamber where monks once climbed steps of solid oak to stand guard. Above this sacred spot is a beautifully painted ceiling. The building finally became a cathedral in 1877, on the inception of St Albans as a city. Additions since then include a choir stall (1905) and a font (1933).

8 WAX HOUSE GATE
This white-plastered archway supports a group of red-brick houses above. It is all that remains of an imposing 15th-century entrance to the abbey.

9 CLOCK TOWER
Formerly the centrepiece of medieval St Albans, this 77ft tower once summoned apprentices to work by the sound of its 'curfew bell'. It is built of flint and rubble and was constructed during the years 1402–11. A restoration was carried out by Sir Gilbert Scott in 1866.

10 FLEUR-DE-LYS INN
Constructed between 1420 and 1440, this plaster and timber tavern was largely rebuilt during the 16th and 17th centuries to include a courtyard. Later additions were granaries, stables and a hayloft.

11 KINGSBURY WATER MILL MUSEUM
The building consists of two distinct storeys. The ground floor is Georgian and made of

red brick, and supports a timber-framed upper construction that is probably Elizabethan. Much of the mill machinery dates from the 16th and 18th centuries, but a major restoration was undertaken in the 1970s. The most interesting of the many exhibits is a collection of agricultural equipment and implements. There is also an art gallery here.

12 ST MICHAEL'S BRIDGE
This is the oldest bridge in Hertfordshire. Made of red brick, it was constructed in 1765 to span the River Ver.

13 ROMAN THEATRE
Built in AD 155, the theatre was unique in Britain in its day. It consisted of a stage with surrounding seating space for nearly 6,000 people. Audiences over the years witnessed cock-fighting and bear-baiting as well as more conventional dramatic and musical productions. Sadly, all that remains today is an outline of flints in the grass to give visitors some idea of the theatre's former overall structure.

14 ST MICHAEL'S CHURCH
The church was founded in 948 on the ruins of a Roman forum and has been added to over many periods. Its outstanding features include two carved sandstone doors, a Saxon nave, Norman aisles, 14th-century brasses, an octagonal 15th-century font and a Jacobean pulpit with finely carved bookrests. Monuments include one to Sir Francis Bacon.

PARKING: *Verulamium Museum, Fishpool St, Abbey Mill La.*

EARLY CLOSING: *Thu.*

MARKET DAYS: *Wed & Sat.*

OPENING TIMES:

Hypocaust Bungalow: open all year.

St Albans Cathedral: open all year.

Clock Tower: Easter–Sep; Sat–Sun.

Kingsbury Water Mill Museum: open all year.

Roman Theatre: open Mar–Oct. (Nov–Feb until 2pm).

Verulamium Museum: open all year. Mon–Sat all day. Sun pm only.

46 | ST ANDREWS

ROUTE DIRECTIONS

*Start at car park at north end of Golf Place. Follow road along north side of Old Course (**1**), and shortly – being careful not to interfere with play – turn l. onto path across fairways. At end of path, turn r. into The Links, then turn r. into Gibson Pl to cross bridge over burn and immediately l. onto footpath alongside burn. Turn r. onto Links Crescent and cross it by footbridge. Then straight on up footpath on far side and r. before park wall. Follow path alongside wall, then keep forward along Kennedy Gardens, and at far end turn l. along Donaldson Gardens. Turn r. at T-junction into Hepburn Gardens. Beyond junction with Buchan Gardens, about 25 yards after school sign, turn l. down wide pathway. Turn l. at foot of hill, through gate and along Lade Braes (**2**) walk following burn. At far end, go through gate, straight on at 'Lade Braes' sign, then l. and r. onto Argyle St. Go through archway of West Port (**3**) into South St passing Madras College (**4**) and the Town Hall (**5**). Turn r. through low opening marked 'South Court' (**6**). Pass Byre Theatre, turn l. into Greenside Pl, l. into Abbey St, passing St Leonard's School (**7**), then r. back into South St. Turn l. at end of South St, passing the Pends, then r. through gate into cathedral (**8**) grounds. Return to that gate, turn r. to pass war memorial and go straight on along Gregory La. Turn l. onto East Scores, go straight along The Scores, passing the castle (**9**) and Bow Butts (**10**) then bear r. onto footpath after junction with Murray Park on l. Turn r. to cross footbridge, then l. at far side, and bear r. to return to car park.*

N amed after the patron saint of Scotland, this healthily situated town on the Fife coast is one of the oldest and most fascinating in the country. The cathedral was founded in the 12th century, and was the centre of violent religious disputes at the time of the Reformation. The university, in buildings scattered throughout the town, was established in 1411. Many of its fine architectural features have been restored in recent years, thanks to the activities of bodies like the St Andrews Preservation Trust. For many, of course, St Andrews is famous for one thing only – golf.

1 OLD COURSE

St Andrews is the home of golf, which was being played on the grassy links between the town and the River Eden earlier than 1552. A document of that year confirms arrangements that already existed. Although not the first one in Scotland, the Society of St Andrews Golfers was founded in 1754, and ten years later reduced its course from 22 holes to 18. That became the standard size of golf courses throughout the world. In 1834, with the approval of William IV, the Society changed its name to the Royal and Ancient Golf Club, and in 1897 it became the governing body of the game. The public right of way across the first and eighteenth fairways of the Old

Top: the cathedral ruins

Course is known as Granny Clark's Wynd. To the right can be seen one of the small bridges over the meandering Swilcan Burn. To the left is the Royal and Ancient clubhouse, opened in 1854. Standing on The Links, overlooking the last fairway, are the other golfing clubhouses of the town.

2 LADE BRAES

This series of footpaths in the wooded valley of the Kinness Burn originally ran alongside a mill lade, which has now been covered over. The area is planted with ash and rowan, sycamore and lime. On the far side of the burn are the new University Botanic Gardens.

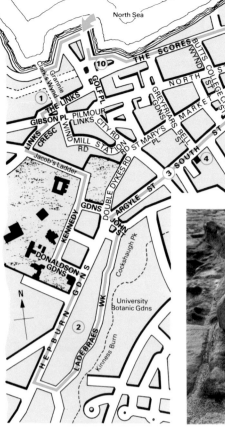

3 WEST PORT
At the entrance to South Street, with its pends and closes and 18th-century houses, the West Port is one of the few surviving city gates in Scotland. It was originally medieval, but rebuilt in 1589 as a copy of the Netherbow in Edinburgh, and restored in 1845.

4 MADRAS COLLEGE
Set back from the street behind open lawns, the elegant Madras College – a school, and not part of the University – was founded in 1832. In front of it is the ruined Blackfriars Chapel. All that survives is the north transept, built in 1525, of a Dominican monastery founded late in the 13th century by Bishop Wishart.

5 TOWN HALL
This civic building in baronial style dates from 1860. On its west side is the unusually laid-out street called Queen's Gardens, with houses to the left and their gardens across on the other side. Facing the Town Hall, across South Street, is Holy Trinity Church, transferred to this site early in the 15th century. It was restored in 1909. Beyond the Town Hall, on the right-hand side of South Street, is the rear wall of St Mary's College, founded in the 16th century on the site of an earlier school called the Pedagogy.

6 SOUTH COURT
In this part of South Street, in the 16th and 17th centuries, wealthy families used to have their town houses, and their

Above: carved corbel in the cathedral

Right: coats of arms dating from the 16th and 17th centuries embellish the elegant architecture of South Court

coats of arms can still be seen on the walls. South Court was given a Saltire Society award for sympathetic restoration in 1977. It leads to the Byre Theatre, which was originally exactly that – a former cow-shed with seating for an audience of only 74. The building on the site today is entirely new.

7 ST LEONARD'S SCHOOL
This girls' school was founded in 1877 and extended in 1961. Its library is in the 16th-century Queen Mary's House, believed to have been where Mary Queen of Scots lodged during her visits to St Andrews. Beyond the entrance to Queen Mary's House are the Pends, a vaulted gateway which once led into the Cathedral precincts.

8 CATHEDRAL
By far the biggest of all the Scottish cathedrals, the Cathedral Church of St Andrew was established in 1160 but not completed until 1318. The building was ruined soon after the Reformation. Its styling moved from Romanesque to Gothic as the long work of building progressed. From 1888 onwards it was the subject of excavation and part-restoration, and many of the finds are now on display in a museum. One of the most striking features of the site is St Rule's Tower, from which there is a good view of the town.

9 CASTLE
Originally the Bishop's Palace, the Castle of St Andrews dates from the early 13th century, although many additions were made in later years. It was the focus of many attacks and sieges, especially in the religious troubles of the 1540s. The great reformer John Knox took refuge here in 1547, but the castle surrendered to a French fleet. Knox and his friends were sent off as galley slaves. The most notorious feature of the long since ruined castle is the Bottle Dungeon, still intact. It is narrower at the top than at the middle or the bottom. There is no means of exit apart from the roof. And no prisoner ever escaped from it.

10 BOW BUTTS
Beyond the castle, the street known as The Scores leads past more fine university buildings and the residence of the Principal. It finishes at a series of grassy mounds topped with the Martyrs' Monument set up in 1842 to the memory of the reformers executed by the church authorities in the middle of the 16th century. The hollow below the monument is still called the Bow Butts. This is where, in medieval times, the townsmen came for compulsory archery practice.

EARLY CLOSING: *Thu.*

PARKING: *North end of Golf Place.*

OPENING TIMES:

Cathedral: open all year.

Castle: open all year. Mon – Sat all day. Sun pm only.

A mile to the north of Salisbury, on the road to Amesbury, is the half-obliterated site of Old Sarum, where castle and cathedral foundations are still visible. In 1198 Peter of Blois, the canon of Sarum, wrote: 'Let us in God's name descend to the plain. There are rich champaign fields and fertile valleys, abounding in the fruits of the earth, and watered by the living stream. There is a seat for the Virgin patroness of our church, to which the world cannot produce a parallel.' However, it was not until April 1220 that Bishop Richard Poore led his people from Old Sarum to lay the foundation stone of a new church, thus establishing Salisbury. The streets of modern Salisbury are still based on the original grid plan of Bishop Poore, and much of the city's stone came from the buildings of Old Sarum. It has the classic layout for an English city, a large market square for commerce and social life, and an even larger cathedral square for spiritual and scholarly pursuits.

ROUTE DIRECTIONS

Start from the NW corner of the market sq (1), and cross over Minster St at the traffic-lights, where the Library (2) is on the r. Turn l. and take the small alleyway beside the estate agency to St Thomas's Church (3). Proceed along the High St, crossing Crane St, to reach the North Gate (4) of Cathedral Close. On rounding Choristers' Sq to the r., Mompesson House (5) is on the r. Follow the road l. into West Wk, where the King's House (6) is on the r. Cross the green to the west door of Salisbury Cathedral (7), which is almost opposite. Leave by the West Door and take the diagonal path across the green to North Wk. Continue to Malmesbury House (8), adjoined by St Ann's Gate (9). Turn l. from here into St John St and go straight along Catherine St. Turn r. into Milford St where the Red Lion (10) is a short way down on the r. Return across Catherine St into New Canal where the Odeon (11) is on the l. Take the next r. at a pedestrian crossing which leads into a short walkway between two buildings, and then r. again into Butcher Row. At the next junction turn l. into Queen's St with Ye House of John à Porte (12) opposite, then with Cross Keys shopping centre to the r., turn l. back into the market sq.

1 MARKET SQUARE

The square is used as a car-park except on Saturday and Tuesday, which are market days. It is a large, tree-lined area with many old and interesting buildings clustered round in a pleasing mixture of architectural styles. Stoby's Fish Restaurant on the south side is of particular interest. Salisbury's markets are famed in the south of England and stallholders come from a wide area to display their wares. The right to hold a market here twice weekly dates back to an ancient charter of 1227.

2 LIBRARY

The building has a large white façade. This frontage, although rebuilt in 1974, gives a clue to the original use of the premises. It was the Market House, built by the Salisbury Market Company during the late 19th century, serving as a corn and wool mart. Such was its volume of trade that a special link with Salisbury station was necessary.

The cathedral was built over a short space of time, and its Early English architecture is marvellously uniform

Plasterwork in Mompesson House

3 ST THOMAS'S CHURCH

The church was dedicated in honour of Thomas à Becket, and it was founded in 1220. The local citizens rebuilt and extended it in the Middle Ages, and the roof and nave date from the Tudor period. A striking painting of Doom hangs above the chancel. The church organ is the one originally presented to Salisbury Cathedral by George II in 1792.

4 NORTH GATE

Of the four gates guarding the entrance to the Cathedral Close, this is the finest. It dates from the 14th century and has a superb coat of arms. There was at one time a portcullis here which the bishops could lower to keep potentially rebellious citizens at bay.

5 MOMPESSON HOUSE

This grand house was built in 1701 in the Queen Anne style and now belongs to the National Trust. It contains baroque plasterwork and original panelling. A carved oak staircase and an important collection of 18th-century English drinking glasses are also to be found inside.

6 KING'S HOUSE

This one-time royal stop-over is a grade one listed building of historical and architectural importance. It was named King's House following several visits paid by James I, and nowadays is the Salisbury and

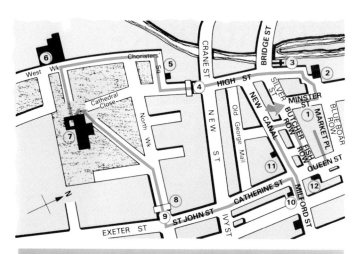

cloisters are the largest of any English cathedral. In the octagonal chapter house the stone vaulting radiates from a single pillar while a fine frieze carved in stone depicts scenes from the Old Testament. One of the many interesting documents in the library is a closely written copy of the Magna Carta.

8 MALMESBURY HOUSE
This building is some 600 years old, but it was refurbished both inside and out in the 17th and 18th centuries. On one wall is a splendid sundial dated 1749. James Harris, a local worthy who organised musical festivals in the borough, was one of its 18th-century owners. The house's interior includes a 'Gothick' library.

9 ST ANN'S GATE
From here, it is believed, George Handel gave his first public performance in Britain. The gate itself was begun in 1331 and served as the north-east entrance to the Close.

10 RED LION INN
This old hostelry has an ivy-clad galleried courtyard, from where the 'Salisbury Flying Machine' left for London each night in the great coaching era.

11 ODEON
The cinema boasts a fine foyer. Behind its 19th-century façade is the hall of the rich merchant John Hulle, with its stained-glass windows and carved wooden ceiling beams.

12 YE HOUSE OF JOHN À PORTE
The house is one of three timber-framed buildings of the 15th century, a block with very pronounced overhanging upper storeys. The one-time resident John à Porte was a rich wool merchant and six times mayor of the city. Inside is Elizabethan panelling and a carved fireplace.

MARKET DAYS: *Tue & Sat.*

PARKING: *Central Car Park, off Castle Street, Salt Lane.*

OPENING TIMES:

Mompesson House: Apr – Oct (ex Thu – Fri); pm only.

King's House: Salisbury & South Wiltshire Museum: open all year. Mon – Sat (& Sun pm Jul – Aug).

South Wiltshire Museum and houses displays of objects from Stonehenge, ceramics and paintings, plus glass and prints of the cathedral, Old Sarum, Salisbury and Stonehenge.

7 SALISBURY CATHEDRAL
The cathedral is the second tallest in Europe, the tip of its spire being 404ft above the ground. It was built in the comparatively short time of 38 years and the spire has a (just discernible) slight twist in it. Near the North Door is a wrought iron clock, made in about 1386 and reputed to be the oldest working timepiece in Britain. Over £1,000 per day is spent on the upkeep of the

For over 700 years the River Avon has reflected the cathedral in its waters

building, hence the necessarily high entrance fee. Inside, there are many fine tombs and stained-glass windows. The

THE CLOSE
Salisbury has the finest cathedral close in Britain. Most of the houses look Georgian, but many have architectural features dating back to the 13th century and the founding of the cathedral. All the houses, including Walton Canonry (right), were built for cathedral functionaries.

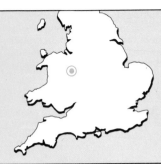

ROUTE DIRECTION

*The walk starts on Pride Hill.
Walk up the hill into Castle St as
far as the library (1), and the
castle (2). Return along Castle St,
passing Council House Court (3),
and turn l. into Windsor Pl
keeping l. into St Mary's Pl. Pass
St Mary's Church (4). At the end,
turn l. for Dogpole, passing the
Guildhall (5), to meet Wyle Cop
(6). Turn r. then next r. up Fish St
passing St Julian's Church (7).
Pass Bear Steps (8) and St
Alkmund's Church (9), then turn
l. into Butcher Row for Abbots
House (10). At Pride Hill, turn l.
and next l. into High St (11).
Turn r. across The Square (12) to
the Music Hall and tourist
information centre. Follow Coffee
House Passage (next to Music
Hall) to meet College Hill and
turn l. Take first r. to visit Clive
House Museum (13). Return to
College Hill and turn l., then next
l. along Swan Hill. Opposite the
Eye, Ear and Throat Hospital,
turn r. into Murivance. Opposite
St Chad's Church (14) enter The
Quarry (15) to visit The Dingle.
Return to the gates and cross into
Claremont Hill. At Barker St turn
l. past bus station to Rowley's
House Museum (16). Cross the bus
station, keeping r. into Hills Lane
and r. along Mardol to return to
starting point.*

F or centuries, Shrewsbury was a strategic focal point on the
uneasy borderlands between England into Wales and was,
consequently, the scene of many violent conflicts. More
peaceful times followed in Tudor and Elizabethan days when the
commercial life of the town flourished. A great deal from this
period remains today in the dozens of historic black and white
houses with which Shrewsbury is so well-endowed. There are
narrow streets and passages, as well as bizarre street names such
as Gullet Passage, that recall urban life in Elizabethan times.

*Top: medieval buildings and a timeless
atmosphere in Bear Steps*

1 LIBRARY
Shrewsbury Grammar School
originally occupied this
building which dates from 1630.
It carries the inscription (in
Greek), "If you love learning,
you will be learned". At the
front is a statue to Charles
Darwin, who was born and
educated in the town.

2 THE CASTLE
The approach to the castle is
past the striking Castle Gates
House, originally built in
Dogpole in the 17th century,
but moved to this site in 1702.
Well placed to defend the river,
the castle was founded in 1067
and mostly rebuilt by Edward I.
Later, in 1787, Telford altered
the fabric to make it a house for
the town's MP. He also added
the gazebo called Laura's Tower
on the original Norman motte.
Exhibitions are now held in the
Main Hall.

3 COUNCIL HOUSE COURT
Law and order in the
borderland between England
and Wales was controlled in the
16th and 17th centuries by the
Council of the Marches and they
would meet, from time to time,
at the Old Council House in
Shrewsbury. Giving little hint
of its former use as a prison, the
ornate Jacobean gatehouse (on
the left) is an imposing entrance
to this historic courtyard.
Straight ahead are two medieval
hall houses at right angles to
each other, where the council
meetings took place. Charles I
and James II both stayed here.

4 ST MARY'S CHURCH
The only truly medieval church
in the town, St Mary's was
probably founded around
AD 960. It has a magnificent
collection of stained glass,
including the Jesse window at
the east end. This dates from
about 1350 and is one of only
eight such windows in England.

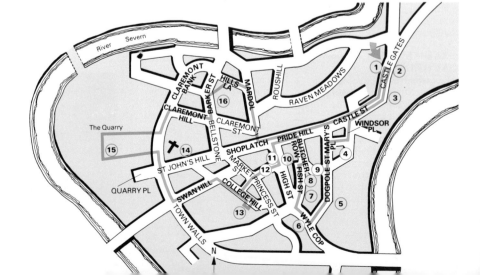

When the spire fell down in 1894, the vicar claimed it was God's judgement on the people of Shrewsbury for planning a memorial to Charles Darwin. The spire was soon replaced. St Mary's Place is a quiet little square with some attractive almshouses and the heavily restored Draper's Hall.

5 GUILDHALL
Originally known as Newport House, this was one of the first houses in classical style to be built in Shrewsbury. The Greek Doric porch, splendidly restored, is a 19th-century addition.

6 WYLE COP
'Hill top' in Welsh, this traditionally busy thoroughfare into the town is packed with fine buildings. Among them are the Lion Hotel, Henry Tudor House (where Henry VII stayed before the Battle of Bosworth), Mytton's Mansion (Nos 65–69), and the Nag's Head Inn (preserving part of a 14th-century hall house).

7 ST JULIAN'S CHURCH
The tower is a prominent landmark in Shrewsbury, contrasting with the spires of St Mary's and St Alkmund's. The church itself is now used as a craft centre.

8 BEAR STEPS
Excellent restoration has uncovered a 14th-century hall with a fine exposed timber trussed roof here. This is now used to house regular exhibitions. At right angles to it, an arcaded range of shops has also been restored and now serves as a coffee shop. This group, set facing St Alkmund's churchyard, is a most charming corner of the town.

9 ST ALKMUND'S CHURCH
Originally built in the 15th century, this church was demolished and rebuilt in 1794. The most striking part of it is the huge east window of painted glass called 'Faith' executed by Francis Egerton in 1795.

10 ABBOT'S HOUSE
This is probably the most authentic looking of all the early timber-framed houses in the town. The shop fronts are as they would have been around 1500, with wide sills and divided doors.

11 HIGH STREET
Two of the most famous houses in Shrewsbury are found in the High Street. Ireland's Mansion is one of the grandest houses in the town – it was built around 1580 by Robert Ireland, a wealthy wool merchant, and is not unduly spoiled by the modern shop fronts which form the ground floor. Opposite it is Owen's Mansion, dating from 1592. The ornate timber-frame and plaster building now houses a bank and a department store.

12 THE SQUARE
Guarding the approach to the former market square is a life-size statue of Lord Clive. Looking down to the far end, there are two interesting buildings on the right side, the 16th-century Plough Inn and 18th-century Woolley's House. In the centre of the square is the Market Hall, built in 1596. Over the open arcades can be seen the arms of Queen Elizabeth I and a figure of Richard, Duke of York. At the far end of the square is the porticoed front of the Music Hall, built in 1839, and now housing the tourist information centre.

A 19th-century print of the market square with the arcaded Market Hall

13 CLIVE HOUSE MUSEUM
Lord Clive was mayor of Shrewsbury in 1762 and represented the town in Parliament until his death in 1774. This attractive Queen Anne house now contains a varied museum, which includes Coalport china, costumes, ornamental ironwork from Coalbrookdale, bicycles and the Regimental Museum of the 1st The Queen's Dragoon Guards.

14 ST CHAD'S CHURCH
This is a fine example of 18th-century Grecian revival building, with a perfectly round nave (one of the few such examples in the country). The galleries are reached by a graceful double staircase and carry tall columns supporting the roof. This unusual church is an elegant contrast to the predominantly medieval buildings in the rest of the town.

15 THE QUARRY
A huge park, The Quarry runs down to the river. Overlooking it from the opposite bank are the buildings of Shrewsbury School.

16 ROWLEY'S HOUSE MUSEUM
The 16th-century timber-framed Rowley's House abuts Rowley's Mansion, which is the earliest brick mansion in Shrewsbury. Rowley's House has been splendidly restored to display the huge collection of finds from the Roman town of *Viroconium* at Wroxeter. There are also displays of Shrewsbury's local history.

EARLY CLOSING: *Thu.*

MARKET DAY: *Wed & Fri.*

PARKING: *Riverside, Murivance, St Mary's Place.*

OPENING TIMES:

The Castle: open all year. Closed Sun Oct–Easter.

Bear Steps: open all year. Mon–Sat.

Clive House Museum: open all year. Mon–Sat.

Rowley's House Museum: open all year. Mon–Sat.

ROUTE DIRECTIONS

Start at the Bargate (1). Walk west along Bargate St, cross Castle Way and turn r. then l. and descend steps by The Inn Centre pub to reach Windwhistle Tower. Turn l. along Western Esplanade to reach a section of the city walls (2). Shortly beyond Catchcold Tower climb steps and turn l. at the Masonic Hall into Albion Place, then turn r. through car park and pass through an arch created in the Bailey Wall into Maddison St. On the l. is a detour down Castle La (3). Return along Castle La and turn l. into Upper Bugle St past the Undercroft (4) Continue to St Michael's Sq (5). Keep forward into Bugle St then turn r. into Westgate St. Beyond the Tudor Merchants' Hall and Westgate (6) climb the steps onto the parapet of the walls and descend by the Pilgrim Fathers Memorial (7). Keep forward along footpath then bear l., and cross Bugle St to reach the Maritime Museum (8). From there keep forward along Town Quay, cross French St and enter Porter's La (9). Cross High St and enter Winkle St (10). From God's House Tower, return along Winkle St and turn r. into High St (11) for the return to the Bargate, passing Holy Rood Church on the corner of Bernard St.

Although much of Southampton was destroyed by bombs during World War II, far more of the old city survives than is realized by the casual visitor. There are still streets with flagged pavements and venerable old buildings, and the magnificent city walls stand to their original height in several places. Southampton has always been, and is still, one of Britain's most important ports, and the constant presence of the sights, smells and noises of shipping and the sea gives the city a unique and pleasurable character.

1 THE BARGATE

Although it is now marooned in the centre of a traffic island, the Bargate retains much of the dignity and some of the imposing power that it must have had when it was the landward entrance to the walled medieval city. The upper floor of the building, once the city's Guildhall, is now a museum housing temporary exhibitions relating to the history of Southampton.

2 CITY WALLS

From Arundel Tower, at the north-west corner of the old walls, there are excellent views south along the line of the west wall. As late as the middle of the 19th century the waters of the River Test lapped against these walls when the tide was in; but some land reclamation took place after 1850, and between the two world wars the whole of this part of the estuary was reclaimed as part of the New Docks scheme. Arundel Tower itself was built in the 13th century, and enlarged in the 19th, while Catchcold, the next tower along, dates from the 15th century and survives almost intact.

3 CASTLE LANE

Half way down this lane is Southampton's old courthouse, a handsome 19th-century building painted white and pale blue. At the end of the lane are the recently excavated bases of two towers that mark the site of the eastern entrance to the long vanished castle which stood where Castle House is today.

Top: the Bargate is one of the finest city gates in Britain

4 THE UNDERCROFT

Set at the junction of Upper Bugle Street and Simnel Street, the Undercroft is the lower room of a medieval house. It is preserved intact, with its early 14th-century fireplace and superb rib-vaulted roof still in their original positions.

5 ST MICHAEL'S SQUARE

The feeling of old Southampton still lingers in and around this ancient market square, which was probably laid out shortly after the Norman Conquest and formed the centre of the city's French Quarter. Miraculously, many of the buildings here escaped the bombing of 1940–2 which wreaked such havoc elsewhere in the city. On the east side is St Michael's Church, Southampton's oldest building. It was founded in about 1070, and parts of the tower, now crowned by a spire that has served as a landmark for shipping since the 15th century, date from that period. Opposite the church is the Tudor House, the city's finest half-timbered building. It now serves as a museum, with exhibits ranging from Tudor furniture to domestic utensils of the 19th century and clothes from the 1920s. Behind Tudor House is a garden that is being laid out as it would have appeared in medieval times, and beyond that, incorporated in the city walls, is an almost intact Norman house. It is one of the finest of its kind in the country.

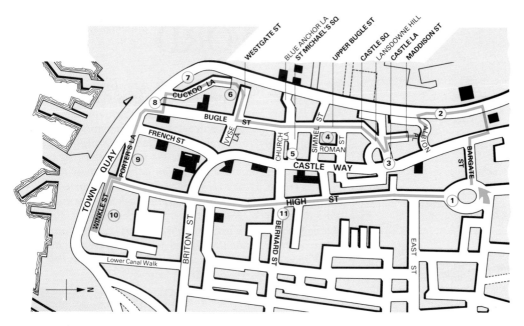

6 WESTGATE AND TUDOR MERCHANTS' HALL

Westgate, built in the early 14th century, once opened directly onto the estuarine waters of the River Test; it now gives access to Western Esplanade and the Arcade, the best preserved stretch of the city walls. On the south side of Westgate is the Tudor Merchants' Hall, which originally stood in St Michael's Square and served as the city's Woollen Cloth Hall. It was sold in 1634 and re-erected in its present position for use as a warehouse.

7 THE PILGRIM FATHERS MEMORIAL

Set in the shadow of the old walls, this tall monument was erected in 1913 to commemorate the sailing of the *Mayflower* and the *Speedwell* from West Quay in 1620. Next to it is the delightful Stella

A model of a sailing boat called a hoy in the Maritime Museum

Memorial to the stewardess of a ship that sank in 1899. Nearby, on the corner of Bugle Street, is Solent House, Southampton's finest early Victorian building.

8 THE WOOL HOUSE MARITIME MUSEUM

The only surviving medieval warehouse in Southampton, the Wool House was built by the monks of Beaulieu Abbey. It became a maritime museum in the 1960s, and at that time the remarkable 14th-century wooden roof was restored to its former glory. Exhibits in the museum include huge models of the steam ships *Queen Mary* and *Capetown Castle* as well as smaller models of many other ships and boats.

9 PORTER'S LANE

On the north side of this lane is so-called Canute's Palace, the ruin of a 12th-century merchant's house that once stood at the water's edge; and at the end of the lane is the city's 14th-century Watergate. It

looks over Town Quay, the centre of Southampton's commercial activity in medieval times and now a ferry terminal.

10 WINKLE STREET

The Hospital of St Julian, a restored 12th-century chapel attached to a quadrangle of almshouses, stands on the north side of this lane near God's House Tower. The city walls were improved and strengthened after an infamous raid on the city by the French in 1388. At that time the South Gate (adjacent to God's House Tower) was modified to carry artillery, and in 1417 God's House Tower itself was built alongside to carry heavy ordnance. As such it is one of the earliest examples of artillery fortification in the world. It now houses the city's archaeological museum, and from the rooftop and windows there are superb views of the docks.

11 HIGH STREET

Long considered one of the finest thoroughfares in England, the High Street had lost many of its lovely old buildings by the 1930s, and much of what remained was destroyed during the blitz. However, some fine buildings still stand, including the shell of the bombed Holy Rood Church. The ruins date from about 1320 and were restored in 1957 as a memorial to merchant seamen lost in the war. Two splendid 18th-century coaching inns, the Star and the Dolphin, also survive amongst Victorian façades and post-war buildings.

PARKING: *Portland Terrace.*

OPENING TIMES:

Bargate Museum: Open all year. Tue–Sat all day. Sun pm only.

Tudor House Museum: as above.

Wool House Maritime Museum: as above.

God's House Tower Museum: as above.

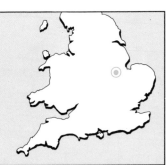

Long before the Romans built their Ermine Street, the tracks of ancient Britons converged on Stamford, it being the only location that guaranteed a year-round crossing of the River Welland. Saxons developed the community and, despite suffering heavily at the hands of the Danes, it prospered. Later, the Normans built a castle beside the river and in time trading developed until Stamford became an important wool town and religious centre. Henry III granted Stamford its charter in 1254 and in the following centuries, despite much damage during the Wars of the Roses, the town emerged with a firm identity. The buildings in Stamford are largely made from beautiful local stone – obtained from nationally-famous quarries like those at Barnack and Ketton – a fact that probably led to its being the first town designated a 'Conservation Area'.

ROUTE DIRECTIONS
Start from Red Lion Sq and walk into All Saints St where Stamford Brewery Museum (1) is on the r. Return to the square and take the second r. into St John's St where St John's Church (2) is on the l. Turn r. into Castle St then l. along Castle Dyke towards the car-park. Cross the footbridge into Vence Wk and continue over a second footbridge. Turn l. into Station Rd where the Burghley Almshouses (3) are on the l. Turn r. at the next junction into High St St Martins. The George Hotel (4) is on the r. and St Martin's Church (5) is further along on the l. Return along High St St Martins and turn r. into Water St. Once past the riverside gardens, turn l. over the footbridge into Albert Rd. At the top turn l. into Wharf Rd then at end turn r. for St Mary's Hill. Turn r. past the town hall into cobbled St Mary's Pl, where St Mary's Church (6) is situated. From here, turn r. into St Mary's St and fork l. at St George's Sq. Then turn l. into St George's St and r. into St Paul's St. Brasenose Gate (7) is down on the r. Return down the opposite side of the street and eventually turn r. past the library into Goldsmith's La. Directly r. in Broad St is the Stamford Museum (8). Head back l. along Broad St where Browne's Hospital (9) is on the r. Fork r. into Crown St which leads back to Red Lion Sq.

1 STAMFORD BREWERY MUSEUM
The brewery was established in 1825, but in 1974 stopped brewing as it was an uneconomical proposition to replace most of the vital machinery necessary for its survival. In 1978 the museum was created. Much of the old brewing and distilling equipment is on display, and an antique beer machine is still in use in the refreshment room.

2 ST JOHN'S CHURCH
A fine example of the Perpendicular style, St John's has many features of interest, including splendidly carved angels on its roof. Several of the windows preserve ancient glass, while the carved screens and brasses are particularly noteworthy.

3 BURGHLEY ALMSHOUSES
These almshouses were originally founded as a hospital by Benedictine monks from Peterborough in the 11th century, and several parts of the building date from that time. In the 16th century Lord Burghley

All Saints Place

altered and enlarged the building to accommodate the aged people of the town.

4 GEORGE HOTEL
On this site there was once a hospital belonging to the Knights of St John of Jerusalem (a military order founded to protect pilgrims on their way to the Crusades). The hotel subsequently built here was one of the original coaching inns, and former waiting-rooms for passengers, labelled London and York, still survive, as do a number of other old features.

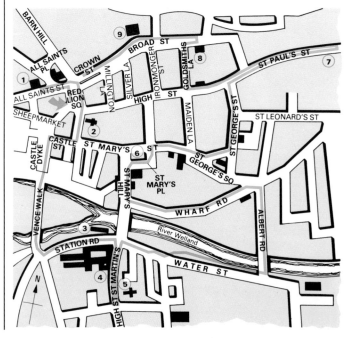

5 ST MARTIN'S CHURCH

Monuments inside this 15th-century church include a magnificent one to Sir William Cecil, the first Lord Burghley, who died in 1598. The windows contain some very fine painted glass of 1450. One of the most interesting is entitled 'Poor Man's Bible'. In the nearby cemetery Daniel Lambert is buried; when he died, aged 39, in 1809, he weighed a massive 52¾ stone. Some of his clothing survives and may be viewed by arrangement with the Stamford Corporation.

6 ST MARY'S CHURCH

St Mary's is the 'mother church' of the town. It has an exceptionally fine broach spire adorned with carvings of the four evangelists. The main body of the church is 13th-century, while the 163ft spire was added a century later. Inside, there are several fine tombs and both the Lady Chapel and the Chapel of the Golden Choir are of particular interest.

In a town given an especially notable skyline by towers and spires, that of St Mary's stands out as being one of the most attractive

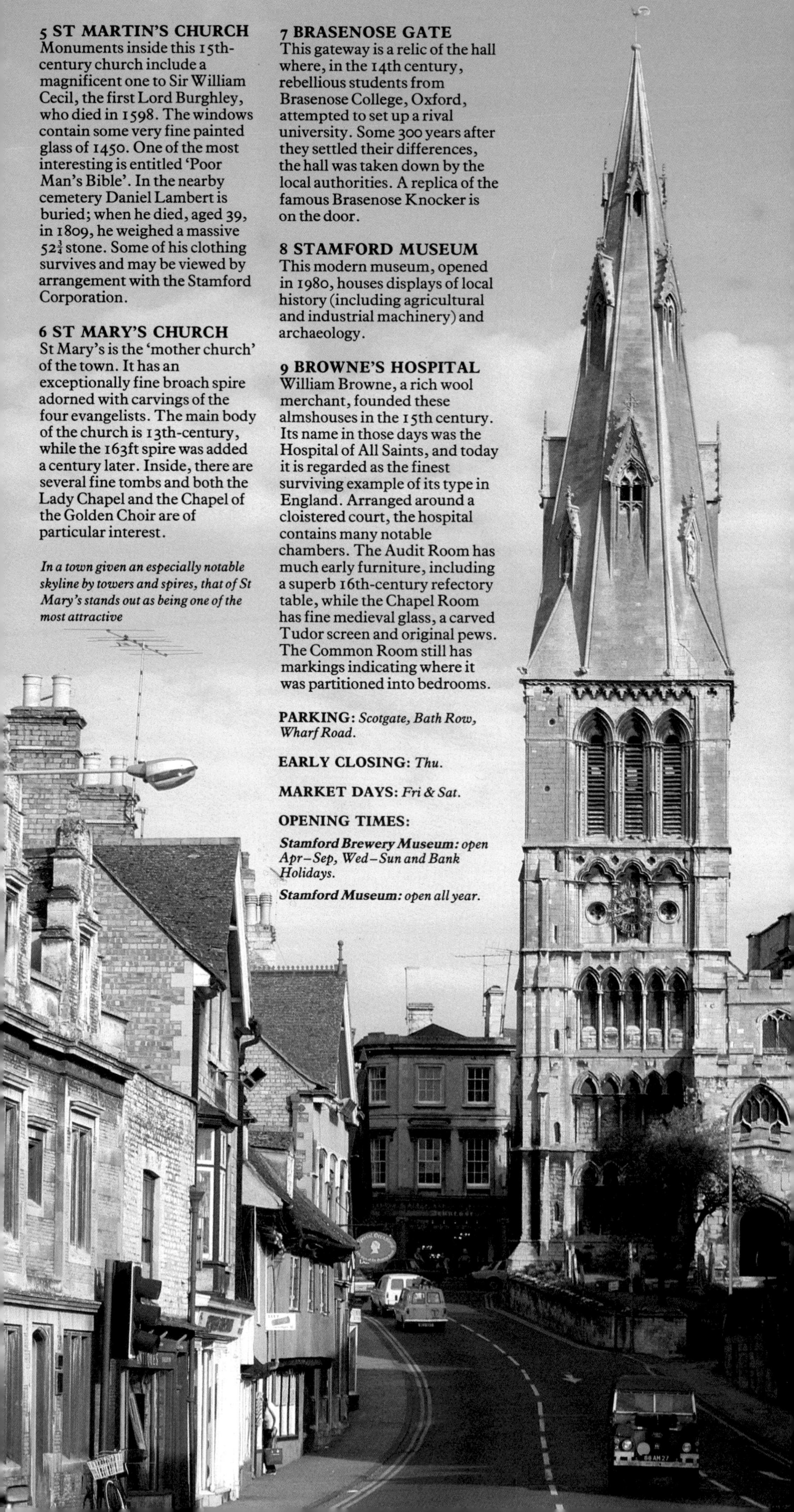

7 BRASENOSE GATE

This gateway is a relic of the hall where, in the 14th century, rebellious students from Brasenose College, Oxford, attempted to set up a rival university. Some 300 years after they settled their differences, the hall was taken down by the local authorities. A replica of the famous Brasenose Knocker is on the door.

8 STAMFORD MUSEUM

This modern museum, opened in 1980, houses displays of local history (including agricultural and industrial machinery) and archaeology.

9 BROWNE'S HOSPITAL

William Browne, a rich wool merchant, founded these almshouses in the 15th century. Its name in those days was the Hospital of All Saints, and today it is regarded as the finest surviving example of its type in England. Arranged around a cloistered court, the hospital contains many notable chambers. The Audit Room has much early furniture, including a superb 16th-century refectory table, while the Chapel Room has fine medieval glass, a carved Tudor screen and original pews. The Common Room still has markings indicating where it was partitioned into bedrooms.

PARKING: *Scotgate, Bath Row, Wharf Road.*

EARLY CLOSING: *Thu.*

MARKET DAYS: *Fri & Sat.*

OPENING TIMES:

Stamford Brewery Museum: open Apr–Sep, Wed–Sun and Bank Holidays.

Stamford Museum: open all year.

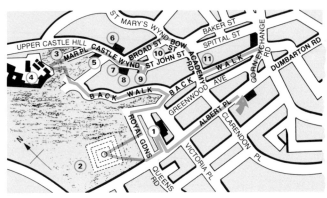

ROUTE DIRECTIONS

Start this walk at Albert Halls. Go west along Albert Place to reach the Smith Art Gallery and Museum (1). Turn r. through gate into King's Knot garden (2). Return to gate, turn sharp l. into Royal Gardens and follow this road as it swings r. Bear l. uphill on broad path at grass islands. Turn sharp l. under the town wall onto Back Walk. Follow the pathway round the back of the cemetary and go forward between wall and railings, then on uphill and l. up steps on to Castle Esplanade (3). Enter castle (4). Return from castle, and follow the cobbled street downhill past the visitor centre. After Portcullis Hotel (5) go down Castle Wynd past Argyll Lodgings (6) and Mar's Wark (7). Turn r. to Church of the Holy Rude (8) and Guildhall (9). Return from Guildhall, turn l. then r. into Broad St. Pass Tollbooth (10) and Mercat Cross. Turn r. into Bow St, go forward up footpath, passing Spittal's House. Cross into Academy Rd, and pass the Old High School (11). Turn l. on to Back Walk and return to Albert Halls via Corn Exchange Rd.

Dominated by its castle and royal palace on a crag-and-tail rock formation, Stirling is on a commanding site linking Lowland Scotland with the Highlands. The North Sea once lapped the foot of the hill. Even when the Romans came, the Carse of Stirling to the west was mostly trackless marshland. And it was knowledge of the terrain around Stirling which helped Robert the Bruce to crush Edward II's army, come to relieve the English-held castle in 1314. His victory at Bannockburn restored Scotland's independence. Parts of this route on to the castle hill follow a Stirling Old Town historical walk.

1 SMITH ART GALLERY

In the heart of a Victorian suburb laid out to a plan drawn up in 1848, the Smith Art Gallery was opened in 1874. Thomas Stuart Smith, who endowed it, left it his own collection of 125 paintings. Since then, many more have been added, as well as local museum displays.

2 KING'S KNOT

Created in the 1620s, this geometrical garden in the then-popular 'knot' style is clearly visible from the castle above. The octagonal centrepiece may have featured in tournaments held here. Certainly, there was a

Above: ornate carving on Mar's Wark

Left: Argyll's Lodging is a magnificent 17th-century mansion

jousting-ground on the far side of Dumbarton Road, in what is still called the King's Park, a royal property since at least the 12th century.

3 CASTLE ESPLANADE

Originally a parade-ground, the Esplanade is a splendid view-point towards the north and east. Over the lower-lying Gowan Hills, site of an old execution ground, the outlook is down to the meanders of the River Forth. Beside one of the windings is the ruin of Cambuskenneth Abbey, founded in 1147. Silhouetted against the skyline of the Ochil Hills, on Abbey Craig, is the 220ft tower of the Wallace Monument, completed in 1869 in memory of the hero of the Battle of Stirling Bridge, where an English army was defeated 572 years before.

4 STIRLING CASTLE

Although the exact date of the building of the oldest part of the castle is not known, it certainly occupied this hilltop site earlier than 1124. The castle was a favourite residence of the Scottish monarchs, right up to the time of James VI, who became James I of the United Kingdom at the time of the Union of Crowns in 1603. Mary Queen of Scots was crowned here in 1543. Some of the most important buildings are the Palace, the Chapel Royal and the Great Hall. The castle includes the regimental museum of the Argyll and Sutherland Highlanders. A fascinating collection of 16th-century oak medallions known as the Stirling Heads is also on display. From the Queen Anne Garden there is an extensive view over the Carse of Stirling, and down to the King's Knot.

Stirling Castle is built on a great spur of rock that has been fortified for many centuries

5 PORTCULLIS HOTEL

From 1788, for almost 100 years this building served as the Grammar School of Stirling. Among its rules was one which instructed all the pupils, throughout the 12-hour school day, to speak only in Latin. The road beside the hotel leads to an impressive stone pyramid erected in the 19th century in memory of the Covenanters – who fought for the Presbyterian cause in the 17th century – and to the Valley Cemetery, opened at the start of the 17th century on ground which had once been used for tournaments.

6 ARGYLL LODGING

This splendid town mansion was built in 1630 for the 1st Earl of Stirling, but takes its name from a later owner, the 1st Marquis of Argyll. For many years it served as an army hospital, and is now Stirling Youth Hostel.

7 MAR'S WARK

Only the frontage remains of this ambitious Renaissance-style palace built in the 1570s for the Earl of Mar, Keeper of Stirling Castle and Regent of Scotland during the childhood of James VI. There are carved rhymes on the lintels, and heraldic sculptures. Almost certainly, the building was never completed.

8 CHURCH OF THE HOLY RUDE

This 15th-century church, one of the finest in Scotland and fully restored in the 1930s, features a lofty nave with timbered ceiling. But it was not always as it is seen today. In 1656 a theological dispute led to the building of a wall to divide it in two, and thereafter there were separate congregations of the East Church and the West Church. The wall was removed only at the restoration. James VI was crowned here in 1567, when John Knox, leader of the Reformation in Scotland, preached the sermon.

9 GUILDHALL

Completed in 1639, this fine building was set up in accordance with the will of John Cowane, a wealthy member of the Merchant Guildry of Stirling. As Cowane's Hospital it housed a number of Guild members 'decayed' by reason of ill health or ill fortune. At the beginning of the 18th century it became the chief meeting place of the Guild, as it remains today. The interior was rebuilt in 1852 and contains many Guild relics. Cowane's statue is above the door. Beside the Guildhall is a bowling green opened in 1712 and still in use, guarded by a pair of Russian cannons captured at Sebastopol.

10 TOLBOOTH

One of many restored buildings in Broad Street, this was built in 1704 to act as the town hall and town jail. From it, in 1820, John Baird and Andrew Hardie, two leaders of the Scottish Radical Rising, were led out to be executed beside the Mercat Cross. The present cross is a replacement one set up in 1891, but it is topped by the stone unicorn which crowned the original. The town council carried out much of the restoration work on the old houses in Broad Street.

11 HIGH SCHOOL

The old High School building stands in Academy Street. At the south end is where the Hospital of the Seven Incorporated Trades of Stirling stood from 1751 to 1907. Behind the High School, the Back Walk, opened in the 18th century, leads down alongside the surviving town wall. This section of it incorporates a powder magazine.

MARKET DAY: *Thu.*

EARLY CLOSING: *Wed.*

PARKING: *Albert Place, Dumbarton Road.*

OPENING TIMES:

Smith Art Gallery: open all year.

Stirling Castle: open all year. Closed Sun am Oct–Mar.

Landmark Visitor Centre: open Easter–Oct.

Church of the Holy Rude: open all year. Closes early pm Nov–Apr.

Guildhall: as above.

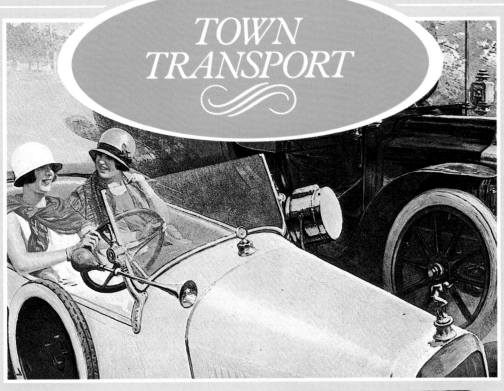

TOWN TRANSPORT

Fulminating in the midst of yet another traffic jam, today's town traveller may muse with envy on imagined gracious journeys through peaceful streets in times past. Yet a century ago, such a journey would almost certainly have been even more frustrating. As well as an early motor car or two, horsedrawn carriages, omnibuses and trams jammed the streets. Congestion was made worse by bad road surfaces overlaid by tram tracks and liberally spread with horse droppings. Add a number of penny farthing bicycle enthusiasts, and picture the resulting chaos!

In the really good old days, before industrialisation and the consequent enormous growth in the size of towns, most ordinary people were pedestrians. The wealthy, reluctant to soil their elegant attire, preferred horseback. Rich ladies were transported in sedan chairs. Originating in France around 1770, these ornate boxes were usually carried by footmen. They soon became fashionable in London society.

Around this time carriages also became popular with the well-to-do. Perched high on elaborate springing, with enormous back wheels, the phaeton was *the* vehicle in which to be seen. Light-weight carriages in the phaeton mould were strictly for visiting or driving around the park, but in 1784, horse-drawn vehicles took on a new dimension with John Palmer's fast, well-built mail coaches. These opened up long-distance travel, the first coach running from London to Bath. But the stage coaches were expensive and only a minority of the populace could afford to use them.

Goods fared better than people: great canals were built by early engineers such as Thomas Telford, James Brindley and others. The canal era began around 1750 and continued through the first quarter of the 19th century. By 1830, Britain had over 4,000 miles of navigable waterway. Horse-drawn barges carried coal to Manchester and pottery to Liverpool. In 1803 the Surrey Iron Railway, an iron track covering nine miles from Wandsworth to Croydon, was opened. The horse-drawn trucks were strictly for goods only. A similar arrangement for passengers began to operate in Swansea four years later.

Horse-drawn vehicles
Early in the 19th century, horse-drawn vehicles were still only available to the favoured few. Even

Top: motor cars transformed towns and society
Above: a sedan chair

so, the variety of models rivalled the motor cars of today. The gig, a two-wheeled open cart of dashing proportions, was clearly the forerunner of the modern sports car. The brougham, a cab mounted on elliptical springs, was a compact, closed carriage, comparable in quality with a Rolls-Royce. The landau, a three-in-one carriage, could be used open, half-closed or completely closed – the prototype of today's convertible.

In 1818 the 'dandy-horse' began to appear in London streets. This simple vehicle consisted of a crossbar and two wheels. The rider sat astride and pushed himself along with his feet on the ground! From 1870 London streets were full of Hansom cabs for hire. Pulled by one horse, they were rather unstable, having two very high wheels. The driver sat high up on a seat at the rear and received instructions from his clients through a trap door in the roof.

Ordinary working people could not afford the luxury of cabs, but the need to get people to their place of work following the Industrial Revolution led to the development of public transport. In 1825 the world's first public steam railway, from Stockton to Darlington, was opened, when George Stephenson's locomotive reached a speed of 12 mph. The line was a great commercial success, but the reliability of new-found steam trains was poor enough to prevent their more widespread use until several years later.

Introducing the omnibus
George Shillibeer transformed road transport with his two 22–seater three-horse omnibuses

which began regular timetabled services in London in 1829. Horse-drawn buses became the most popular form of urban transport, and Thomas Tilling's private company vied for passengers with the London General Omnibus Company. Both these companies ran buses which carried passengers on an upper deck. They were called 'knifeboard' omnibuses, because the people on the top deck sat back to back on a long bench called the knifeboard.

By the 1870s, priority was being given to public transport with the introduction of trams which ran on tracks in the road. The first tram in this country, a single-decker horse-drawn vehicle, was designed by an American, G. F. Train. In 1861 it was run on three experimental tracks in London. Horse-drawn double-decker trams were soon introduced in other cities.

By 1863, steam railways had plunged underground. The Metropolitan Railway in London ran in roofed trenches below street level. Baker Street became the world's first underground steam railway station.

Trolleys and trams

In 1883, a battery electric tramcar ran at Kew. The accumulators were cumbersome and as electric current became available, this type of tram became obsolete. Steam trams, popular for a time in Europe around 1890, were never received favourably in this country. A separate locomotive pulled a trailer car. The attendant noise and smoke which filled the streets provoked public hostility and hastened the demise of this version of the tramcar. Britain's first electric tram, drawing current by means of an overhead trolley and trolley pole, appeared in Leeds in 1891. The prototype had been invented in the USA in the 1880s. Electric trams became an extremely important means of urban transport. As well as being smokeless and less noisy than the steam trams, they were cheaper to run. London County Council electric trams, operational from 1903, were roofless double-deckers, considered to be safer than covered trams. Following World War I, new Feltham class trams were ordered by the LCC. They were fast, comfortable, roomy and completely enclosed. Birmingham Corporation trams were among the longest-surviving of that genre, remaining in service until 1953, by which time trolleybuses and motor omnibuses had taken over.

In London, tramcars had been challenged by the world's first electric tube railway from as early as

*Early bicycles took
many outlandish forms*

1890. This was the City and South London line, which ran in steel tube tunnels carrying the running track and current rails.

The first trolleybus was seen in Britain in 1909. It was similar in design to buses already produced in Germany and France, the only difference being the twin trolleys introduced in this country. These early trolleybuses could run either on or off rails. By the 1930s, trolleybuses had become very popular vehicles in Britain and by virtue of their great mobility they soon replaced tramcars in many towns and cities. Sadly these clean, inexpensive vehicles are no longer to be seen and the diesel motor bus is the remaining form of public road transport. The earliest motor buses had appeared in Britain around 1904. The body still basically resembled that of a horse-drawn omnibus, the driver in a similar position but gripping a steering wheel in place of reins.

Private motoring

The first motor cars, looking like car-carriage hybrids, were on the road in the 1890s. In the early days of motoring, the speed limit in towns was 2 mph (4 mph on country roads). By law, a man had to walk in front carrying a red flag by day, and a lantern at night. Gradually, cars and road surfaces improved, but private motoring remained a rarity until after World War I.

No one could deny the need for a taxi when a quick dash is essential, but at other times buses or the Underground, if there is one, are a better method of urban transport than the motor car, which causes so much congestion and pollution in our towns. It is paradoxical that as long ago as 1899 Camille Jenatzy, a Belgian, built a bullet-shaped car driven by an electric motor. In 1983 manufacturers the world over are racing to produce the ideal electric city car. They could soon be widely available. It may be the beginning of yet another revolutionary change in the character and look of our towns.

Private carriages were for the rich only

ROUTE DIRECTIONS

Start from the front of the Royal Shakespeare Theatre (1). Walk to the River Avon and then l. along the riverside. Cross the footbridge turning l. around the side of the canal basin, passing on the r. the Gower Memorial Statue of Shakespeare (2). Turn l., leaving the gardens onto Bridge Foot passing the end of Waterside (for The World of shakespeare (3)) then up Bridge St. At top cross to r. then forward into Henley St passing on the r. Shakespeare's Birthplace (4) and the Shakespeare Centre (5). At the end walk around to r. and cross to the Motor Museum (6). Return along Henley St then turn r. into Meer St to market place and around to l. into Wood St. At end turn r. into High St with the tourist information centre across on the l. then Harvard House (7) on the r. Pass Sheep St into Chapel St with the Town Hall (8) then the Shakespeare Hotel on the l. Also on the l. is New Place (9) then on the r. the Falcon Hotel. Go forward into Church St passing on l. the Guild Chapel (10), then the King Edward VI Grammar School and Guildhall. At end go l. into Old Town passing Hall's Croft (11), then keep forward for Holy Trinity Church (12). Return onto Old Town then turn r. into the Gardens of the Royal Shakespeare Theatre (9 am to sunset) and forward along the pathway towards the river, then pass the brass rubbing centre. Leave the gardens, then go up the second set of steps through the gardens onto Waterside to pass the Royal Shakespeare Company Gallery and return to the start.

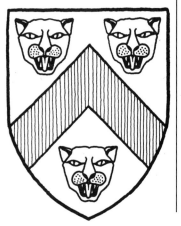

There is, of course, no escaping the fact that Stratford is where William Shakespeare was born and died. His name is everywhere, as are statues, memorials and plaques to his memory. But even without the lure of the bard Stratford would be an outstanding town, for its streets of lovely old houses make it one of the best townscapes in England.

1 ROYAL SHAKESPEARE THEATRE

Opened in 1932 as an international memorial to the world's most famous dramatist, this red-brick building was considered controversial for its time and attracted much criticism. It is set among attractive meadows and gardens and its riverside terraces are a particularly attractive feature. As a theatre it boasts superb facilities for actors and audiences. The adjoining picture gallery and museum contains portraits of Shakespeare and famous Shakesperian actors, as well as many other fascinating theatrical mementoes.

2 GOWER MEMORIAL STATUE

Overlooking the canal basin and commanding the approach to Stratford over ancient Clopton Bridge, this statue of Shakespeare was erected in 1888. It was a gift to the town from its maker, Lord Ronald Gower, who had taken twelve years over its design and modelling. The statue of the bard is flanked by figures of Falstaff, Lady Macbeth, Prince Hal and Hamlet.

3 THE WORLD OF SHAKESPEARE

The 25 life-size tableaux in this auditorium are designed to depict everyday life in Shakespeare's England. Each tableau is accompanied by dramatic lighting, appropriate Tudor music and spoken commentaries. Among the experiences which can be relived are the London Plague and the journey which Elizabeth I made from London to Kenilworth in 1575.

Top: The Royal Shakespeare Theatre and the River Avon

Above: A lovely knott garden stands on the site of New Place

4 SHAKESPEARE'S BIRTHPLACE

This 16th-century half-timbered house is where Shakespeare was born in 1564. It was originally in two parts – workshop and dwelling place – and part of a terrace. The adjoining buildings were demolished in 1857 to diminish the risk of fire, and at the same time the house was restored to its appearance as recorded in a drawing made in 1769. Since 1847, when the house came under the stewardship of the Birthplace Trust, every care has been taken to preserve and enhance as many of its original features as possible. The living part of the house is equipped with appropriate Elizabethan and Jacobean furniture, and the workshop serves as an excellent museum.

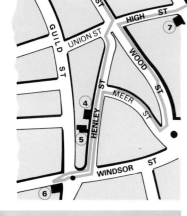

cars and motorcycles displayed in suitable settings. The speciality of the museum is exotic sports and grand touring cars, and among these are a prototype Rolls-Royce Phantom I, once loaned to Lawrence of Arabia, and a polished aluminium Rolls-Royce used by Edward VIII on a state tour of India.

7 HARVARD HOUSE

American visitors will find this half-timbered house particularly interesting. It was built in 1596 by Thomas Rogers, whose daughter married Robert Harvard of Southwark in 1605. Their son, John, emigrated to America, where he died in 1637 at the age of 30. He left a bequest which founded the now world-famous Harvard University. The house in Stratford was purchased in 1909 by Edward Morris of Chicago and donated by him to the university. Displays inside relate to the founder and his life and times.

8 TOWN HALL

Built of cream-coloured stone, this handsome Palladian building was erected in 1767. On its Sheep Street façade is a statue of Shakespeare presented by David Garrick, the famous 18th-century actor. Sheep Street itself is lined with timbered buildings.

9 NEW PLACE

Shakespeare left Stratford to make his fortune in London, and by 1597 he was wealthy enough to resettle permanently in the town of his birth, and to buy one of its most substantial houses. Unfortunately it was destroyed by a disgruntled owner in the late 18th century after he had had a row with the local authority, but its foundations can still be seen. These are set in gardens which have been laid out with plants and flowers that Shakespeare would have known. The gardens are entered through New Place Museum, a timbered building which contains furniture, archaeological exhibits and many items of local historical interest. Shakespeare died at New Place on 23 April 1616, aged 52.

5 THE SHAKESPEARE CENTRE

Next to the Birthplace is this stark brick building, opened in 1964 to commemorate the 400th anniversary of the birth of the poet. In the entrance vestibule is a huge bronze statue of Shakespeare, symbolising his giant influence over the world. The reading room is dominated by a carved wood panel inscribed with the names of the bard and many of his distinguished contemporaries. The Centre has a dual purpose; it is the headquarters of the Birthplace Trust and also an educational centre in which students can study more than 30,000 publications held in the library. An associated records office holds documents and records relating to Shakespeare and every aspect of Stratford.

6 STRATFORD MOTOR MUSEUM

Housed in what was once a combined Victorian church and school, this museum has vintage

10 THE GUILD CHAPEL

Originally this was the meeting place of members of the Guild of the Holy Cross, a powerful body composed of prominent citizens. It was founded before 1269, but in the 15th century the chapel was enlarged by the addition of a nave and west tower. A considerable number of wall paintings are preserved in the interior.

11 HALL'S CROFT

One of Stratford's best half-timbered houses, this was the home of Shakespeare's daughter Susanna and her husband, Dr John Hall. One room is equipped as an Elizabethan surgery with exhibits illustrating medical practice in the 16th century. A spacious walled garden surrounds the house, which was bought by the Birthplace Trust in 1949.

12 HOLY TRINITY CHURCH

Most of this riverside church dates from the 12th century. Its stone spire was built in 1763 to replace a wooden one. Shakespeare is buried beneath the chancel steps. The bust of the bard holding a quill pen dates from the time of his death. Also buried here are his wife Anne, his eldest daughter, Susanna, her husband Dr Hall, and Thomas Nash, husband of Shakespeare's grand-daughter Elizabeth Hall. Photographs of the parish register show entries of Shakespeare's baptism and burial. Other items of interest include the misericords in the choir stalls, the Clopton Chapel and a chained Bible.

EARLY CLOSING: *Thu.*

MARKET DAY: *Fri.*

PARKING: *Waterside Lane, off Rother St, Warwick Rd.*

OPENING TIMES:

Royal Shakespeare Theatre Gallery: open all year. Mon – Sat all day; Sun pm only.

The World of Shakespeare: open all year.

Shakespeare's Birthplace: open all year. Sun pm only Nov – Mar.

Stratford Motor Museum: open all year.

Harvard House: open all year. Weekdays all day; Sun pm only.

New Place: open all year. Weekdays all day; Sun pm only. Closed Sun Nov – Mar.

Hall's Croft: open all year. Weekdays all day; Sun pm only. Closed Sun Nov – Mar.

ROUTE DIRECTIONS

Start the walk at Five Arches (1) and walk along South Parade with the town wall on the r. On the l. at the junction with Upper Park Rd are the War Memorial Gardens (2). Continue for a short way along South Parade, then turn r. into Town Wall Arcade to reach Upper Frog St. Turn l., reach White Lion St, turn r. and then l. into the Norton. By the tourist information centre descend a zigzag path to the r. to reach North Beach. Turn r. along North Walk, and walk along the l. side of the Sluice to reach the Harbour (3). Pass St Julian's Seamen's Church and reach Castle Sq. Take the footpath to the l. round Castle Hill (4). On the far side of the headland is Tenby Museum (5). Continue on the footpath back to Castle Sq. Go forward in the square, then bear r. along Bridge St, and keep l. into Harbour Court. Reach the Tudor Merchant's House (6) and then turn l., climbing the steps up Quay Hill. Turn r. into Tudor Sq, keep forward into the High St, with St Mary's Church (7) on the left. Go through the churchyard and leave by the south gate, cross St Georges' St and enter St Mary's St. At the end turn r. into Paragon. Turn l. and r., passing the entrance to the Imperial Hotel, and pass through an arch of the town wall, Belmont Archway, to reach St Florence Parade. Turn l. then r. along the Esplanade (8). At the end turn r. into Victoria St, then r. into Southcliffe St, then l. into St Florence Parade to return to the start point.

Two beaches of golden sand enclosed by rocky headlands and overlooked by a tumble of Georgian and Victorian houses help to make Tenby one of the most delightful of Welsh towns. Ancient town walls and a medieval street plan add an historical dimension. Fishing boats in a picturesque harbour complete the picture of a perfect seaside resort.

1 FIVE ARCHES

Originally this great bastion of stone was built as the west gate of the wall which surrounded the town. Three of the five apertures in the structure were erected in recent times for the convenience of traffic. The town walls were built in the 13th century and considerably strengthened in the 16th when fears of a Spanish invasion were at their height. They are unique in Wales in that they have two tiers of arrow-slits.

Fishing is popular along the rugged cliffs and little coves around Tenby

2 WAR MEMORIAL GARDENS

Favoured as it is by a gentle climate, South-western Wales can grow plants which cannot withstand the colder weather elsewhere, and Tenby is especially sheltered, so that palm trees thrive here. Some can be seen in these pleasant and well laid-out gardens.

3 THE HARBOUR

The Harbour is given its particular charm by the higgledy-piggledy rows of brightly painted houses which surround it. Fishing boats still make use of the sheltered waters here, but as in most harbours today the majority of vessels are pleasure craft. The Sluice is a little loop of the harbour used for the winter maintenance of boats. Around the Sluice are three-storeyed buildings which were built as fish markets and net stores. Overlooking the harbour is St Julian's Seaman's Church, a largely reconstructed building where the last special fisherman's services were held in Wales. Dotted along the harbour wall are bollards which are actually cannons used by land batteries against Parliamentary ships in 1643.

Tenby became fashionable in the 19th century, and was visited by Lord Nelson and Lady Hamilton

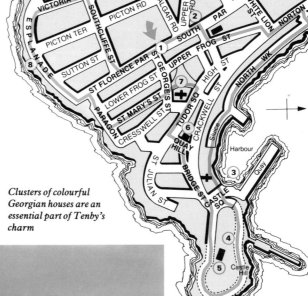

Clusters of colourful Georgian houses are an essential part of Tenby's charm

4 CASTLE HILL

Stretches of broken walls and foundations are all that remain of Tenby Castle. It was once a powerful fortress on a natural promontory that was easily defended. The surviving remains probably date from about 1153, but there was a castle here before that. On the north side of the promontory is the lifeboat station on its raised slipway, while to the south, and only 500 yards offshore, is St Catherine's Island, on which stands a fort built in 1864 to protect the approaches to Milford Haven.

5 TENBY MUSEUM

Built partly into the remaining walls of the castle, the museum contains displays relating to the archaeology, geology, natural history and medieval history of the area. Especially interesting are the Smith collection of animal remains and the Lyons collection of shells.

6 TUDOR MERCHANT'S HOUSE

In its heyday, Tenby undoubtedly had a number of substantial houses like this, but all the others have long since disappeared, leaving the Tudor Merchant's House as a very special survivor. It was probably built in the 15th century, and considerably altered and extended in the 16th century. It is from this time that the windows and many other features date. In the late 1960s removal of old lime wash revealed the house's original painted wall decorations. These took the form of a repeated pattern of trailing flowers and were applied when the plaster was still wet. The house contains furniture and fittings from many periods.

7 ST MARY'S CHURCH

This is one of the largest and most handsome parish churches in Wales. It was enlarged by the addition of chapels and a north aisle during the 15th century – an indication of the town's prosperity at that time. At the same time the beautiful wagon roof in the chancel was added. This is especially noteworthy for its carved and painted bosses. There are many interesting tombs in the church, including one to a 15th-century cleric which depicts him as a shrouded skeleton. In St Thomas' Chapel are elaborate tombs to two merchant families prominent in Tenby in the 15th and 16th centuries. A tablet in the church commemorates Robert Recorde, the inventor of the equals sign, who was born in the town in 1510.

8 ESPLANADE

Overlooking South Beach, the Esplanade is lined with handsome Victorian and Edwardian buildings, nearly all of which are hotels. From here there are marvellous views across to Caldey Island, the site of a monastery on and off for more than a thousand years.

EARLY CLOSING: *Wed.*

PARKING: *Upper Park Rd, Lower Park Rd.*

OPENING TIMES:

Tenby Museum: open all year; closed Fri pm, and Sun, Oct–May.

Tudor Merchant's House: Open Easter–Sep. Mon–Fri and Sun pm.

125

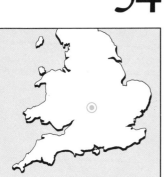

T he ancient town of Warwick was founded in AD 914 by Ethelfleda, daughter of Alfred the Great. She built a fortress on the rise here from which to ward off Danish marauders. Later came the castle, idyllically situated alongside the tree-lined River Avon. Despite a disastrous fire in 1694 which destroyed most of the medieval town, a handful of ancient buildings survive. These contrast pleasantly with the Georgian houses that eventually followed. Modern Warwick, beyond the old wall, has managed to develop as an industrial and university town while successfully merging with the delightful surrounding countryside of the very heart of England.

ROUTE DIRECTIONS

Begin the walk by the Castle Hill/Mill St junction. Walk up the drive and turn r. up the steps to Warwick Castle (1). On leaving the castle turn l. then l. again into Castle La. Turn r. and cross Castle St to Ocken's House (2). Continue to the Court House (3). Next, turn l. into the High St where Lord Leycester's Hospital (4) is along on the r. Turn r. under the Westgate archway into Bowling Green St. Take the second r. opposite the West Gate Arms into Market St, which leads into the Market Pl, for the Warwickshire Museum (5). Keeping to the l. of the square, turn l. then r. into Barrack St. Take a r. turn next to pass into Northgate St where Shire Hall (6) is on the r. Further along on the l. is St Mary's Church (7). Walk on into Church St and turn l. at the junction into Jury St. At the crossroads, pass under Eastgate to find Landor House (8). Walk along the r.-hand side of Smith St and cross over St Nicholas Church St to St John's House (9). From here go l. along St Nicholas Church St, passing St Nicholas Church (10) on the l. and return to the starting point.

1 WARWICK CASTLE

The present castle was mostly built in the 14th century on the site of a Norman fortification. Its many splendid features include Guy's Tower, the Gatehouse and the 147ft Caesar's Tower, a grim fortification used as a gaol for French prisoners as early as 1356. The Bear Tower and Clarence Tower were built by order of the Duke of Clarence, the peer whom Shakespeare wrote was 'drowned in a butt of Malmsey wine'. Inside, within the castle armoury, is a helmet said to have belonged to Oliver Cromwell. The many state rooms are eclipsed by the Great Hall, a grandiose place with many classical paintings and furniture, plus Cromwell's macabre death-mask. The extensive library was painstakingly restored following a fire in 1871. The delightful gardens surrounding the castle were designed by Capability Brown.

2 OKEN'S HOUSE

This 16th-century structure was the birthplace of Thomas Oken, a Warwick bailiff and local worthy. Nowadays the building is a doll museum with exhibits spanning the years 1750–1950.

3 THE COURT HOUSE

Robert Dudley donated the land on which this building stands in exchange for the buildings now forming part of Lord Leycester's Hospital. Francis Smith constructed the house in the 1720s on then-popular classical lines and incorporated an ornate colonnaded façade. The building is now the home of Warwick Town Council and is also the town's tourist information centre. It houses a collection of 17th-century civic regalia.

4 LORD LEYCESTER'S HOSPITAL

This is perhaps the most interesting building to survive the fire of 1694. The collection of buildings dates from the 12th to the 16th centuries and has been used as a guildhall, council chamber and grammar school. Westgate, part of the ancient town wall, is incorporated in the complex. Founded in 1571 by Robert Dudley, Earl of Leicester (a favourite courtier of Elizabeth I), the hospice was a home for those wounded while in the service of the fighting gentry. The accommodation was for a master and 12 'brethren'. Although the quarters have been much modernised, they are still occupied in the same manner today and the inmates occasionally wear the original Elizabethan costume. The group of buildings surrounds a small but attractive courtyard.

The Beauchamp Chapel, St Mary's

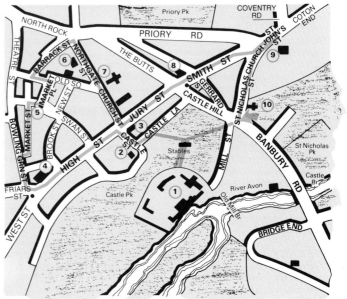

5 WARWICKSHIRE MUSEUM

The museum is located in the Market Hall, which was built in 1670. Originally standing on arches, it provided undercover space for stalls, but in the 19th century the archways were railed off to provide an open space for the stocks, which were on wheels. The unfortunate culprits were made to pull them into position before being fettered. The museum itself covers all aspects of social and natural history in the town and in the county.

6 SHIRE HALL

Forming a complex with the old county gaol and the Judge's Lodging, the Shire Hall is a handsome, single-storey structure designed in the mid-18th century by Sanderson Miller. It consists of one huge room, 93ft long, flanked by two octagonal court rooms. The grim looking gaol was built at the end of the 18th century.

7 ST MARY'S CHURCH

Most of this famous church was rebuilt after the Fire of Warwick in 1694. The style used in the rebuilding was Gothic, which blended with the chancel and Beauchamp Chapel, both of which had survived the blaze. It is the Beauchamp Chapel which makes this church so outstanding. It was built between 1443 and 1464 and has superb vaulting, brilliant stained glass and the best mid 15th-century sculpture in the country. Forming the centrepiece of the chapel is the monument to Richard Beauchamp, Earl of Warwick. Other monuments here are to members of the Dudley family, the subsequent earls. The soaring chancel roof is a perfect example of Perpendicular architecture.

8 LANDOR HOUSE

Taking its name from Walter Savage Landor, 19th-century poet and scholar who was born in Warwick, this house was built in 1692.

9 ST JOHN'S HOUSE

An early 17th-century mansion, it now houses a branch of the county museum. Special displays include those of folk life, costume, craft and musical instruments. On the first floor is the Museum of the Royal Warwickshire Regiment.

10 ST NICHOLAS CHURCH

Although the present church was not built until 1780, it is locally believed that there has been a religious site here for nearly a thousand years.

EARLY CLOSING: *Thu.*

MARKET DAYS: *Sat.*

PARKING: *Castle La, Castle Hill, Market St.*

OPENING TIMES:

Warwick Castle: open all year.

Oken's House: open all year.

Lord Leycester's Hospital: open all year.

Warwickshire Museum: open all year. Mon–Sat all day (Sun pm May–Sep only).

St John's House: open all year. Wed–Sat all day (Sun pm May–Sep only).

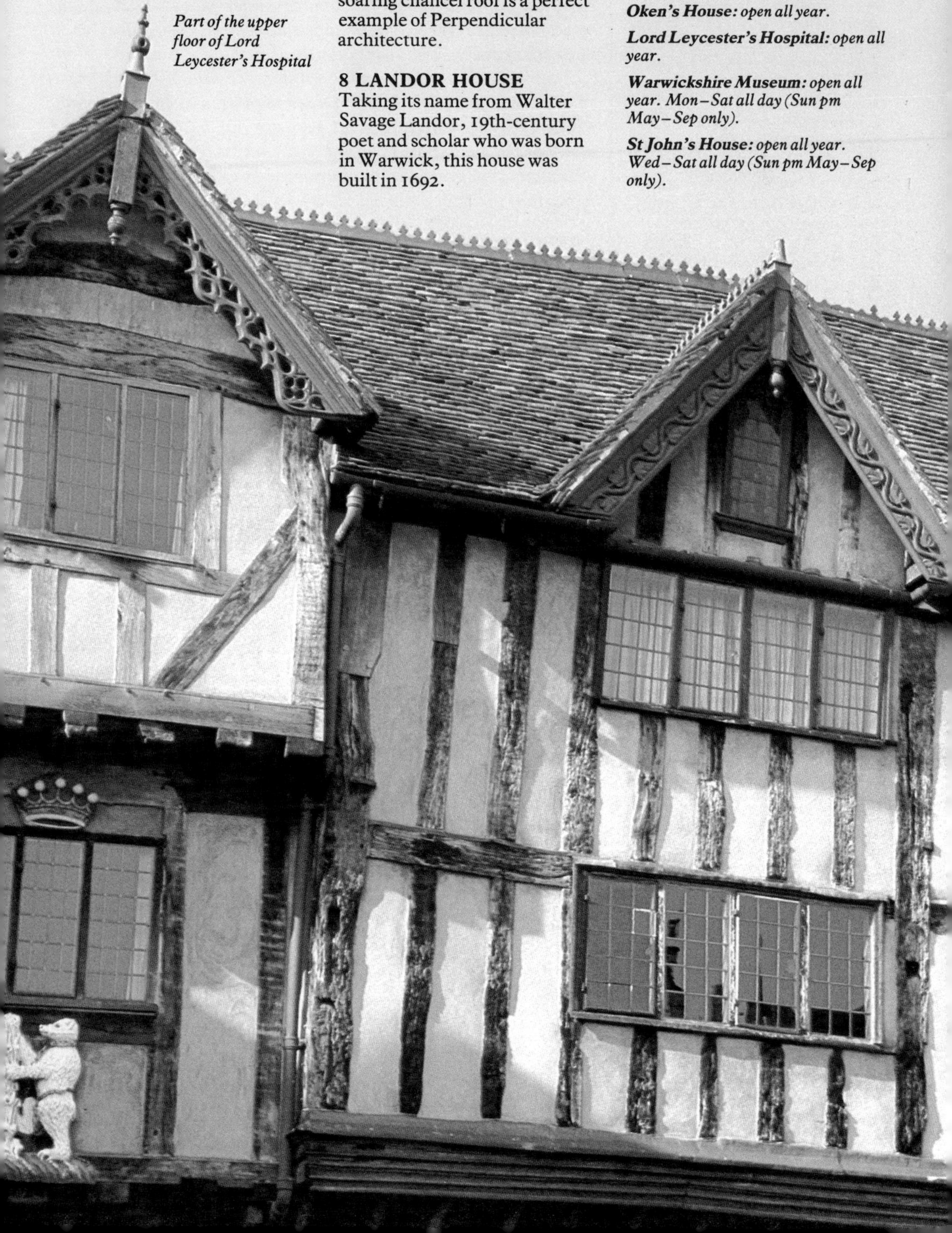

Part of the upper floor of Lord Leycester's Hospital

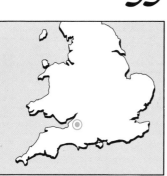

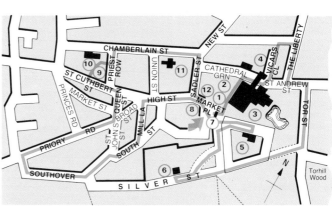

ROUTE DIRECTIONS

Start at the north-east corner of the Market Pl at the Penniless Porch (1). Turn r. into Cathedral Close (2). Pass by the porch of Wells Cathedral (3) and turn l. into The College of Vicars (Vicars Close) (4). At the end, bear r. From here turn r. into The Liberty, then l. into St Andrew's St and immediately r. into Tor St. By the entrance to Torhill Wood cross over and turn r. then follow the footpath until the moat of the Bishop's Palace (5) is reached. Continue forward into Silver St where the Bishop's Barn (6) is on the r. From here, return to the moat and walk along the footpath to its northern end. Pass through the Bishop's Eye (7) into the Market Pl once more. From this standpoint, the Crown Inn (8) is to the r. of the Town Hall. Turn l. here into the High St, then l. again into Mill La. Next, bear r. into South St and follow the pavement round into Southover. At the end turn r. into Priory Rd. Take the second l. into Queen St, pass the end of Priest Row and walk into St Cuthbert St. Cross over to St Cuthbert's Church (9) and, on leaving, turn r. and pass through the churchyard to the Almshouses (10). Return to Priest Row and turn l. At the junction turn r. into Chamberlain St to pass the Church of SS Joseph and Teresa (11) on the r. At the end turn r. into Sadler St then l., past a Commemorative Plaque (12), into the Market Pl to complete the walk.

The cathedral clock, one of the earliest of its kind in the world

The City of Wells, known as the capital of the Mendips, has a population of under 9,000, making it one of England's smallest cities. Its cathedral was built in the second half of the 12th century in a then new wholly English style. However, a bishop's seat for Somerset was established here as early as 909 and although authority later moved to Bath, the episcopal seat returned on the appointment of Bishop Jocelyn in the 13th century. The eventual title of Bishop of Bath and Wells was introduced to satisfy public opinion. Today, Wells is home to small local industries, chiefly paper-making and dairy farming. Much of its rich architectural heritage has been retained, and many of the old buildings have been beautifully restored in recent years, while newer buildings have been built in sympathetic styles in parts of the city.

1 THE PENNILESS PORCH
This gate into the close was so called because it once attracted beggars and paupers who sought alms from people visiting the cathedral. It was built in 1450.

2 CATHEDRAL CLOSE
Many of the buildings that stand around the close have histories that stretch back to at least the 15th century, but these ancient origins are often disguised by later façades. Of particular interest is the series of buildings

on the north side of the green. The Deanery dates from the 15th century, but has windows installed at the close of the 17th century. Next to it is the Chancellor's House; Tudor with an 18th-century facing. It houses Wells Museum.

3 WELLS CATHEDRAL
One of the loveliest of Britain's cathedral's, Wells was begun in about 1180, and completed during a second, astonishingly creative, building period which ended in 1340. On the west front is the greatest array of British 13th-century sculpture to be found anywhere. To the south of the building are the cloisters and above the East Cloister is one of the largest medieval libraries in England. It was fully restored in 1686 and houses documents and archaic papers some of which are 1,000 years old. The Chapter House, added in the early 14th century, is a delightful octagonal structure, as is the Lady Chapel at the eastern end. Perhaps the most eye-catching feature of the cathedral is the astronomical clock. Made as early as the 1390s, it features a 6ft dial and moving models of knights that joust every quarter of an hour.

4 THE COLLEGE OF VICARS
Known more recently as Vicars Close, this is believed to be the oldest intact 14th-century street in Europe. The college itself was

The ceiling of the Chapter House is an astonishing tracery of stone ribs

founded in 1348 and finally disbanded only in 1934. It consists of terraced houses. No. 22 has been restored to its original appearance. The Close is to this day occupied by vicars and employees of the cathedral.

5 BISHOP'S PALACE
This is one of the oldest inhabited houses in England. Its outer walls date back to 1206 and give the building the appearance of a castle. The moat which surrounds the palace receives water from the wells in the Bishop's Garden, from which the city derives its name. Swans in the moat ring a bell near the bridge when hungry.

6 THE BISHOP'S BARN
Built in the 15th century, this cross-shaped barn is 110ft long and is used for social events.

Houses in Vicars Close

7 BISHOP'S EYE
One of Bishop Bekynton's many improvements to the close, this gateway, built in 1450, leads into the Market Place.

8 THE CROWN INN
A 17th-century tavern with a black and white frontage. From one of its windows William Penn, the pioneer Quaker, is said to have preached to a crowd of 2,000 in 1685 before being arrested.

9 ST CUTHBERT'S CHURCH
This fine example of Perpendicular architecture is the largest church in Somerset and at one time was the focal point of Wells.

10 ALMSHOUSES
An interesting 15th-century building donated to the city by Bishop Bubwith. It was probably unique in that it doubled as both an almshouse and a guildhall, the latter being identifiable today by its bell-turret and high roof.

11 CHURCH OF SS JOSEPH AND TERESA
Rather out of step geographically, the design of this Roman Catholic church was taken from a small wayside chapel in Norfolk.

12 COMMEMORATIVE PLAQUE
This tablet is dedicated to Mary Bignal Rand, a native of Wells who captured a gold medal for the long jump in the 1964 Tokyo Olympics.

EARLY CLOSING: *Wed.*

MARKET DAY: *Sat.*

PARKING: *Market Pl.*

OPENING TIMES:

Wells Museum: open all year. Mon–Sat, Apr–Sep, all day. Sun pm only Jun–Sep. Oct–Mar pm only.

Bishop's Palace: open Easter–Oct, Thu and Sun. Open daily Aug.

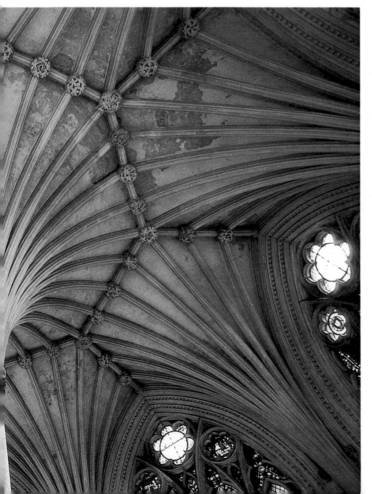

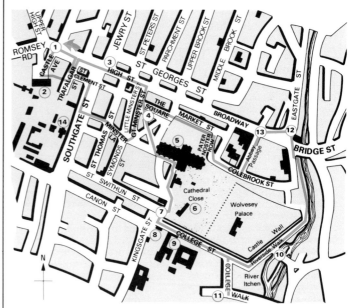

ROUTE DIRECTIONS

*Start at Westgate (1) and go l. up
Castle Ave to Great Hall (2).
Walk down steps, l., to Trafalgar
St, turn l. then shortly r. into High
St (3). At City Cross go r. under
archway to museum (4) and then
bear l. to the Cathedral (5). Walk
through Inner Close (signed
College and Water Meadow) past
Pilgrims' Hall (6) to Kingsgate
(7). Go through arch to College St
past Jane Austen's House (8) and
Winchester College (9) and bear l.
to Riverside Walk (10) with views
of Wolvesey Palace. (Footpath
from end of College Walk leads
through meadows to St Cross
Hopsital (11).) Opposite City
Mill (12), emerge into Broadway
(13) and turn l. past King Alfred
statue to Abbey Passage l. by
Town Hall. Turn r. up Colebrook
St and by Wessex Hotel take path
through Cathedral Green to The
Square. At end of Square, turn l.
up Gt Minster St, then r. up
Minster La to St Thomas St. Go
up St Thomas Passage opposite to
Southgate St and Serle's House
(14). Turn r. to St Clement St and
l. for return to Trafalgar St to
complete the walk.*

For 200 years before the Norman Conquest Winchester was
the true capital of England, a Saxon city built on the site of
the Roman town of Venta Belgarum, where Alfred the
Great held court and Cnut lies buried. It is one of England's great
cathedral cities, and the home of the oldest public school in the
country, Winchester College, founded in 1382.

1 WESTGATE
The Westgate, dating from the
12th to 14th centuries, is one of
the two surviving gates of the
medieval city and stands on
what is thought to be the site of
the old Roman gate. It is now
part of the City Museum and has
a fascinating collection of
weights and measures, arms and
armour. Carvings on the walls of
the Upper Chamber date from
the 17th century when the room
was used as a prison.

2 GREAT HALL
The 13th-century Great Hall is
all that survives of the Norman
castle. It is a great aisled hall
with a timbered roof supported
by eight columns of Purbeck
marble. High on the west wall is
the famous Round Table, a
massive circle of oak measuring
18ft across and weighing $1\frac{1}{4}$
tons; it is known to be more than
500 years old, but may be more
ancient still.

3 THE HIGH STREET
An attractive mixture of styles,
from half-timbered Elizabethan
to bow-fronted Regency,
characterises the broad High
Street. Projecting over the street

*No one knows for sure when the
Round Table was made. It is
almost certain, however,
that King Arthur never
sat at it*

above Lloyds Bank is the Jacobean Town Clock, supported on an intricately carved wooden beam. The bank stands on the site of the old Hall of Court, later known as the Guildhall, and a curfew bell is still rung here on weekdays at 8 pm. Opposite is God Begot House, a 16th-century timber-framed and gabled building.

4 CITY MUSEUM
Displayed on three floors of this fascinating museum are exhibits ranging from Roman mosaic pavements to medieval implements and objects relating to 19th-century life in the city.

5 CATHEDRAL
St Swithun, Bishop of Winchester in the 9th century and King Alfred's tutor, is the cathedral's patron saint. The site of his shrine, destroyed at the Reformation, can be seen in the Retrochoir. The present cathedral, preceeded by earlier minsters, dates from 1079, but the beautiful vaulted Gothic nave is 14th-century and is largely the work of Bishop William of Wykeham, who also founded Winchester College. Part of the area on which Old Minster stood is marked out on the north side of the cathedral. Around the chancel screen lie the mortuary chests of Anglo-Saxon kings and bishops, and of Cnut and his wife Emma. There are many other tombs, including Bishop Fox's, which has a figure of him depicted as a rotting corpse. A particularly interesting memorial is that of deep-sea diver William Walker, which stands near the entrance to the Lady Chapel. When, early in this century, the east end of the cathedral was found to be sinking, he went down into the peat bog beneath the foundations and, working only with his hands in complete darkness, replaced the medieval timbers with concrete.

6 PILGRIMS' HALL
The Inner Close has many fine buildings, only one of which, the 14th-century Pilgrims' Hall, now part of Pilgrims' School, is open to the public.

7 KINGSGATE
Above the 14th-century gate is the charming little church of St Swithun, reached by a stone staircase beside the archway. There were originally five gates to the medieval city, but this and the Westgate are the only two which survive.

8 JANE AUSTEN'S HOUSE
At the top of College St, on the right near Kingsgate, a plaque identifies the modest 18th-century house (not open) where Jane Austen spent her last months and where she died.

9 WINCHESTER COLLEGE
Founded in 1382 by William of Wykeham, the college is one of the country's leading public schools, and the earliest planned foundation. Wykeham also founded New College at Oxford to provide for the higher education of its pupils. The chapel, hall and cloisters can usually be visited.

10 RIVERSIDE WALK
A delightful riverside walk follows the River Itchen, skirting the old wall of Wolvesey Castle. Bishop Henry of Blois, half-brother of King Stephen, built the castle as a bishop's palace in the 12th century, and the ruins – the castle was destroyed by Cromwell – can be seen from the riverside, as can the new Bishop's Palace, which dates from 1684. Slight remains of the Roman wall can be seen here.

11 ST CROSS HOSPITAL
(*detour*)
A short detour from the main route leads along College Walk and across the watermeadows to the fine medieval almshouse of St Cross Hospital. Here the brethren still dispense the wayfarer's dole of bread and beer. The dole was originally intended to provide food and drink for 100 poor men daily but is now restricted to a gallon of beer and two loaves each day.

Half-timbered houses glimpsed through the south-eastern entrance to the cathedral precincts

12 CITY MILL
A mill has stood on this site over the River Itchen since the 12th century. It is a delightful brick and tile building, built in the 18th century, and in use as a working mill until quite recently. It now belongs to the National Trust and is used as a youth hostel.

13 THE BROADWAY
The statue of King Alfred by Hamo Thornycroft, erected in 1901, dominates the eastern end of the High Street. Winchester was Alfred's capital and remained the first city in the kingdom until the Norman Conquest. The Town Hall, a large Victorian Gothic building, contains the city art gallery and a tourist information centre. The Abbey Gardens, just past St John's Hospital, are the site of the Nunnaminster, the great Anglo-Saxon church of the Benedictine convent of St Mary, founded in 900 by Alfred and his queen, Ealhswith, and destroyed at the Reformation.

14 SERLE'S HOUSE
This distinguished 18th-century mansion was the home of Colonel William Serle, who commanded the South Hampshire Militia, later incorporated into the Royal Hampshire Regiment, from 1804 to 1826. It is now the Regimental Museum.

EARLY CLOSING: *Thu.*

MARKET DAYS: *Wed, Fri, Sat.*

PARKING: *Friarsgate, Upper Brook St, Tower St.*

OPENING TIMES:

Westgate: open all year. Mon–Sat am and pm; Sun pm only.

Great Hall: open as above.

City Museum: open as above.

Winchester College: open as above.

St Cross Hospital: open all year.

Serle's House: open all year, Mon–Fri.

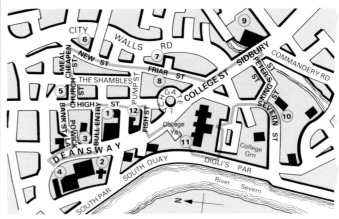

ROUTE DIRECTIONS

The walk starts from the Guildhall (1) in the High St. Walk north up High St and in 40 yards l. down Bull Entry (signed to Riverside Walk). Meet Deansway and turn r. to pass St Andrew's Spire (2) and Countess of Huntingdon's Chapel (3). Reach All Saint's Church (4), then return along Deansway and turn l. up Powick La leading to Bank St. Cross High St and walk down Church St passing St Swithan's Church (5), continue forward into Mealcheapen St to the cornmarket. Turn r. down New St to pass King Charles House (6) leading into Friar St in which are Greyfriars (7) and Tudor House Museum (8). At the end turn l. into College St then cross City Walls Rd into Sidbury to The Commandery (9). Cross Sidbury turning r. then l. and into St Peter's St and King St keeping l. into Severn St. The Royal Porcelain Works and Museum (10) are to the l. Return along Severn St keeping l. past King St through Edgar Tower to College Green and the Cathedral (11). Return to College Green and, turning r. then r. again, go down through Water Gate to the River Severn. Return through Water Gate and go forward through gardens and follow path round north side of Cathedral into Cathedral Close and College Yard. Turn l. into Deansway, then r. up Fish St and l. along High St passing St Helen's Church (12) to return to starting point.

Many people have only ever seen brief glimpses of Worcester as they rush along the ring road on the way to Wales. But the city deserves much more than that, despite the fact that planners did their best to destroy its superb array of ancient buildings in the 1960s. Much that was beautiful and irreplaceable has gone for ever, but a very great deal survives. The cathedral towers over all, but it does not detract from the beauty of such building as the Guildhall and Greyfriars.

1 GUILDHALL

There are few finer examples of early Georgian architecture in the country than this exuberant symbol of civic pride. It is built of brick, but it is the stone dressings and decorations which give it its unique appearance. Statues of Charles I, Charles II and Queen Anne surround the central doorway, while directly above the door is a carving of Oliver Cromwell's head – apparently held up by the nails which pierce the ears – a sign of Worcester's detestation of the Roundhead cause. Crowning all this decoration is a superb pediment with a coat of arms, axes, maces, arrows and many other weapons.

2 ST ANDREW'S SPIRE

Dating from the 15th century, the 245-foot high tower and spire are all that now remain of the original church. It is known as 'Glover's Needle' – a tribute to the glove-making trade that used to be so important in Worcester.

3 COUNTESS OF HUNTINGDON'S CHAPEL

When it was new in 1815 this was a focal point of the city's residential area. It has since been allowed to fall into decay, but is now being restored as a concert hall and music teaching centre. Its elegant interior still retains the original furnishings.

4 ALL SAINTS' CHURCH

The original 11th-century church was badly damaged in the Civil War, but it was beautifully restored in 1739–42. Inside can be seen a rare chained bible of 1608 and some fine monuments.

5 ST SWITHUN'S CHURCH

It is sad to see this, one of the finest Georgian churches in Britain, labelled as redundant. A great deal of restoration work has been carried out, however, and the interior is most impressive. The pulpit is a three-decker built of oak, surmounted by a sounding board carrying a gilded pelican. The altar is of superb wrought iron, and an unusual feature is the mayor's chair built in beneath the pulpit. Just beside the church, St Swithun's Hall was founded in the reign of Elizabeth I as a school.

6 KING CHARLES HOUSE

'Love God and honor ye King' is the motto inscribed over the doorway of this unusual half-timbered house. Charles II was pursued here after his defeat at the Battle of Worcester in 1657, but just managed to escape.

Built in 1721, the Guildhall is one of Worcester's most sumptuous buildings

7 GREYFRIARS
Friar Street is full of impressive 16th-century timbered buildings, and, of them all, Greyfriars is the most outstanding. It was once the guest house of the Greyfriars Friary and was built about 1480.

8 TUDOR HOUSE MUSEUM
A very informative and well-organised display of everyday life in Victorian and Edwardian days has been created in this 500-year-old building.

9 THE COMMANDERY
A comprehensive exhibition of many aspects of Worcester's history, life and industry has been assembled in the excellently restored buildings of the Commandery. It was originally a medieval hospital but subsequently passed into private hands. It became the Royalist Headquarters during the Civil War and much fierce fighting took place all round it. The Great Hall is a superb medieval room with timber walls, a fine hammerbeam roof, a beautiful oriel window and a 17th-century gallery. The painted chamber has 15th-century wall paintings depicting St Michael and the Martyrdom of St Erasmus. There are displays of the city's history from Roman times with special exhibits on such themes as the River Severn and education.

10 ROYAL WORCESTER PORCELAIN COMPANY
It is not necessary to be a connoisseur of porcelain to enjoy the priceless and exquisite collection of Royal Worcester porcelain on display in the Dyson Perrins Museum (adjoining the Royal Worcester Porcelain works). C. W. Dyson Perrins had already put Worcester on the international map when he invented Worcester Sauce, and his profits enabled him to build up an unrivalled collection of every type of Worcester porcelain from outrageous, monster pieces to the simplest everyday items. In between these are many other colourful pieces. Tours of the factory are arranged at regular intervals when all the aspects of ceramic manufacture and painting can be seen.

11 CATHEDRAL
Entering the cloisters on the south side, walk all round them before going into the cathedral. On the north side there is a collection of the bells which formed the original peal, and some good roof bosses in the north and south walks should not be missed. Just off the cloisters is the Chapter House, a circular, Norman building with a central pillar. It is the earliest building of this type left in England. Outside the cathedral, much of what is first seen belongs to the 19th-century restoration work of Sir George Gilbert Scott and A. E. Perkins. The original fabric of the cathedral dates back to the 11th century and the 14th-century reconstruction. The nave is mostly 14th-century work and part of the north choir transept dates from the 13th century, as do the choir and Lady Chapel. Prince Arthur's Chantry, to the right of the high altar, is a richly decorated little chapel with some very fine tracery. The crypt, however, is the main survival of the 11th-century

The cathedral from the river

cathedral and is a superb example of Norman architecture. South of the cathedral, towards the river, are some of the remains of the monastic buildings that used to stand here. On reaching College Yard, it is possible to see across Lychgate the new statue of the composer Edward Elgar, whose work is frequently performed in the Three Choirs Festival which takes place regularly in Worcester Cathedral, alternating with Gloucester and Hereford.

12 ST HELEN'S CHURCH
The County Record Office (holding the marriage bond of William Shakespeare and Anne Hathaway) now occupies this church, whose foundation (in AD680) is the oldest in the city.

MARKET DAY: *Sat.*

EARLY CLOSING: *Thu.*

PARKING: *Deansway, City Walls Road.*

OPENING TIMES:

Guildhall: open all year, Mon–Fri.

Greyfriars: open May–Sep, first Wed of month, pm only.

Tudor House Museum: open all year, except Thu and Sun.

Commandery: Open all year, Tue–Sat; also Sun pm Apr–Sep.

Dyson Perrins Museum: open Apr–Sep Mon–Sat; Oct–Mar Mon–Fri.

Royal Worcester Porcelain Company Factory Hours: open all year, Mon–Fri.

St Helen's Church, County Record Office: open all year, Mon–Fri.

133

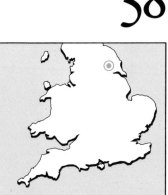

ROUTE DIRECTIONS

Start the walk at the Castle Museum (1) and Assize Courts and take the path with Clifford's Tower (2) to the r. Cross Tower St into St George's Gardens and on to the South Esplanade. Turn r. and follow the bank of the River Ouse along to King's Staith. Pass the King's Arms and ascend steps to Low Ousegate. Cross Bridge St, turn r., then l. into a lane for Riverside Inn. Then turn r. and l. into Coney St. Pass St Martin-le-Grand Church (3) and walk through St Helen's Sq into Lendal (a lane on the l. leads to the Guildhall and Mansion House (4)). Cross Museum St and pass through the gates into Museum Gdns. Take the path bearing r. to pass the Yorkshire Museum (5). To the l. is the Multangular Tower (6). Continue past the ruins of St Mary Abbey, and keep r. to pass through the gates into Marygate, where St Olave's Church (7) is located. At the end of Marygate turn r. for Bootham Bar (8). Ascend the city walls (9) above Gillygate, walking in a north-east direction around the Deanery Gdns to Monk Bar (10). Descend into Goodramgate, then turn r. into College St passing St William's College (11) for the Treasurer's House (12). Return and bear r. along Queen's Path into Minster Yard, walking round the south side of the Minster (13), From the West Door, cross and turn l. into High Petergate passing St Michael-le-Belfrey Church (14), then r. along Stonegate. Continue and turn l. into Little Stonegate and Swinegate, then turn r. through a doorway into an alley leading to St Sampson's Sq and the Roman Bath Inn. From here, turn l. into Church St to King's Sq, turn r. then bear. r. and l. into the Shambles (15). At the end turn l. then r. into Fossgate and at the Merchant Adventurers' Hall (16) turn r. through a doorway into an alley which leads, via a garden and steps, to Piccadilly. Turn r. then l. into Coppergate and l. again into Castlegate. Pass St Mary's Heritage Centre (17) on the l. then at the end of the street cross the car park and return to Castle Museum and Assize Courts to finish the walk.

O ne of the finest cities in Europe, York has buildings and architectural details spanning every age from Roman times up to the present day. History is brought to life in many ways in the city – the sights and smells of Viking times have been recreated at the Heritage Centre, unsurpassed medieval stained glass flickers and glows in the minster and many of the churches, and shoppers walk along medieval streets to buy goods in Tudor, Georgian and Victorian shops.

1 YORK CASTLE MUSEUM

Without doubt the most popular and well-known feature of this excellent museum is Kirkgate – a cobbled street of reconstructed shops complete with vehicles, street furniture, shop signs and window displays. It has recently been extended by the addition of Half Moon Court, which has such attractions as a gas lit pub, an early garage and even a working water mill. Other parts of the museum house collections of domestic and agricultural equipment, toys, costumes, and early crafts.

2 CLIFFORD'S TOWER

William the Conquer built two wooden castles in York to subjugate the citizens after the north country had risen against him. Clifford's Tower was built towards the end of the 13th century, on the site of one of the wooden castles. There is no other castle in England with a plan like it.

3 ST MARTIN LE GRAND CHURCH

Beautiful 15th-century stained glass is what makes this church outstanding. The church was badly damaged during World War II and much of it was demolished. Extensive restoration in the 1960s repaired what could be saved and left the rest open to the sky.

4 GUILDHALL AND MANSION HOUSE

A lane from St Helen's Square leads to the River Ouse and these two fine buildings. The Guildhall was built in 1447 but

Top: York Minster and one of the fine houses in Minster Yard

very badly damaged in World War II. It has been restored to its original appearance, preserving as much as possible of the old stone and timber work. The Mansion House is a handsome stone and brick building built in 1726 as a residence for the mayor.

5 YORKSHIRE MUSEUM

The museum is built in the grounds of St Mary's Abbey, of which extensive ruins can still be seen. Parts of the monastic building are actually incorporated into the museum's structure. The objects gathered here make up a vivid and detailed picture of life in York from earliest times.

6 MULTANGULAR TOWER

Built in the 4th century, this tower is one of the most impressive examples of Roman military architecture surviving in Britain. Attached to it is a length of Roman wall that stands, apart from missing parapets, to its original height.

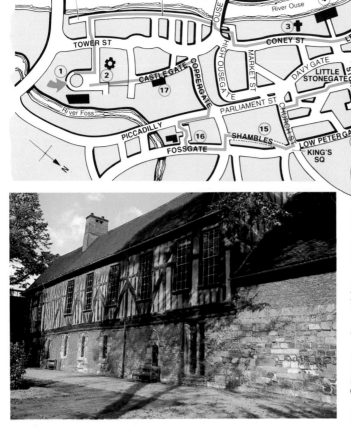

Parts of the Merchant Adventurers' Hall date from the early 15th century

7 ST OLAVE'S CHURCH
Founded before the Norman Conquest, much of the church of St Olave dates from the 18th century, when it was largely rebuilt after having been used as a gun emplacement during the Civil War.

8 BOOTHAM BAR
Although refaced in 1719 and again in 1832, this city gate still retains its original Norman archway. The figures on the parapet are replacements for lost originals.

9 CITY WALLS
York's city walls are the longest and best preserved in England. They were originally built in Roman times but have been remodelled, repaired and rebuilt throughout the subsequent centuries. They are pierced by numerous gates and towers, of many different periods, giving the city a visible pattern of defensive work spanning twenty centuries.

10 MONK BAR
This gate retains the original machinery used to raise and lower the portcullis.

11 ST WILLIAM'S COLLEGE
Half-timbered above and stone below, this handsome building stands in the Minster precincts and was originally built as a dwelling for a church official. It was enlarged in the middle of the 15th century and has been altered several times since. Many of the timber details were remodelled in the 19th century.

12 TREASURER'S HOUSE
Now dating mostly from the 17th and 18th centuries, the Treasurer's House was originally built in about 1100 for the Minster's treasurer. That post ended with the Dissolution of the Monasteries in 1547, after which there was no more treasure to guard. The present lovely building was rescued from near dereliction in 1899, was subsequently stocked with furniture and decorations that are as lovely as the house, and now belongs to the National Trust.

13 THE MINSTER
Among the largest churches in Europe, York Minster must be considered one of the master works of western architecture. It is especially famous for its stained glass, some of which dates back to 1150 and is thought to be the earliest glass in England. The best of the glass is from the 15th century and much of it was made in the workshops of one John Thornton. As it stands today, the Minster is almost entirely Gothic in design, most of the work having been started after 1200. However, the fascinating undercroft museum tells a complex, much older story. Here can be seen Roman foundations, parts of an 11th-century burial ground and many details of Norman architecture.

14 ST MICHAEL-LE-BELFREY CHURCH
Dwarfed by the vast bulk of the Minster, St Michael's is actually one of York's largest churches. Again, there is superb stained glass here from the 15th and 16th centuries; especially notable is a whole series of saints. Guy Fawkes was baptised here.

15 THE SHAMBLES
York has very many picturesque streets, but the Shambles is one of the prettiest, and is certainly the most well-known. It is lined with half timbered buildings, some with overhanging stories so prominent that they almost touch the building opposite.

16 MERCHANT ADVENTURERS' HALL
The barn-like central hall of this building is its most outstanding feature. This is on the half-timbered first floor, while the stone ground floor contains an undercroft and a chapel.

17 ST MARY'S HERITAGE CENTRE
Probably Britain's finest heritage centre, this was set up in 1975 to provide a venue in which York's story could be told using the latest audio visual techniques. It is housed in the old church of St Mary's.

EARLY CLOSING: *Wed.*

PARKING: *Castle, Piccadilly, North St.*

OPENING TIMES:

York Castle Museum: open all year.

Clifford's Tower: open all year.

Guildhall: open all year, except Sat and Sun Nov–Apr and Sun pm May–Oct.

Yorkshire Museum: open all year. Weekdays all day; Sun pm only.

Treasurer's House: open Apr–Oct.

Merchant Adventurers' Hall: open all year. Weekdays.

St Mary's Heritage Centre: open all year. Weekdays all day; Sun pm only.

135

ACKNOWLEDGEMENTS

Maps by K.A.G., Basingstoke, England

The publishers gratefully acknowledge the following for the use of photographs and illustrations:

Automobile Association Publications Division Photographic Library

British Tourist Authority

Mary Evans Picture Library

Westminster Abbey by Jeremy Marks, Woodmansterne Ltd
St Paul's Cathedral by Nicholas Servian FIIP, Woodmansterne Ltd

The Alan Sorrell painting of Roman Silchester is Crown Copyright and is reproduced with the permission of the Controller, H.M.S.O.